Exam Ref 70-779
Analyzing and Visualizing
Data with Microsoft Excel

Chris Sorensen

Exam Ref 70-779 Analyzing and Visualizing Data with Microsoft Excel

Published with the authorization of Microsoft Corporation by:
Pearson Education, Inc.

ISBN-13: 978-1-5093-0804-0
ISBN-10: 1-5093-0804-0

Library of Congress Control Number: 2018943933
1 18

Trademarks

Microsoft and the trademarks listed at *https://www.microsoft.com* on the "Trademarks" webpage are trademarks of the Microsoft group of companies. All other marks are property of their respective owners.

Warning and Disclaimer

Special Sales

For information about buying this title in bulk quantities, or for special sales opportunities (which may include electronic versions; custom cover designs; and content particular to your business, training goals, marketing focus, or branding interests), please contact our corporate sales department at corpsales@pearsoned.com or (800) 382-3419.

For government sales inquiries, please contact governmentsales@pearsoned.com.

For questions about sales outside the U.S., please contact intlcs@pearson.com.

Editor-in-Chief	Brett Bartow
Senior Editor	Trina MacDonald
Development Editor	Rick Kughen
Managing Editor	Sandra Schroeder
Senior Project Editor	Tracey Croom
Editorial Production	Backstop Media
Copy Editor	Liv Bainbridge
Indexer	Julie Grady
Proofreader	Katje Richstatter
Technical Editor	Daniil Maslyuk
Cover Designer	Twist Creative, Seattle

I dedicate this book to my wife, Joely, my daughter Camryn, and my son Murphy. Their love, support and encouragement had no bounds through what was one of the most challenging projects I have ever worked on.

—Chris Sorensen

Contents at a glance

Contents

Chapter 2   Model data   87

Chapter 3   Visualize data   171

Acknowledgements

I would like to thank the first two members of the Iteration Insights team, Jane Wood and Emily Gu, for their enthusiasm and contributions as we worked on this project as a newly formed company. They helped make this book possible as we worked days, nights, and weekends for months to bring it all together. I would also like to thank Trina MacDonald for her encouragement, support, and belief in our team through the process of writing this book. Writing a book of this magnitude would not be possible without the contribution of the editing staff of Daniil Maslyuk, Troy Mott, Rick Kughen, and Christina Rudloff, who sifted through the many versions of our materials to ensure technical and grammatical accuracy. Their insights and contributions were appreciated.

About the author

CHRIS SORENSEN, MCSE (Data Management and Analytics) and MCT, is the Founder and President of Iteration Insights Ltd. He is a consultant, architect, educator, and coach who has been working in the Analytics space for nearly 20 years. Over his career, he has provided strategic and architectural advisory services to many clients and most recently he has been involved with leading numerous Power BI and Excel PowerPivot projects. He has evangelized both Excel and Power BI with Microsoft since July 2015. Follow him on both Linkedin and Twitter as @wjdataguy.

Introduction

The 70-779 exam is designed for both Business Intelligence developers and Business power users that have used Excel for many years to help support Analytics in an organization. The book is an even split between the skills needed to Consume and Transform Data, Model Data, and then Visualize Data.

In the Consume and Transform Data chapter the focus is on the sources that Excel can connect with for data, and then how to transform data using the Power Query Editor. It is important to understand the M language that underlies the Power Query Editor and is generated when performing transform tasks using the GUI.

The chapter on Modeling Data turns the focus to the Excel Data Model to build the necessary relationships that glue the data model together, and the how to optimize it for reporting. Next, we look at how to extend the model and make it easy to consume for users by utilizing DAX, KPIs, and Hierarchies.

When Visualizing data, we spend time considering PivotTables and PivotCharts as the two primary methods in Excel for presenting data. Lastly, you will spend time investigating how to interact with Power BI as an additional means for distributing content to users.

This book covers every major topic area found on the exam, but it does not cover every exam question. Only the Microsoft exam team has access to the exam questions, and Microsoft regularly adds new questions to the exam, making it impossible to cover specific questions. You should consider this book a supplement to your relevant real-world experience and other study materials. If you encounter a topic in this book that you do not feel completely comfortable with, use the "Need more review?" links you'll find in the text to find more information and take the time to research and study the topic. Great information is available on MSDN, TechNet, and in blogs and forums.

Organization of this book

This book is organized by the "Skills measured" list published for the exam. The "Skills measured" list is available for each exam on the Microsoft Learning website: *http://aka.ms/examlist*. Each chapter in this book corresponds to a major topic area in the list, and the technical tasks in each topic area determine a chapter's organization. If an exam covers six major topic areas, for example, the book will contain six chapters.

Microsoft certifications

Microsoft certifications distinguish you by proving your command of a broad set of skills and experience with current Microsoft products and technologies. The exams and corresponding certifications are developed to validate your mastery of critical competencies as you design and develop, or implement and support, solutions with Microsoft products and technologies both on-premises and in the cloud. Certification brings a variety of benefits to the individual and to employers and organizations.

> **MORE INFO** **ALL MICROSOFT CERTIFICATIONS**
>
> For information about Microsoft certifications, including a full list of available certifications, go to *http://www.microsoft.com/learning*.

Check back often to see what is new!

Microsoft Virtual Academy

Build your knowledge of Microsoft technologies with free expert-led online training from Microsoft Virtual Academy (MVA). MVA offers a comprehensive library of videos, live events, and more to help you learn the latest technologies and prepare for certification exams. You'll find what you need here:

http://www.microsoftvirtualacademy.com

Quick access to online references

Throughout this book are addresses to webpages that the author has recommended you visit for more information. Some of these addresses (also known as URLs) can be painstaking to type into a web browser, so we've compiled all of them into a single list that readers of the print edition can refer to while they read.

Download the list at *https://aka.ms/examref779/downloads*

The URLs are organized by chapter and heading. Every time you come across a URL in the book, find the hyperlink in the list to go directly to the webpage.

Errata, updates, & book support

We've made every effort to ensure the accuracy of this book and its companion content. You can access updates to this book—in the form of a list of submitted errata and their related corrections—at:

https://aka.ms/examref779/errata

If you discover an error that is not already listed, please submit it to us at the same page.

If you need additional support, email Microsoft Press Book Support at *mspinput@microsoft.com.*

Please note that product support for Microsoft software and hardware is not offered through the previous addresses. For help with Microsoft software or hardware, go to *http://support.microsoft.com.*

Stay in touch

Let's keep the conversation going! We're on Twitter: *http://twitter.com/MicrosoftPress.*

Important: How to use this book to study for the exam

Certification exams validate your on-the-job experience and product knowledge. To gauge your readiness to take an exam, use this Exam Ref to help you check your understanding of the skills tested by the exam. Determine the topics you know well and the areas in which you need more experience. To help you refresh your skills in specific areas, we have also provided "Need more review?" pointers, which direct you to more in-depth information outside the book.

The Exam Ref is not a substitute for hands-on experience. This book is not designed to teach you new skills.

We recommend that you round out your exam preparation by using a combination of available study materials and courses. Learn more about available classroom training at *http://www.microsoft.com/learning*. Microsoft Official Practice Tests are available for many exams at *http://aka.ms/practicetests*. You can also find free online courses and live events from Microsoft Virtual Academy at *http://www.microsoftvirtualacademy.com*.

This book is organized by the "Skills measured" list published for the exam. The "Skills measured" list for each exam is available on the Microsoft Learning website: *http://aka.ms/examlist*.

Note that this Exam Ref is based on this publicly available information and the author's experience. To safeguard the integrity of the exam, authors do not have access to the exam questions.

CHAPTER 1

Consume and transform data by using Microsoft Excel

As a business intelligence professional, chances are you have spent a lot of time wrangling with data that comes in many shapes and sizes and from a multitude of different sources. This is a challenge that most analysts face daily. Data is scattered, and sometimes not managed properly, which complicates the process of making data easily accessible for analytics. The task of consuming and transforming data in Excel has long been one of the hardest, and yet most important, skills for a data analyst to master as they prepare data sets for consumption and presentation. After all, it is all about the data. If your data is of a poor degree of quality or it is not structured properly, it can lead to challenges when using your data for meaningful and reliable analysis.

> **IMPORTANT**
> ## *Have you read page xix?*
> It contains valuable information regarding the skills you need to pass the exam.

For years Excel professionals have relied upon their mastery of advanced Excel functions such as: VLOOKUP, IF, FIND, CLEAN, and SUBSTITUTE, on top of traditional data import means.

In this chapter, start by looking at the different sources that Excel can connect into using the newly organized Get & Transform Data functionality. Once you have connected to a source, we turn your attention to transforming the data and performing any cleansing that is deemed appropriate for making your data sets easier to navigate and ultimately more reliable.

The focus of this chapter is to connect, transform, and cleanse data into individual tables using what is now known as Get & Transform. In Chapter 2 "Model data," we dive deeper into the Data Model and discuss data modeling best practices, optimization techniques, and how to set up your model for a rich end-user self-service experience. In Chapter 3 "Visualize data," you focus on using the data in the data model for reporting within Excel.

Skills in this chapter:

- Skill 1.1: Import from data sources
- Skill 1.2: Perform data transformations
- Skill 1.3: Cleanse data

Skill 1.1: Import from data sources

One of the great things about Power Query, which is part of the Get & Transform functionality, is that the process of connecting to source systems and cleansing data has been made substantially easier to perform and maintain over traditional Excel techniques.

The first stop when getting data is to become familiar with the Excel 2016 ribbon. In this section, you focus on connecting to data sources via the **Get & Transform Data** group in the **Data** tab. When you connect to any source, you have many options. First, you can just create a query, which is a stored definition. You can load data into an Excel table, or you can also choose to load to the Data Model. Which method you choose depends on how you will be using your data. For purposes of the exam, we focus on loading data to the Excel Data Model.

> **This section covers how to:**
> - Connect to and import from databases, files, and folders
> - Connect to Microsoft SQL Azure and Big Data
> - Import from other Excel workbooks
> - Link to data from other sources

Connect to and import from databases, files, and folders

Databases and files are some of the most common data sources used when connecting to data for analytics purposes. In this Skill, we also connect to a folder structure, which is a very convenient way to acquire data from multiple files that share the same format.

Excel can connect to the following database sources:

- SQL Server database
- Access database
- SQL Server Analysis Services database
- Oracle database
- IBM DB2 database
- MySQL database
- PostgreSQL database
- Sybase database
- Teradata database
- SAP HANA database

Analytics in Microsoft Excel—Then

Before diving into the new methods that are available in Excel for making the overall process of data analysis easier (which is the focus of this book), we need to look at how Excel used to work.

Traditionally, you had to combine data you were acquiring from external systems into single objects, such as an Excel data table, so you could use PivotTables to slice and dice or to build other objects such as PivotCharts. This method typically posed a few problems.

- First, you would often end up with mixed grains of data in a table (for example, an order total repeating with each order line item) that would need to be known by the consumer at analysis time to prevent producing incorrect results.

- Second is that you typically needed to do some sort of workaround to deal with the one million row limit in Excel. This often involved aggregating data (e.g. from day-level to month-level), which causes loss of granularity, and this meant your analysis could only go to the month level, and your users would be asking for day-level analysis. The very nature of analytics is that you ideally want the lowest level of detail in your models to support "the next question" that users inevitably ask. Million-plus row datasets are now a reality.

- Third is that combining, transforming, and cleaning data is a challenge. Pure Excel functions, such as VLOOKUP(), typically do not perform well with larger datasets. Mixed into this problem is that to do more complex transformations, users often found themselves injecting VBA or SQL into their solutions that drove up complexity.

- Lastly, the sources that were available were limited. Today, businesses want to mashup data from many different internal and external systems. This is no easy task with traditional Excel methods.

Analytics in Microsoft Excel—Now

In Excel 2010, a new feature—called Power Pivot—was introduced along with Power Maps, Power Query, and Power View. Microsoft was making a concerted effort to improve analytical capabilities within Excel. When Power Pivot was introduced, Excel expert Bill Jellen declared it as the greatest thing to happen to Excel in 20 years. That is high praise!

Suddenly, the 1,048,576-row limit in Excel was gone and you can now import considerably larger data sets into PowerPivot, which is also known as the Excel Data Model. More on this in Chapter 2 in the section named "Understanding the Excel data model.." And data did not have to be mashed into a single table as it had before so PivotTables could query the data. Also, Microsoft introduced Power Query, which made importing, transforming, and cleansing data much easier and more performant.

A Data Model is a new approach for integrating data from multiple tables, relating those tables, and building a queryable model within an Excel workbook. Within Excel, Data Models are used transparently, providing tabular data that can be consumed by PivotTables and PivotCharts. The engine that drives this is known as xVelocity which is the same in-memory engine that drives SQL Server Analytics Services Tabular models.

Connecting to sources

Now, explore the different sources you can acquire data from using Excel Get & Transform. To connect to a data source, Click the **Data** tab and then on the **Get & Transform Data** group, click **Get Data**.

The menu options shown in Figure 1-1 categorize the data sources into the following groupings. **From File** > **From Database** > **From Azure** > **From Online Services** and **From Other Sources**.

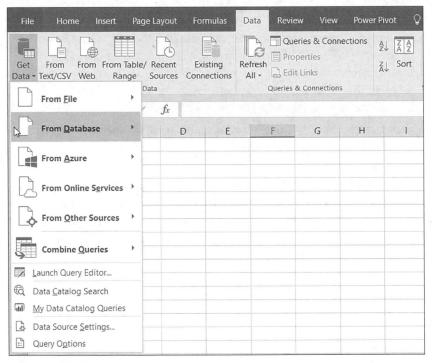

FIGURE 1-1 The Get Data Function

There are three ways to analyze data in Excel. You can import data into Excel using the Data Model, or you can use traditional Excel means, such as an Excel table. If you are using Analysis Services, you also have the option to connect directly into the database and query information live. This allows you to interact with the data without importing it into the spreadsheet, which keeps workbook size down and might also improve performance.

The examples in this guide indicate which data sources to use when following the hands-on examples. In Skill 1.1, you use many different data sources. Following along is optional, but doing so helps reinforce the concepts. In Skills 1.2 and beyond, you move to your local file system and use files that are available on the book's companion site, which simplifies the overall process.

EXAM TIP

The data connectors that are available in Get & Transform Data are important. You do not need to know the details of each system they connect to, but you should know enough about the specifics of the connector from the Get & Transform perspective regarding what can be configured and where common problems lie.

Connecting to SQL Server

One of the most popular enterprise relational database management systems in use today is Microsoft SQL Server. In this example, we connect to an AdventureWorks2016 Database to obtain the following two tables:

- [AdventureWorks2016].[Sales].[SalesOrderHeader]
- [AdventureWorks2016].[Sales].[SalesOrderDetail]

> **NOTE DOWNLOADING THE ADVENTUREWORKS DATABASES**
>
> Throughout the book, you will be interacting with AdventureWorks data through a SQL Database and both Analysis Services Multidimensional and Tabular models. The files and installation instructions are available on the GitHub sites listed below:
>
> The AdventureWorks SQL Database files named AdventureWorksDW2016.bak and Adventure-Works2016.bak can be downloaded from *https://github.com/Microsoft/sql-server-samples/releases/tag/adventureworks*.
>
> The AdventureWorks Multidimensional and Tabular Models named adventure-works-multidimensional-model-full-database-backup.zip and adventure-works-tabular-model-1200-full-database-backup.zip can be found at *https://github.com/Microsoft/sql-server-samples/releases/tag/adventureworks-analysis-services*.

To Connect to a Microsoft SQL Server database, follow these steps:

1. Select **Data** > **Get Data** > **From Database** > **From SQL Server Database**. You are then presented with the window in Figure 1-2. Your **SQL Server Database** dialog may be contracted and if so, click **Advanced Options** to mirror Figure 1-2. Now type the name of your **Server** and leave all other defaults. Do not click **OK** until you have read the following discussion of the options in this dialog.

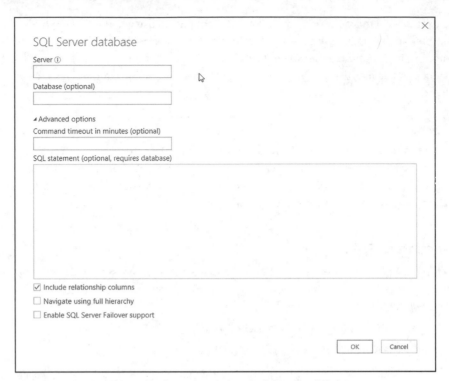

FIGURE 1-2 The SQL Server Database connection configuration dialog

There are several configurations that can be made in the dialog:

- **Server** Here you specify a mandatory server name that you wish to connect to with an option to include the port number.

- **Database (Optional)** If you know the name of the database you want to connect to, type the name here. If you leave the field blank, when you move to the **Navigator** dialog as shown in Figure 1-6; you are allowed to choose from a list of databases for which your credentials have access.

If you expanded the Advanced options, you can configure a few more properties:

- **Command Timeout In Minutes(Optional)** This allows the SQL query to time out should the query not return in the allotted timeframe.

- **SQL Statement (Optional, Requires Database)** In this text box, you can write a Native Database Query. This can be very helpful in situations in which you already have a complex query written that you know cannot be written in the Query Editor, or when you simply do not want to repeat the work. If you choose this option, you are prompted to add a value in the **Database** field. This query may cross databases, despite the Database field indicating a single database.

- **Include Relationship Columns** If chosen, you can subsequently choose the **Select Related Tables** option in Figure 1-7. If not, the metadata that drives the relationships is not included and no related tables are found, even if you know referential integrity exists at the database layer. The default for this option is selected.

- **Navigate Using Full Hierarchy** If chosen, you can navigate the Hierarchy of SQL Server objects from the server down to databases, then schemas, and finally objects within schemas. If disabled, you navigate from server to databases, and then all objects from all schemas. The default for this selection is cleared.

- **Enable SQL Server Failover Support** If chosen, your query can take advantage of local high availability through the server-instance level. The default selection is cleared.

> **NEED MORE REVIEW?** **IMPORT DATA FROM DATABASE USING NATIVE DATABASE QUERY**
>
> For more information, see the following article, "Import Data from Database using a Native Database Query."
>
> *https://support.office.com/en-us/article/Import-Data-from-Database-using-Native-Database-Query-Power-Query-f4f448ac-70d5-445b-a6ba-302db47a1b00.*

2. When you are done configuring the options in Figure 1-2, Click **OK**. If this is your first time connecting to this source, the dialog box in Figure 1-3 appears. Here you enter the credentials to connect to the database. If you are using your Windows credentials, make the appropriate selection. If you are going to connect using SQL Server Credentials, click the **Database** tab and Figure 1-4 appears, where you can enter those credentials. Click **Connect** after you have specified the credentials.

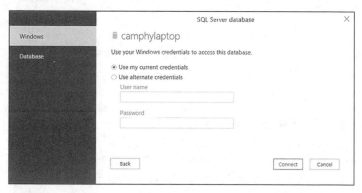

FIGURE 1-3 SQL Server Database Windows-based credentials

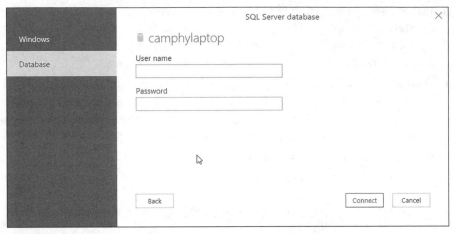

FIGURE 1-4 SQL Server Database SQL User credentials

3. If this is the first time connecting to the specified source, you might be presented with a subsequent dialog box that prompts you to select the authentication mode for the connection. The database in this example does not support encryption, so the dialog shown in Figure 1-5 appears. If you have the option presented to you (in this example we do not) and you do not want to connect using an encrypted connection, clear this check box, and then click **Connect** or **OK**.

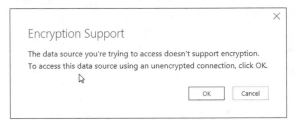

FIGURE 1-5 Encryption Support dialog

> **NEED MORE REVIEW? ENCRYPTED CONNECTIONS**
>
> If your connection supports encryption and you clear the Encrypt connection check box, or your database does not support encryption, as in Figure 1-5, data is transferred from SQL Server to Excel in plain text. A malicious user might be able to intercept and examine unencrypted data.

4. You are brought to the **Navigator** dialog as shown in Figure 1-6. Because you did not type a database name in Figure 1-2, you see the server name followed by a list of databases. Expand out the **AdventureWorks2016** database and find the two tables that you named at the beginning of the Connect to a Microsoft SQL Server database exercise.

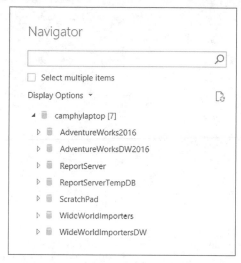

FIGURE 1-6 SQL Server Object Navigator at the server and database level

5. Navigate down the tree to the specific object that you need, as in Figure 1-7. Notice that SQL tables, views, table valued functions, and scalar functions are visible in the object hierarchy. Also, examine your options on this screen:

- The search box as highlighted by the first callout bubble (callout area 1) is useful if you know the name or part of the name of the object that you want to find, and you have a large number of objects.

- Callout area 2 shows the two tables you want. The problem is that at this point, you can only select one table. To solve this, click the **Select Multiple Items** check box that appears in callout area one; doing so allows you to choose multiple tables. You can now select the tables you wanted.

- In callout area 3, notice that you can select **Select Related Tables**. If you selected **Include Relationship Columns** in Figure 1-2, this function performs as expected. This uses any referential integrity that is in the database to help determine what the related tables are. You do not need to choose this option as you only need the two tables mentioned in the opening of the exercise.

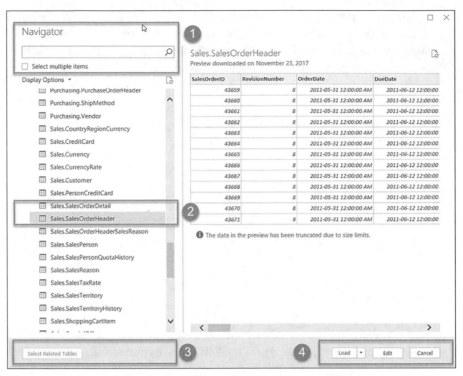

FIGURE 1-7 SQL Server Object Navigator expanded to the objects you want

6. Now that you have the two tables chosen, you can explore the options available in callout area 4 of Figure 1-7. If you are ready to transform and cleanse the data in the selected tables, click the **Edit** button to open the Query Editor. Do not click **Edit** now, because we will do that in Skills 1.2 and 1.3. In this section, we explore the **Load** button. Click on the drop-down arrow on the right side of the **Load** button to open the dialog box shown in Figure 1-8.

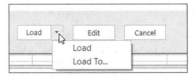

FIGURE 1-8 Load Options

7. From here, click **Load** to open the **Import Data** dialog in Figure 1-9. Choose whether to load your data and where to store it in the **Import Data** dialog box. The first three radio buttons under **Select How You Want To View This Data In Your Workbook** (**Table**, **PivotTable Report**, and **PivotChart**) all load data directly into the Excel workbook. Notice that if you select one of the first three radio buttons, you also have the option of loading data to the data model by checking **Add This Data To The Data Model**. Be aware that if you choose one of the first three options and check the **Add This To The**

Data Model option, you double up the data in your workbook because it is stored in both the object chosen by your radio box selection and the data model. It is not recommended to load data to both locations; in fact, now you are encouraged to load to the data model. You also have the **Only Create Connection** radio box, which will *not* load the data anywhere. For our example, choose **Only Create Connection** and click **OK** to create the connection in Excel as shown in Figure 1-10.

8. Once you have reviewed the figures below, you can close your Excel spreadsheet.

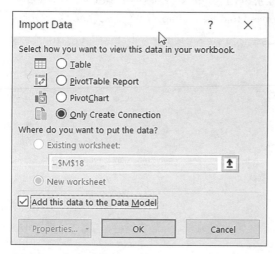

FIGURE 1-9 Import Data options

NOTE **DEFAULT QUERY LOAD SETTINGS**

The default query load settings can be configured in the Query Editor. Refer to the article below that discusses the default behavior and configuration options:

https://support.office.com/en-us/article/Add-a-query-to-an-Excel-worksheet-Power-Query-ca69e0f0-3db1-4493-900c-6279bef08df4#setdefault.

FIGURE 1-10 Queries & Connections Listing

Microsoft Access

Access is a popular desktop management system in many organizations. To connect to an Access database follow the steps below:

1. To connect to Access, select the **Data** tab > **Get Data** > **From Database** > **From Microsoft Access Database**.

2. You are presented with a Windows **Import Data** dialog box where you can navigate to the database file to which you want to connect. Choose the AdventureWorks2014 Access database in the book supplied folder at \Chapter 1\Access\ and click Open

3. Once you have chosen the database, you are presented with the **Navigator** dialog box as shown in Figure 1-11.

4. You may click Cancel.

FIGURE 1-11 Access Database Object Navigator

If you had tried to connect to an Access database with a password, you would have encountered the error displayed in Figure 1-12.

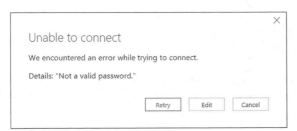

FIGURE 1-12 Unable to connect to a password-enabled Access Database

Analysis Services

Analysis Services provides dimensional data that is well suited for business reports and client applications such as Power BI, Excel, Reporting Services, and other data visualization tools. Data in Analysis Services can be structured in one of two ways:

- Multidimensional OLAP cubes
- Tabular models

You have two options for analyzing data in Analysis Services. First, you can use a live online connection which enables you to slice and dice data in the cube in a PivotTable or PivotChart without loading the data into your workbook. Second, you have the option to import the data from the cube into your workbook.

If you installed the Tabular and Multidimensional Adventure works databases as directed earlier in the Note titled *Downloading the Adventure Works databases*, you can follow along with this example. Follow these steps to Connect to Analysis Services using a live connection:

1. Click **Get Data** > **From Database** > **From Analysis Services**.

2. On the opening screen of the **Data Connection Wizard** in Figure 1-13, choose a **Server Name** and add type your **Log On Credentials**. In the **Server Name** field, you can either choose to connect to a tabular or multidimensional instance of Analysis Services. Click **Next** once you are finished.

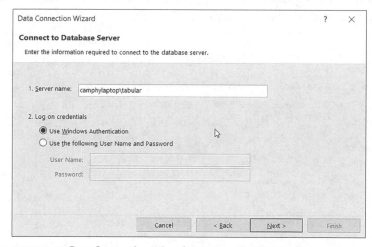

FIGURE 1-13 Data Connection Wizard to connect to SSAS Server

3. In this example, you connect to a tabular instance, which means you will see the **Data Connection Wizard** screen in Figure 1-14, where you choose the database to which you want to connect. Choose **Adventure Works Internet Sales Model** and click **Next**.

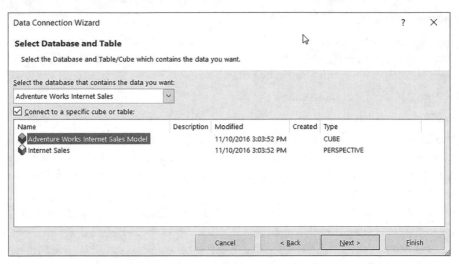

FIGURE 1-14 Select Database and Table/Cube to connect to

4. Next, you Save Data Connection File and Finish in the dialog shown in Figure 1-15. Do-ing saves your data as an Office Data Connection File. You provide both a **File Name** and a **Friendly Name** along with any **Search Keywords**, which help with searchability. Also, click **Authentication Settings** to modify those settings if needed. Once you have the values configured, click **Finish** and the Import Data dialog will appear, as shown in Figure 1-16.

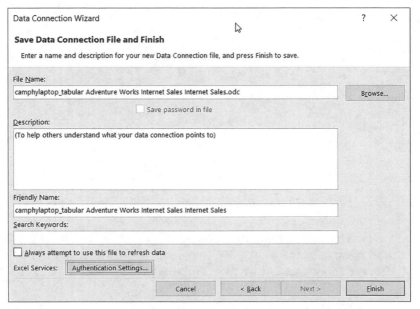

FIGURE 1-15 Save Data Connection File and Finish

NEED MORE REVIEW? OFFICE DATA CONNECTION FILES

See the following article for more information on Office Data Connection Files: *https://support.office.com/en-us/article/Create-edit-and-manage-connections-to-external-data-89d44137-f18d-49cf-953d-d22a2eea2d46*.

NEED MORE REVIEW? CONNECTING TO AZURE ANALYSIS SERVICES

For more about Azure Analysis Services, see the article at *https://docs.microsoft.com/en-us/azure/analysis-services/analysis-services-odc*.

5. In the Import Data dialog as shown in Figure 1-16, notice that you cannot select to store data in a table or the data model. Recall that with a live connection, no data is stored in the workbook.

6. Click Cancel.

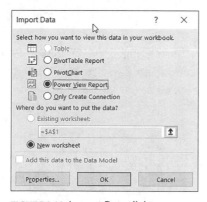

FIGURE 1-16 Import Data dialog

Now that you have completed the live connection, you can do the steps to import data into the workbook:

1. Click **Get Data** > **From Database** > **From SQL Server Analysis Services Database (Import)**.

2. You are presented with the **SQL Server Analysis Services Database** dialog in Figure 1-17. Here you are required to enter a **Server** with an optional port number and an optional **Database**. Also, you have an option to create an MDX or DAX query depending on the type of server to which you are connecting. Once you are done, click **OK**.

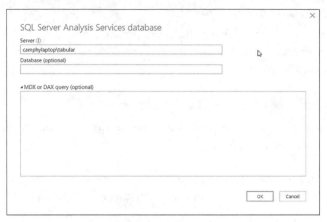

FIGURE 1-17 SQL Server Analysis Services database connection

3. If this is your first time connecting to this resource, you are prompted to enter credentials. Enter them and select **Connect.**

4. In the **Navigator** dialog in Figure 1-18, you navigate the objects on the server to which you are connected. From this point, choose to **Load** to the default location, **Load to** a select location, or **Edit** to begin transforming the data. You can click **Cancel** at this point, as this is as far as we will go.

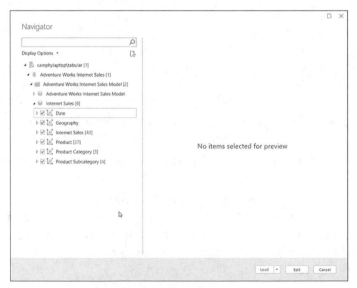

FIGURE 1-18 Analysis Service Object Navigator

Oracle

Follow these steps to connect to an Oracle database:

1. To get data from an Oracle Database, click the **Data** tab > **Get Data** > **From Database** > **From Oracle Database**. To connect, you first need to ensure that you have Oracle client software v8.1.7 or greater on your computer. If not, you receive the error shown in Figure 1-19.

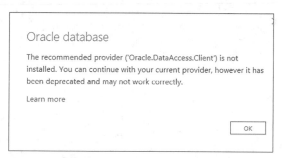

Oracle database

The recommended provider ('Oracle.DataAccess.Client') is not installed. You can continue with your current provider, however it has been deprecated and may not work correctly.

Learn more

OK

FIGURE 1-19 Oracle client error

2. Once you have resolved the driver issue, you can continue to the **Oracle database** dialog box, as shown in Figure 1-20. Here you configure the options much like when configuring an SQL Server connection. Examine the options below and click **OK** when you have it configured properly.

   - **Server** Specify the Oracle Server. If a SID is required, it can be specified as Server-Name/SID.

   - **Command Timeout In Minutes (Optional)** This allows the SQL query to time out should the query not return in the allotted timeframe.

   - **SQL Statement (Optional)** If you want to import data using native database query, specify your query here.

   - **Include Relationship Columns** If chosen, this allows you to choose the **Select Related Table** option as shown in Figure 1-7. If not, the metadata that drives the relationships are not included and no related tables are found, even if you know referential integrity exists at the database layer. The default selection is unchecked.

- **Navigate Using Full Hierarchy**   If selected, you can navigate the Hierarchy of SQL Server objects from the server down to the databases, then schemas, and finally objects within schemas. If it is not selected, you navigate from the server to the databases, then all objects from all schemas. The default selection is unchecked.

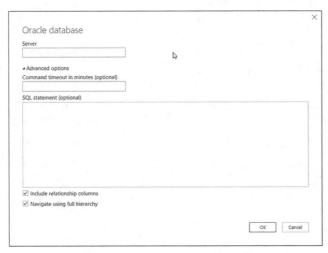

FIGURE 1-20 Oracle Connection Configuration

3.   If the database requires credentials, enter them in the **Access A Database** dialog box.

4.   Click **Connect**.

5.   There is no need to save your work.

Other Database Management Systems

Excel can connect to many other Database Management Systems (DBMS) outside of SQL Server, SQL Server Analysis Services, Oracle, and Access. The pattern to connect repeats through the various DBMS. As seen in the Oracle example, one of the first roadblocks you might encounter is not having the correct drivers installed to allow Power Query to make the connection. This error comes even before you have a chance to specify server names and credentials.

> *NOTE* **INFORMATION ON HOW TO CONNECT TO OTHER DATABASE MANAGEMENT SYSTEMS**
>
> For more information on how to connect to other database systems, read the following article:*https://support.office.com/en-us/article/Import-data-from-external-data-sources-Power-Query-be4330b3-5356-486c-a168-b68e9e616f5a*.

Text/CSV

Text and CSV data are very common file types when doing analytics.

Follow these steps to connect to a Text/CSV source:

1. To get data from a text file, click the **Data** tab > **Get Data** > **From File** > **From Text/CSV**.

2. When prompted with the Windows **Import Data** file dialog box, navigate to \Chapter 1\ Advanced Example 1\Append Examples\United States Sales.txt. This is a tab-delimited file. You are then presented with the dialog shown in Figure 1-21. Note the following options that you may configure. When complete, click Cancel.

   ■ **File Origin**   Power Query detects the File Origin.

   ■ **Delimiter**   Power Query detects the delimiter in use. Available delimiters are:

      ■ Tab

      ■ Comma

      ■ Colon

      ■ Equals Sign

      ■ Semicolon

      ■ Space

      ■ Custom

      ■ Fixed

   ■ **Data Type Detection**   This is where you choose if and how Power Query performs data type detection. The options are:

      ■ Based on first 200 rows; this is the default

      ■ Based on entire dataset

      ■ Do not detect data types

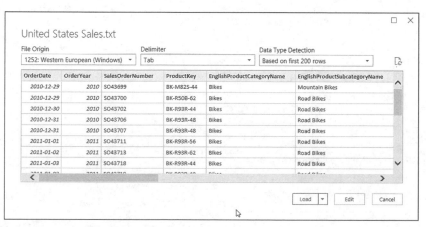

FIGURE 1-21 Text file configuration

Connect to XML

XML or eXtensible Markup Language has been around for many years and is now a common format for moving and storing data. It was designed to be both human- and machine-readable. Follow these steps to Connect to an XML source:

1. Click the **Data** tab > **Get Data** > **From File** > **From XML**.

2. Find the file in **\Chapter 1\XML JSON\XML Internet Orders.xml**.

3. When you click **Open**, the **Navigator** appears, as shown in Figure 1-22. Here you can choose which node you would like to process.

4. When complete, click Cancel.

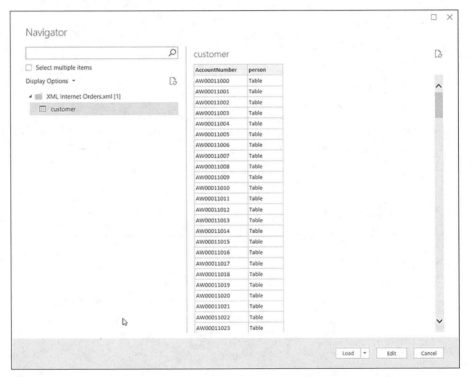

FIGURE 1-22 XML Navigator

Connect to JSON

JSON (or JavaScript Object Notation) is a lightweight data-interchange format that is easy for humans to read and write. It is also easy for machines to parse and generate. It has an advantage over XML in that similar data volumes tend to be much smaller when wrapped into JSON.

Follow these steps to Connect to a JSON source:

1. Click the **Data** tab > **Get Data** > **From File** > **From JSON**.

2. Find the file in \Chapter 1\XML JSON\JSON Internet Orders.json.

3. When you click **Import** in the **Import Data** dialog box, the **Query Editor** appears, as shown in Figure 1-23.

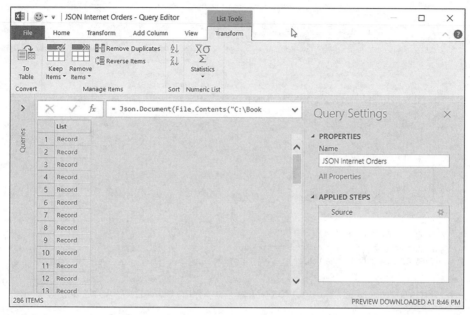

FIGURE 1-23 Initial Query Editor with JSON source

Connect to a folder

It is very common in business scenarios to have multiple files that are divided up among users in the organization and that are all structured in the same way. The only difference is the data they contain. Corporate budgeting is a very good example of this. File structures are tightly controlled by the managers of the budget process. This control around the structure enables the final data extraction process to occur without error.

In situations like this, the folder connector is a very useful way to use multiple files in one operation, placing them into a single table. The number of files can go up or down, and Power Query grabs all the files that are in the folder. The criteria for this:

- All files must reside in the same folder.
- All files must share the same structure.

Follow these steps to Connect to a Folder source:

1. Click the **Data** tab > **Get Data** > **From File** > **From Folder**.

2. In the **Folder** dialog, click **Browse**.

3. In the **Browse For Folder** dialog box, navigate to the folder at \Chapter 1\Folder\. Once you have the folder, click **OK**.

4. In the **Folder** dialog, now click **OK**.

5. When this is complete, you will be presented with the dialog shown in Figure 1-24 where you can see the six files that are in the folder. Click **Combine** > **Combine & Edit** to bring them into one table.

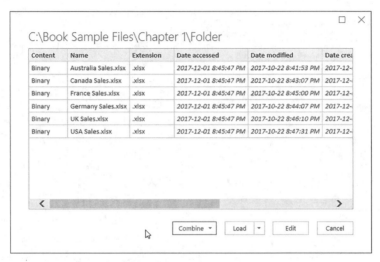

FIGURE 1-24 Files in the folder that was chosen

6. From here you are brought to the **Combine Files** dialog in Figure 1-25. Here you choose:

- **Example File**   Choose which file to use as the sample file.

- **Select The Object To Be Extracted From Each File**   I have chosen Sheet 1 from our example.

- **Skip Files With Errors**   This option allows you to skip any files that contain errors.

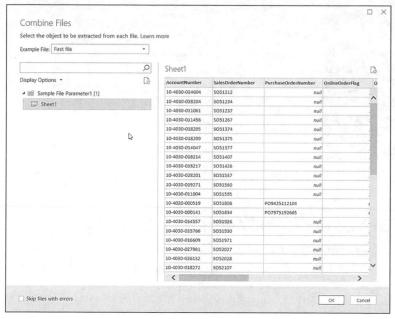

FIGURE 1-25 Combine Files dialog box

7. Click **Cancel** at this point. In Skill 1.2, you go through an end-to-end example on how to perform these steps along with Transforms.

Connect to a SharePoint folder

Fundamentally, connecting to a folder and a SharePoint folder are similar. SharePoint typically provides a more flexible and portable means for sharing files than a traditional file share or folder. Follow these steps to Connect to a SharePoint Folder source:

1. Click the **Data** tab > **Get Data** > **From File** > From SharePoint Folder.

2. On the **SharePoint folder** dialog, enter the root URL for the SharePoint Site, not including subfolders. Click **OK** when done.

3. In the next screen, select **Anonymous** > **Windows** > or **Microsoft Account** as seen in Figure 1-26. Here you can also indicate at which level in the SharePoint environment the permissions will apply. There are three levels where permissions can be applied in this example.

4. You may click Cancel.

FIGURE 1-26 SharePoint site folder configuration

Connect to Microsoft SQL Azure and Big Data

Azure data sources are growing in popularity due to their total cost of ownership, their scalability, and their flexibility. These sources are used by more and more organizations, so the need to easily access data increases. Excel can connect to the following Azure sources:

- Azure SQL Server
- Azure SQL Data Warehouse
- Azure Data Lake Store
- Azure HDInsight
- Azure BLOB
- Azure Table Storage

> **NOTE AZURE SUBSCRIPTION**
>
> If you choose to try any of the examples in this section, you need access to Azure. For this, you can set up a free trial account at the following location: *https://azure.microsoft.com/ en-ca/free/*.

Azure SQL and Azure SQL Data Warehouse

Connecting to Azure SQL and Azure SQL Data Warehouse is similar to connecting to SQL Server. To connect, you need to use the fully qualified name of your server, which is available in your Azure portal. The format is: *<your database name>.database.windows.net*. Additionally, you need to ensure that the firewall rules are correctly configured to access the databases once they are set up.

Azure Data Lake

Azure Data Lake is a scalable cloud-based data storage and analytics service. It gives users fast and efficient alternatives to deploying and managing big data infrastructure. Data of all shapes and sizes can be stored within Azure Data Lake, and if data processing is needed, you can take advantage of Azure Data Lake Analytics.

In this example, use the same example that is used throughout the book to show bringing in data from files and folders.

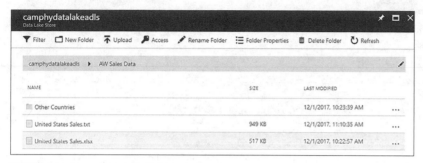

FIGURE 1-27 Azure Data Lake folder explorer

Follow the steps below to Connect to Azure Data Lake:

1. To get data from an Azure Data lake, click the **Data** tab > **Get Data** > **From Azure** > **From Azure Data Lake Store**.

2. You are presented with the **Azure Data Lake Store** dialog box shown in Figure 1-28. To connect, enter the following information and then click **OK**:

    ▪ **URL**   *adl://<your data lake store name>.azuredatalakestore.net/*

    ▪ The URL can be:

        ▪ The root directory of your data lake store

        ▪ A specific folder

        ▪ A single file

FIGURE 1-28 Azure Data Lake Store URL dialog box

3. You are then prompted to connect with an organizational account that has access to the resource as shown in Figure 1-29. Sign in with those credentials and click **Connect** when you are done. You are presented with the dialog shown in Figure 1-30.

FIGURE 1-29 Azure Data Lake Store Sign in dialog Box

4. You may click **Cancel.**

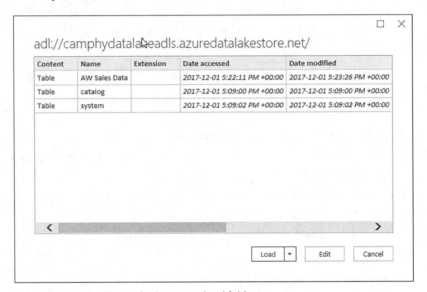

adl://camphydatalakeadls.azuredatalakestore.net/

Content	Name	Extension	Date accessed	Date modified
Table	AW Sales Data		*2017-12-01 5:22:11 PM +00:00*	*2017-12-01 5:23:26 PM +00:00*
Table	catalog		*2017-12-01 5:09:00 PM +00:00*	*2017-12-01 5:09:00 PM +00:00*
Table	system		*2017-12-01 5:09:02 PM +00:00*	*2017-12-01 5:09:02 PM +00:00*

FIGURE 1-30 Azure Data Lake Store root level folder

NEED MORE REVIEW? **CONNECTING EXCEL TO AZURE DATA LAKE STORAGE**

Consult the following article for more details on how to work with Azure Data Lake:

https://blogs.msdn.microsoft.com/azuredatalake/2017/07/19/analyze-data-in-azure-data-lake-store-using-familiar-and-powerful-Excel-2016/.

Import from Excel workbooks

Data can be imported from workbooks external to the one that you are working in, as well as data from within your current workbook. For example, you can have tables and ranges in your workbook that you want to import. Now, it is time to see this option in an example.

Follow these steps to **Get Data** from a **Table/Range**:

5. With Excel closed, open the workbook at **\Chapter 1\Excel\Table Range Example.xlsx** as you would normally open and xlsx file.

6. In this file, you can see two objects: an Excel table named tblSales and a Named Range, rngRegions.

7. First, highlight any part of the Excel table and then click **Get Data** > **From Other Sources** > **From Table/Range**. The Query Editor appears where you can perform any shaping. Click **Close & Load** to move back to Excel.

8. Now highlight the entire range and click **Get Data** > **From Other Sources** > **From Table/Range**. You are are taken to the Query Editor where you can perform any shaping. Click Close & Load to move back to Excel.

9. Notice how both the query names have been picked up from the name of the Excel object that you have imported.

Link to data from other sources

There are many other data sources to which Power Query can connect. Below are the categories of other sources and the specific sources to which you can connect.

From Online Services

With the popularity of online applications, more and more data now resides in cloud-based solutions. For example, in a CRM-based Analytics scenario, some customer data might reside in Dynamics 365 CRM, and additional information might reside in Facebook. Power Query allows you to mash these sources together to help enable a 360-degree view of your customer. Get & Transform functionality makes it easy to connect to the following online sources:

- SharePoint Online List
- Microsoft Exchange Online
- Microsoft Dynamics 365 (online)
- Facebook
- Salesforce Objects
- Salesforce Reports

From Other Sources

There are many other connectors available, such as the following:

- Web
- Microsoft Query
- SharePoint List
- OData Feed
- Hadoop File (HDFS)
- Active Directory
- Microsoft Exchange
- ODBC
- OLDB
- Blank Query

Power Query can connect to Web sources

When doing analytics, you might find the need to acquire data from external sources to augment solutions. For example, you might need population data as part of your work. If your organization does not have this available internally, you can get it yourself and mash it in. For this example, look at getting population data from Wikipedia by following these steps to connect to a Web source: **Get Data** > **From Other Sources** > **From Web**.

1. You are presented with the **From Web** dialog box shown in Figure 1-31. If you choose the Basic option, you are asked to provide type URL. For this demo use the following URL and click OK: *https://en.wikipedia.org/wiki/List_of_countries_by_population_(United_ Nations)*.

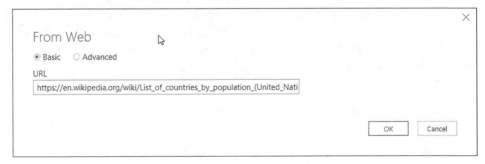

FIGURE 1-31 Web URL configuration dialog box

2. In the Access Web content dialog shown in Figure 1-32, you configure credentials to access the data. You can choose Anonymous, but you also have the following options to choose from, depending on the location of the web resource you are trying to connect to:

- Anonymous
- Windows
- Basic
- Web API
- Organizational account

FIGURE 1-32 Web Content configuration dialog box

3. Also, note that you need to use Select Which Level To Apply These Settings To. If you click the drop-down box in the Access Web Content dialog box shown in Figure 1-32, you can see three levels where security can be applied: the root of Wikipedia, the next level down in the folder structure (wiki), or the actual web page itself. This is discussed more in the section on Privacy Levels in Power Query. For now, leave it at the root level, and click Connect.

4. You should now see the Navigator window as shown in Figure 1-33. Power Query inspects the web page for suitable structures to import and has found three objects that are listed. Click through each to see what they look like. You need to select Countries And Areas Ranked By Population In 2017. Note that when you have this highlighted, you can toggle between the Table View and Web View on the right of the window. This is helpful in situations in which there are many options, and you want to preview what you are selecting.

5. Go ahead and click Edit to move the Query Editor to do further processing, or you may click Cancel.

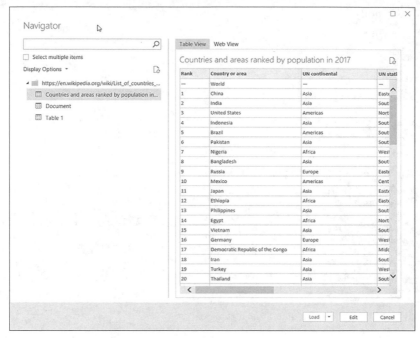

FIGURE 1-33 Web Page Object Navigator

Blank Query

You can use the Blank Query to create advanced queries that use the M language within Power Query. M provides a wide variety of formulas that are used to build complex expressions and transformation steps.

When you choose a Blank Query, you are immediately taken to the Query Editor where you can begin to build out your query using the various wizards, or you can go directly into the Advanced Editor to code your steps. More information about the Advanced Editor is provided in Skill sections 1.2 and 1.3.

Privacy Levels

Now that you have worked with several data sources, it is worth discussing Privacy Levels. Privacy Levels are rules that define isolation levels between data sources. These rules might affect performance of queries, and in some cases, your queries are not executed at all if Privacy Levels conflict between sources.

To view the current Privacy Levels in your workbook, click **Get Data** > **Data Source Settings**. Note, this can be done from the Query Editor as well. You should see the Data source settings dialog shown in Figure 1-34. From there, you select the multidimensional source and click Edit Permissions. Note that you can also change the Credential used at this point. You have the option to change Privacy Level to the following values:

- None
- Public
- Organizational
- Private

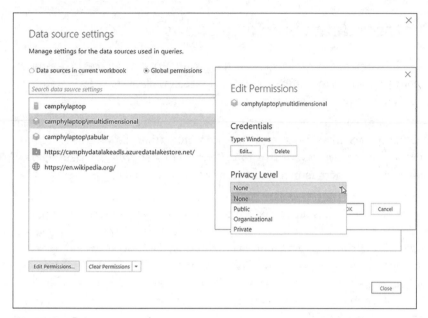

FIGURE 1-34 Data source settings

To view the settings on how your workbook treats privacy levels, click **Get Data** > **Query Options**. The Query Options dialog will appear as shown in Figure 1-35.

FIGURE 1-35 Privacy settings in Query options

Skill 1.2: Perform data transformations

Now that you have seen examples of how to connect to the vast array of data sources that are available in Excel, let's shift attention to the different methods that are available to users to transform data using the Query Editor, which is the primary focus of Skill 1.2 and Skill 1.3.

Rarely is data in the state that you need it to be in for production quality reporting. If it is, count yourself lucky. If not, the Query Editor has a very rich set of features that allows users to perform transformations and cleansing activities with ease. You often hear this referred to as Data Shaping, which has become the more modern term for Extract Transform and Load (ETL).

The front-to-back process of importing data, performing transformations, and then visualizing data is highly iterative, and tools such as Excel are well-suited to enable fast iterations. Data can be taken from front to back, and as it is used at each stage, feedback can be provided that can be pushed back into earlier steps that make later steps in the process easier. For example, maybe your model has no easy way in the first iteration to perform analysis by Year. As this feedback is provided, the data shaping process can create a Year column, so that is available in the Data Model for end users. This is a simplistic example, but it is a very common way to iterate on improving models for widespread usage.

This section covers how to:

- Design and implement basic and advanced transformations
- Apply business rules
- Change data format to support visualization
- Filter data
- Format data

Design and implement basic and advanced transformations

In this skill section, we review the methods available in the Query Editor for performing basic and advanced transformations of your data. The bulk of time in data shaping is spent taking data tables and fields that come in many shapes and sizes and preparing them for easy to use and consistent analytics. Many times, when performing analysis, you are merely happy getting any data, no matter how good or bad it is. You then take advantage of techniques available to standardize and cleanse the data for use.

For the most part, the visual tools available in the ribbon and menu options more than cover your transformation needs. However, as you become more advanced with using the Query Editor you might start diving into the M language that is available for scripting steps by typing code versus using the GUI commands. The Power Query M formula language is optimized for building highly flexible data mashup queries. It's a functional, case-sensitive language which can be used with Power BI Desktop, Power Query in Excel, Get & Transform in Excel 2016, Power Apps, and now SQL Server Analysis Services 2017. Through this Skill, M scripts are highlighted as they are output from transformations using the GUI because this a great way to gain familiarity with the language. This is done by first showing the individual lines of code that are generated with each step. Then you are introduced to the Advanced Editor for viewing and maintaining the entire script that has been generated by applying transformation steps to your data.

> **NOTE QUERY EDITOR AND POWER QUERY**
>
> Originally, Query Editor was called Power Query, and to this date, still shows up in documentation on many sites, including the Microsoft Office support site. As of the time of this writing, the two terms are used interchangeably, and questions on the exam might show using either term.

Importing data to support basic transformations

Let's start off with basic transformations by importing data from sources that do not need much in the way of transformations. This approach is very common when bringing in data from a Data Warehouse where many of the transformation steps that need to be performed on data have already been handled by the warehouse team. However, even well-formed data warehouses occasionally do not have all the data for analysis in the state an analyst requires. Perhaps something was never incorporated into the warehouse, or maybe a business rule changed, or occasionally, unaccounted data sneaks into the warehouse. For these examples, import FactInternetSales and DimCustomer from the AdventureWorksDW2016 SQL Server databases.

Perform take these steps to make the connection to the data source:

1. Click **Data** tab > **Get Data** > **From Database** > **From SQL Server Database**.

2. In the SQL Server database dialog, configure the following options as below and in Figure 1-36, and then click OK.

   - **Server**   Your server name
   - **Database**   AdventureWorksDW2016

   Leave all other items as their defaults

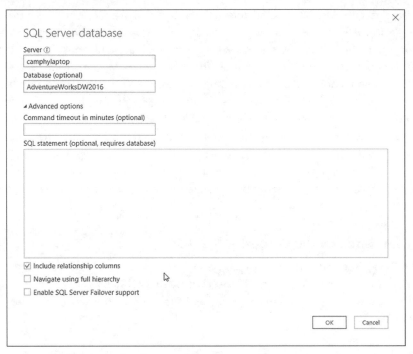

FIGURE 1-36 SQL Server Database configuration

3. In the Navigator dialog (as in Figure 1-37), you can check the Select Multiple Items check box so you can choose the FactInternetSales and DimCustomer tables that you want to bring in. Next, click the drop-down on the right side of the **Load** button and choose **Load To**.

4. Make the following selections in the **Import Data** dialog, and then click OK:

   ■ **Select How You Want To View This Data In Your Workbook** Ensure that Only Create Connection is selected.

   ■ **Add This Data To The Data Model** Ensure that this option is not selected.

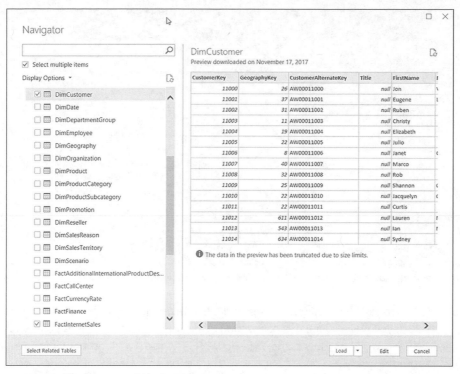

FIGURE 1-37 The data source Navigator

5. Once you have completed this, you have only created a connection to the targeted data source. At this point, no data has been brought into any Excel objects, which is fine for now because you are only working on transformations. Once the data is ready for consumption, you can load it to a consumable location. You should now see the screen in Figure 1-38. Both tables show up under Queries and are in a state of Connection Only. If you do not see the **Queries & Connections** pane on the right side of the screen, go the **Data** tab and in the **Queries & Connections** group, click the **Queries & Connections** command. This will toggle the pane on and off.

> **NOTE ONLY CREATE CONNECTION**
>
> Depending on the size of the data that you are loading, choosing to only create the connection in the Import Data dialog can help avoid a potentially lengthy load process when you are in the early stages of data shaping. Later when you are working in the Query Editor and want to save your work, you can close and load the work.

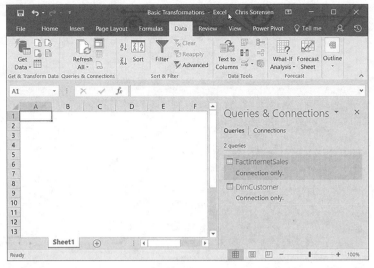

FIGURE 1-38 Excel window showing connections and queries

6. Now, look at a few options that are available from the Excel window shown in Figure 1-38. If you hover over either connection in the Queries & Connections pane, you can view the "peek" window as shown in Figure 1-39, which is a snapshot of information about the query. As you will see later in this section, this window also contains many functions that are available in the Query Editor window, as shown later in this section.

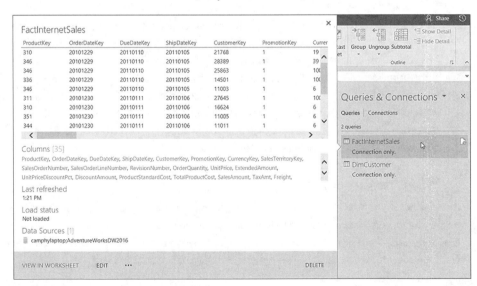

FIGURE 1-39 Query and connection peek window

7. Other options that are available in the pane can be found by right-clicking on one of the queries, as shown in Figure 1-40. As with the peek menu in Figure 1-39, many of the commands in this window can also be performed in the Query Editor.

8. Now that you have explored some of the options in the Excel window, right-click **FactInternetSales** and click **Edit** in the context menu to open the Query Editor (see Figure 1-40). This takes you directly to the highlighted query in the Query Editor, as shown in Figure 1-41.

9. Save your Query Editor work by clicking **Home** tab > **Close Group** > **Close & Load**. This will close the Query Editor and send you back to Excel.

10. Save your workbook as Chapter01Exercise01.xlsx as it will be used in subsequent demos.

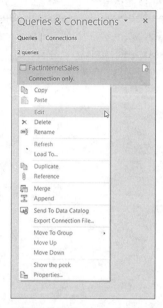

FIGURE 1-40 Query and context menu

Query Editor Overview

Before you begin the process of transforming data, review the parts of the **Query Editor** in Figure 1-41.

1. **Ribbon** This is where Data Shaping tasks are located. They are grouped into like functionality by tab and then by tab groupings. Keep in mind that many of the data-shaping tasks are also available in other locations.

2. **Queries pane** This lists the objects that you build over the course of shaping data. Also—as you will see soon—as this list of queries grows, you can add Groups, which are folders where similar objects can be placed. This will be demonstrated shortly.

3. **Formula bar**   As you build data-shaping steps, the resulting M code that is generated for that step is displayed here. If you cannot see the formula bar as shown, click **View** tab > **Layout** group > **Formula** bar. You can also use the formula bar to type in your own custom M transformations.

4. **Query settings pane**   Shows the name of the query and the Applied Steps that have been taken to transform the data. This will be discussed in detail as you build examples up.

5. **Data preview pane**   Displays a preview of the data resulting from your query. It is in this window where you select columns that you are looking to shape. To help with performance, the Query Editor takes a snapshot of the data and caches it. If you need to refresh the cache, you have a few options. If you want to refresh only the query you have selected, you can click the **Refresh** Preview command from the Home tab, Query group above the formula bar shown in Figure 1-41. If you want to refresh the preview for all your queries, select the **Home** > **Query** group > **Refresh Preview** drop down, and choose Refresh All. Note that in this example, you can see that the last Data preview for FactInternetSales was from November 17, 2017, as shown in the very bottom right side of the screen in Figure 1-41. This is also indicated above the formula bar as shown in Figure 1-42.

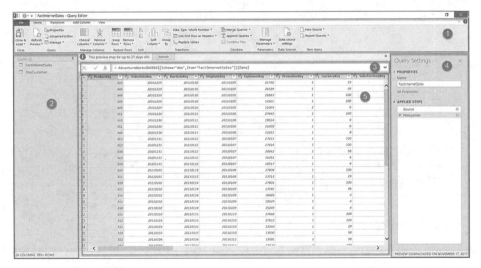

FIGURE 1-41 Query Editor

FIGURE 1-42 Data preview cache age indicator

Perform basic transformations

Now that you have reviewed the Query Editor landscape, let's perform some transformations on the FactInternetSales table, and then we'll look at the DimCustomer table. Ensure that the FactInternetSales query is selected in the Queries pane and that the Query Settings pane is open. If not, it can be toggled on and off from **Home** > **View** > **Query Settings**.

Let's pick up from the Importing data to support basic transformations steps where you imported FactInternetSales and DimCustomer. Note that you have already performed two steps, which are listed in the Query Settings pane under APPLIED STEPS. These came from the initial screens that you ran through to make the connection. The first step named Source shows the server you connected to and the second shows that you are bringing the FactInternetSales table from the dbo schema in the database named AdventureWorksDW2016. To view this metadata, click the gear icon to the right of each step.

Depending on your source, the Query Editor may attempt to recognize header rows and data types as well. Because you are connecting to a SQL Server, both can be determined through database metadata, so this step does not need to be performed.

1. The next thing you notice is that there are lots of columns in this table, many of which are not needed for this analysis; you should remove the unneeded columns. There are a few options for doing this. Follow the steps below to remove columns that you do not need: Ensure that you are in the Query Editor, which was the last step in the previous exercise.

2. With the FactInternetSales table selected in the Queries pane, click **Home** > **Manage Columns** > **Choose Columns** command drop-down. From here, you have two options available. The first option is to choose Go to column, which allows you to select a column from a list of sorted columns in the query. This is good for when you have a large table and want to get to a column without scrolling through the Data preview pane. The second option is Choose Columns, which allows you to choose only the columns you want to keep by selecting them in the dialog box. Click Choose Columns and then in the Choose Columns dialog box, ensure only the following columns are checked and click OK when complete:

   - CustomerKey
   - SalesOrderNumber
   - SalesOrderLineNumber
   - OrderQuantity
   - UnitPrice
   - UnitPriceDiscountPct
   - DiscountAmount
   - SalesAmount
   - TaxAmt
   - Freight
   - OrderDate

3. Notice That you now have a third step named **Removed Other Columns** as shown in Figure 1-43.

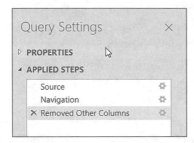

FIGURE 1-43 Query Settings

4. This step name may be meaningful now, but will it mean something to the next developer? Likely not. In instances like this, you should document your steps by highlighting the step you want to document, right-clicking on it to open the context menu, and then choosing Properties. You are then presented with the Step Properties dialog box shown in Figure 1-44; here, you can rename the step to something more meaningful and can also add a description, which is very useful for complex transformations. Click Cancel, as we will leave the default values.

5. Note if you just want to change the name of the step, you can do that by right-clicking the step name in the Applied Steps portion of the Query Settings pane, and then selecting Rename in the context menu. This enables the step name in Applied Steps to be directly edited.

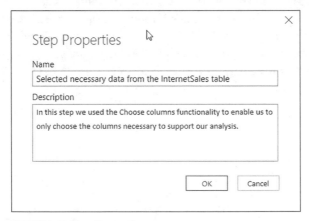

FIGURE 1-44 Step Properties

6. Look at the M code that was generated after you finished choosing the columns that you wanted. The code is in Listing 1-1 and can be viewed in the Formula bar in the Query Editor.

7. Save your Query Editor work by clicking the **Home tab** > **Close group** > **Close & Load**. This will close the Query Editor and send you back to Excel.

8. Save your workbook as **Chapter01Exercise01.xlsx** because it will be used in subsequent demos.

LISTING 1-1 Code generated by the Choose Columns step

```
= Table.SelectColumns(dbo_FactInternetSales,{"CustomerKey", "SalesOrderNumber",
  "SalesOrderLineNumber", "OrderQuantity", "UnitPrice", "UnitPriceDiscountPct",
  "DiscountAmount", "SalesAmount", "TaxAmt", "Freight", "OrderDate"})
```

EXAM TIP

M questions are on the exam. As opposed to having a separate section that calls out how to write M, I have chosen to demonstrate by example. As Applied Steps are created in the Query Editor, highlight the M code that is generated by the engine. This allows you to perform a function using the GUI, so you become familiar with the M code.

With the Chapter01Exercise01.xlsx file that you have created still open, let's explore the Query Editor further. Now that you have only the data you want to look at in the Data preview pane, review the data types that you have so far. The highlighted area of Figure 1-45 is one place where you can go to determine the data type for each column. The data types determine what type of operations you can perform on the column, and how much storage is required in the model.

FIGURE 1-45 Data Types for each column

Clicking on the highlighted area in Figure 1-45 reveals a list of different supported data types, as shown in Figure 1-46. If you see the ABC123 icon displayed (not seen here), this signifies the Any data type has been set for the column. The data types can also be changed in the **Home** tab in the **Transform** group in the **Data Type** drop-down. Note that some data types exist only in Query Editor and are converted once you load the data. An example of this is the percentage data type, which is available in Query Editor, but once you load the data, it is converted to a decimal.

FIGURE 1-46 Possible Data Types context menu

As you can see, when you move into the section on DAX in Chapter 2.2, the available Data Types in the Query Editor contains two data types that are not available in Data or Report view: These are **Date/Time/Timezone** and **Duration**. When a column with these data types is loaded into the Data Model and viewed in Data or Report view, the following occurs. A Date/Time/Timezone data type is converted into a Date/Time, and a column with a Duration data type is converted into a decimal number. Follow these steps to change a data type:

1. Open the **Chapter01Exercise01.xlsx** file and start the Query Editor if you do not already have it open.

2. Change the Data Type for UnitPriceDiscountPct from a Decimal to a Percentage by highlighting the column in the Data preview pane and then navigating to the Home tab in the and the Transform group in the Data Type drop-down. Choose Percentage.

3. Observe the resulting M code in the Formula bar as shown in Listing 1-2.

LISTING 1-2 M Code generated the change in data type

```
= Table.TransformColumnTypes(#"Removed Other Columns",{{"UnitPriceDiscountPct",
Percentage.Type}})
```

If you need to rearrange the position of your columns, you have several options. First, you can select **Move** from the **Transform** tab, or right-click the column header and select **Move** from the context menu. Move provides you with options to move the column to the:

- Beginning of your query
- End of the query
- Left
- Right

Alternatively, you can drag and drop the columns where needed. Follow these steps to move the OrderDate column in FactInternetSales to the beginning of the Query:

1. Select the OrderDate column header in the Data preview pane.

2. Drag it into position at the beginning of the query column in the Data preview pane.

3. Observe the resulting M code in the Formula bar as shown in Listing 1-3.

LISTING 1-3 M Code generated by the Move columns steps

```
= Table.ReorderColumns(#"Changed Type",{"OrderDate", "CustomerKey",
  "SalesOrderNumber", "SalesOrderLineNumber", "OrderQuantity", "UnitPrice",
  "UnitPriceDiscountPct", "DiscountAmount", "SalesAmount", "TaxAmt", "Freight"})
```

4. Now let's add some extra columns to the FactInternetSales table to support analysis. In this example, you are going to add some additional date and time columns by taking advantage of some built-in functions. You need to add a year, month name, and month number to support analytics. Perform the following steps to add columns: Select the OrderDate column in the Data preview pane.

5. Go to the Add Column tab, From Date & Time group, and select Date as shown in Figure 1-47. Here you have several functions that you can perform on a Date Time column to easily extract parts of the date into new columns.

FIGURE 1-47 Date Transforms

6. Next choose **Year** > **Year**. This adds a new column at the end of the table with the value of year. The M code is shown in Listing 1-4. For each row in the table, this M code has determined the year value and has added it into the newly added Year column. If you do not like the name that the new column was given, you can edit the M code by changing the value in the "Year" to some other value; alternatively, you can do it in an additional step and perform a rename. Before you do that, add the other columns.

LISTING 1-4 M Code generated by adding the Year column

```
= Table.AddColumn(#"Reordered Columns", "Year", each Date.Year([OrderDate]),
  type number)
```

7. Repeat steps 1-3 two times, once to add a Month, which gives you a month number, and once to add a Month Name. When you are done, the table should look like the something like table shown in Figure 1-48. Recall that these additional columns will appear at the end of your table.

FIGURE 1-48 Snapshot of current exercise steps

> **NOTE DATE AND TIME TRANSFORMS**
>
> If you want to transform Date and Time, you can do this either from the Transform tab or the Add Columns tab, but they produce different results. Choosing from the Transform tab transforms an existing column in place; choosing from the Add Column tab adds an additional column.

8. Now that you are done, take note of the data types. Year and month are both decimal formats, and the Month name is text format. Make the following changes to the data types:

   - **Year** should be a Whole Number
   - **Month** should be a Whole Number
   - **Month Name** can remain as Text

9. Now move the three columns to the beginning of the query by using the Move functionality. To do this, press the Control key and click on the three new columns. Now right-click to be presented with the context menu where you can choose **Move** > **To Beginning**.

The last thing that you want to do with FactInternetSales is to give the query a name, and give some of its columns better names. Follow these steps to rename a query and columns:

1. First, rename the query to a friendlier name, such as InternetSales. This is important because this name shows up in the data model once you choose **Load To The Data Model**. In the Query Settings pane under Properties, change the Name value to InternetSales as shown in Figure 1-49. Note that you can do this from the Queries pane by right-clicking on the Query and choosing Rename from the context menu.

FIGURE 1-49 Query Settings Query Name

2. Now rename the following columns according to Table 1-1. You can do this by right-clicking on the column names in the Data preview pane and choosing **Rename.** Do the same by clicking **Transform tab** > **Any Column group** > **Rename**, or more easily by double-clicking on the column name in the Data preview pane and simply typing a new name. The resulting M code for this step is in Listing 1-5.

TABLE 1-1 Renaming InternetSales columns

Original column name	New column name
Month	Month Number
Month Name	Full Month Name

LISTING 1-5 M Code generated by adding the Year column

```
= Table.RenameColumns(#"Reordered Columns1",{{"Month", "Month Number"}, {"Month
Name", "Full Month Name"}})
```

3. Finally, look at the cumulative result of the M code for all the transforms by going to the Advanced Editor from either the View or Home tabs while the InternetSales query is selected. The sample of the Advanced Editor is shown in Figure 1-50. Your code might be different depending how you did the above steps. Also, note that the dialog box does not explicitly title it as the Advanced Editor.

FIGURE 1-50 Advanced Editor

LISTING 1-6 All M Code applied to Fact Internet Sales

```
let
    Source = Sql.Databases("localhost"),
    AdventureWorksDW2016 = Source{[Name="AdventureWorksDW2016"]}[Data],
    dbo_FactInternetSales =
AdventureWorksDW2016{[Schema="dbo",Item="FactInternetSales"]}[Data],
    #"Removed Other Columns" = Table.SelectColumns(dbo_FactInternetSales,{"CustomerKey",
"SalesOrderNumber", "SalesOrderLineNumber", "OrderQuantity", "UnitPrice",
"UnitPriceDiscountPct", "DiscountAmount", "SalesAmount", "TaxAmt", "Freight",
"OrderDate"}),
    #"Changed Type" = Table.TransformColumnTypes(#"Removed Other
Columns",{{"UnitPriceDiscountPct", Percentage.Type}}),
    #"Reordered Columns" = Table.ReorderColumns(#"Changed Type",{"OrderDate",
"CustomerKey", "SalesOrderNumber", "SalesOrderLineNumber", "OrderQuantity",
"UnitPrice",
"UnitPriceDiscountPct", "DiscountAmount", "SalesAmount", "TaxAmt", "Freight"}),
    #"Inserted Year" = Table.AddColumn(#"Reordered Columns", "Year", each
Date.Year([OrderDate]), type number),
    #"Inserted Month" = Table.AddColumn(#"Inserted Year", "Month", each
Date.Month([OrderDate]), type number),
    #"Inserted Month Name" = Table.AddColumn(#"Inserted Month", "Month Name", each
Date.MonthName([OrderDate]), type text),
    #"Changed Type1" = Table.TransformColumnTypes(#"Inserted Month Name",{{"Year",
Int64.Type}, {"Month", Int64.Type}}),
    #"Reordered Columns1" = Table.ReorderColumns(#"Changed Type1",{"Year", "Month",
"Month Name", "OrderDate", "CustomerKey", "SalesOrderNumber", "SalesOrderLineNumber",
"OrderQuantity", "UnitPrice", "UnitPriceDiscountPct", "DiscountAmount", "SalesAmount",
"TaxAmt", "Freight"}),
    #"Renamed Columns" = Table.RenameColumns(#"Reordered Columns1",{{"Month", "Month
Number"}, {"Month Name", "Full Month Name"}})
in
    #"Renamed Columns"
```

Now, look at performing some transformations on the DimCustomer table. In the next steps you will:

- Remove unneeded columns.

- Merge columns.

- Extract values from existing columns.

First, remove columns that are not needed for analysis. With the DimCustomer query selected in the Queries pane, select the following columns by highlighting the first one, pressing the Control key, and then highlighting the remaining columns. Alternatively, you can make changes column by column (the resulting code will be the same). Either way, once you have one column (or all columns) chosen, you can right-click and select Remove Columns from the context menu or do the same from the Manage Columns group on the Home tab, which is shown in Figure 1-51. The resulting M code is shown in Listing 1-7.

- GeographyKey

- NameStyle

- TotalChildren

- NumberChildrenAtHome
- EnglishEducation
- SpanishEducation
- FrenchEducation
- EnglishOccupation
- SpanishOccupation
- FrenchOccupation
- HouseOwnerFlag
- NumberCarsOwned

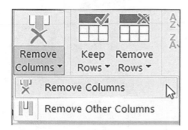

FIGURE 1-51 Remove Columns Options

LISTING 1-7 All M Code applied by removing columns from DimCustomer

```
= Table.RemoveColumns(dbo_DimCustomer,{"GeographyKey", "NameStyle", "TotalChildren",
 "NumberChildrenAtHome", "EnglishEducation", "SpanishEducation", "FrenchEducation",
 "EnglishOccupation", "SpanishOccupation", "FrenchOccupation", "HouseOwnerFlag",
 "NumberCarsOwned"})
```

> **NOTE** **REMOVE OTHER COLUMNS**
>
> If you have a table that has many columns and you only want to keep a few, you can use the Remove Other Columns transform, which keeps only the columns you have selected. The M function for this is Table.SelectColumns.

Now that you have only the columns you want, we will extract the username from the email address column and create a new column. This Extract command is used to extract characters from columns and can perform the operations shown in Figure 1-52.

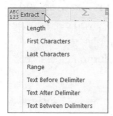

FIGURE 1-52 Extract options

Perform the following steps to extract the username from the email columns:

1. Ensure the EmailAddress column in the DimCustomer query is selected.

2. Click the Add Column tab and find the Extract command under the From Text grouping. From here, choose the Text Before Delimiter option.

3. Configure the values per Text Before Delimiter dialog in Figure 1-53. The result of this is to select all the characters before @ symbol, to start the scan from the beginning of the text field and to skip 0 delimiters. Click **OK** when complete.

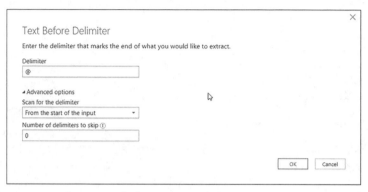

FIGURE 1-53 Extract Text Before Delimiter dialog

4. Find the new column that has been added to the end of the table and rename it to **Username**. The resulting M code for both the extract and rename is shown in Listing 1-8.

LISTING 1-8 M code for the Extract of username and rename of new column

```
= Table.AddColumn(#"Removed Columns", "Text Before Delimiter", each
Text.BeforeDelimiter([EmailAddress], "@", 0), type text)
= Table.RenameColumns(#"Inserted Text Before Delimiter",{{"Text Before Delimiter",
  "Username"}})
```

Lastly, merge the three name columns together using the Merge function by performing the following steps:

1. Ensure that DimCustomer is the selected query in the Query pane.

2. Highlight the FirstName column, press and hold the Control key and then select the MiddleName and LastName fields.

3. Click the Add Column tab and find the Merge command under the From Text grouping. This brings you to the Merge Columns dialog screen in Figure 1-54. Here you can choose the separator that you would like to put between the columns and can give the new column a name. Choose Space as the Separator and name the New Column Full Name (with a space). The resulting M code is shown in Listing 1-9.

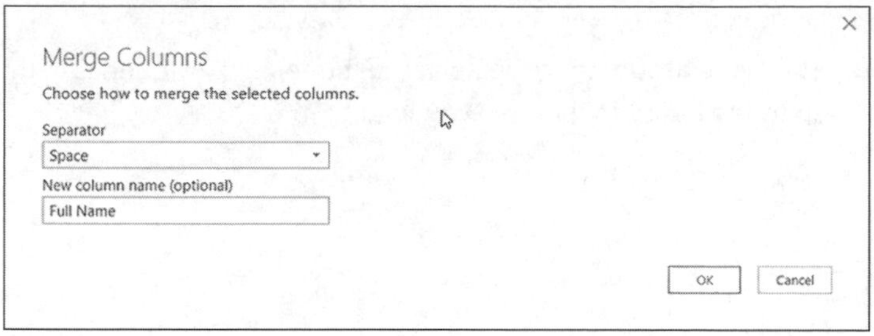

FIGURE 1-54 Merge Columns dialog

LISTING 1-9 M code for the Merging of columns

```
= Table.AddColumn(#"Renamed Columns", "Full Name", each
Text.Combine({Text.From([CustomerKey], "en-CA"), [FirstName], [MiddleName], [LastName]},
"
"), type text)
```

Listing 1-10 contains the resulting combined M code for all of the steps you applied to DimCustomer. You will find this by opening the Advanced Editor.

LISTING 1-10 M code for the Extract of username and Rename of new column

```
let
    Source = Sql.Databases("localhost"),
    AdventureWorksDW2016 = Source{[Name="AdventureWorksDW2016"]}[Data],
    dbo_DimCustomer = AdventureWorksDW2016{[Schema="dbo",Item="DimCustomer"]}[Data],
    #"Removed Columns" = Table.RemoveColumns(dbo_DimCustomer,{"GeographyKey",
"NameStyle",
 "TotalChildren", "NumberChildrenAtHome", "EnglishEducation", "SpanishEducation",
 "FrenchEducation", "EnglishOccupation", "SpanishOccupation", "FrenchOccupation",
 "HouseOwnerFlag", "NumberCarsOwned"}),
    #"Inserted Text Before Delimiter" = Table.AddColumn(#"Removed Columns", "Text Before
 Delimiter", each Text.BeforeDelimiter([EmailAddress], "@", 0), type text),
    #"Renamed Columns" = Table.RenameColumns(#"Inserted Text Before Delimiter",{{"Text
Before Delimiter", "Username"}}),
    #"Inserted Merged Column" = Table.AddColumn(#"Renamed Columns", "Full Name", each
Text.Combine({Text.From([CustomerKey], "en-CA"), [FirstName], [MiddleName],
[LastName]},
 " "), type text)
in
    #"Inserted Merged Column"
```

Now that you have completed what you need to transform both FactInternetSales and DimCustomer, it is time to do some housekeeping by performing the following steps:

1. Rename DimCustomer query to Customer.

2. Start organizing the queries that you have in the Queries pane. Create a new Group in the Query Pane named Fact Queries. Do this by right-clicking in an open space in the Query pane and then select New Group in the context menu per Figure 1-55. In the New Group dialog that opens, configure the following and click OK.

- **Name**   Fact Queries.
- **Description**   This is the group where you place fact queries. Any queries in this folder are moved to the Data Model when you load to it.

FIGURE 1-55 Create a New Group

3. Create a second group with the following values:

- **Name**   Dimension Queries.
- **Description**   This is the group where you place dimension queries. Any queries in this folder are moved to the Data Model when you load to it.

4. Now that you have these two groups created, the queries pane should look like Figure 1-56.

FIGURE 1-56 New Groups in the Queries Pane

5. What you need to do next is to move the InternetSales query to the Fact Queries group and move Customer to the Dimension Queries group. This can be done with a drag and drop, or by right-clicking on either query and selecting Move To Group and then selecting the proper group from the context menu. Note that you can also create a new group from this menu. Once you have done this, the Queries pane looks like Figure 1-57. When you create your first group, a new folder called Other Queries is generated by the Query Editor and this group cannot be deleted because it becomes the default group for new objects.

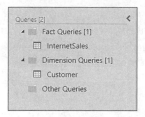

FIGURE 1-57 Queries moved to groups

6. As a final step to this transformation, load this data through to the Data Model. To do this, save your work in the Query Editor; in the Home tab, choose Close & Load. This brings you back into Excel.

7. In the Queries & Connections pane in Excel, right-click on InternetSales and choose Load To from the context menu, which brings you to Figure 1-58. Originally, you had asked to Only Create Connection. Now that you are done with Transforms, check the Add this to the data model check box. When done click OK and notice that the status of the Query in Excel has changed to show the rows loaded.

FIGURE 1-58 Import Data dialog

Another concept called Query Folding is worth pointing out since you are connecting to a relational database management system. Power Query attempts to translate the APPLIED STEPS into the data source's native language where supported. To see whether Query Folding takes place, right-click on any step in the Query Settings pane and choose View Native Query from the context menu. If the step cannot be selected because it is dimmed in the context menu, it means that Query Folding does not take place or has been disabled at some point in the steps. This is the case with InternetSales as it currently stands. Query folding ends after the Removed Other Columns step. Perform the following steps see the entire query run using query folding:

1. Open the Query Editor and select the InternetSales Query.

2. Remove the step that converts UnitPriceDiscountPct to a Percentage data type by clicking the x to the left of the step name or by right-clicking and selecting **Delete** from the context menu.

3. Remove the step that inserts the Month Name and all the step after it by right-clicking the Inserted Month Name step and choosing Delete Until End from the context menu. Now right-click on the last step and highlight the View Native Query. Your screen should now look like Figure 1-59.

FIGURE 1-59 View Native Query

4. Now Click on View Native Query to open the Native Query dialog (Figure 1-60).

```
Native Query

select [_].[OrderDate] as [OrderDate],
    [_].[CustomerKey] as [CustomerKey],
    [_].[SalesOrderNumber] as [SalesOrderNumber],
    [_].[SalesOrderLineNumber] as [SalesOrderLineNumber],
    [_].[OrderQuantity] as [OrderQuantity],
    [_].[UnitPrice] as [UnitPrice],
    [_].[UnitPriceDiscountPct] as [UnitPriceDiscountPct],
    [_].[DiscountAmount] as [DiscountAmount],
    [_].[SalesAmount] as [SalesAmount],
    [_].[TaxAmt] as [TaxAmt],
    [_].[Freight] as [Freight],
    datepart("yyyy", [_].[OrderDate]) as [Year],
    datepart("m", [_].[OrderDate]) as [Month]
from
(
    select [CustomerKey],
        [SalesOrderNumber],
        [SalesOrderLineNumber],
        [OrderQuantity],
        [UnitPrice],
        [UnitPriceDiscountPct],
        [DiscountAmount],
        [SalesAmount],
        [TaxAmt],
        [Freight],
        [OrderDate]
    from [dbo].[FactInternetSales] as [$Table]
) as [_]
```

OK

FIGURE 1-60 Native Query window

5. Click **OK** and then close the Query Editor. When the Query Editor Keep your changes dialog box opens, click **Discard** to remove the changes that you made to get Query folding to work.

Advanced transformations

Now that you have done some basic transformations, it is time to look at some more advanced techniques. In this example, you use multiple text files to build out a star schema that is based on the Fact Internet Sales schema in AdventureWorksDW2016.

To start this exercise, you are going to combine files in a folder named Countries, which contains five Excel workbooks, and then append the combined query to a file with U.S. data. The Countries folder contains a spreadsheet for Internet Sales in each country with which Adventure Works does business. These files share the same structure, and all contain a column named Country, which is set to the country's name. However, the U.S. file does not have a column for country name and it is implied that each row of data is for the U.S. To solve this imbalance, add a custom column to the U.S. file.

Follow these steps to combine the files in the Other Countries folder using a folder import and the Combine Files transform.

1. Open a new blank Excel workbook.

2. Select **Data** tab > Get Data > **From File** > **From Folder**.

3. When the Folder Path dialog box opens, browse to the location where you downloaded the Book Sample file to, then navigate to **\Chapter 1\Advanced Example 1\Append Examples\Other Countries**.

4. A dialog box like the one in Figure 1-61 will appear, showing the five named .xlsx files you want to append. Scroll though and note the metadata that is extracted for each file. Once you are done, select Edit. As a note, you can choose Combine And Edit to open the Query Editor with a fully combined set. In this example, you are looking to show you the details as they are examinable.

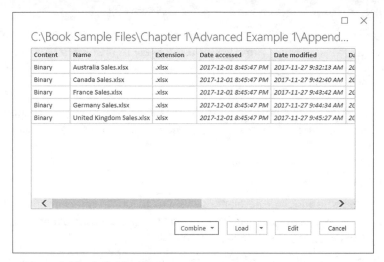

FIGURE 1-61 Files in Folder Source

5. Select the first column named Content as shown in Figure 1-62.

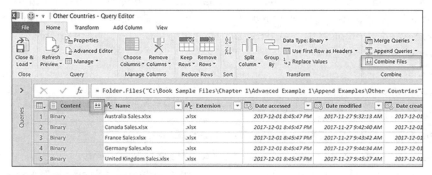

FIGURE 1-62 Combine Files Options

6. Click the icon on the right side of the column header as highlighted in Figure 1-62 OR from the Ribbon Choose the **Home** tab > **Combine Group** > **Combine Files**. Both options move you to the Combine Files dialog in Figure 1-63. In this dialog you make the following selections:

- **Example File** You leave the First file, but you can select any of the files as an example via the drop-down. This provides the template from which all other file structures are compared.

- **Sample File Parameter** Here you choose which object you want to load from the spreadsheet. Select tblSales.

- **Skip Files With Errors** Leave this unchecked. If checked, files that do not match will be skipped.

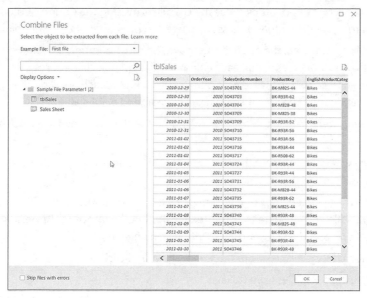

FIGURE 1-63 Combine Files dialog

7. Once you are done, click OK, which completes the process of combining the files into a table called Other Countries. Several other objects are created in the Queries pane that are used to support loading and combining the files from the folder source.

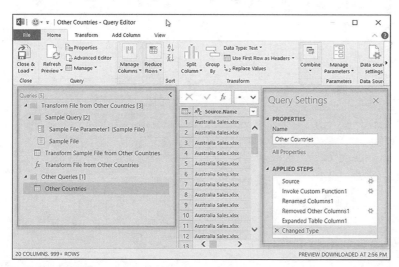

FIGURE 1-64 Results of File combine

8. Remove the column named Source.Name.

Now that you have combined the data for other countries' Internet sales, it is time to Append the U.S. and Other Country queries together with it so that you have the complete picture of Internet Sales across all countries. Since the U.S. file is missing the Country Column, which is contained in the Other Countries data set, you need to prepare that data set first.

For Append to work as expected, the queries must have the same number of columns, with the same names and same data types within each column. If the columns in a source query are different, Append still works, but it will create one new column for each new column in the queries. The source that does not have that column will be assigned a null value.

Perform the following steps to Add the column, rearrange the data set, and then Append the sets:

1. If you are in the Query Editor, from the **Home** tab > **New Query** group > click **New Source** > **File** > **Excel**.

2. When the Import Data dialog box opens, browse to the location where you downloaded the Book Sample file and navigate to **\Chapter 1\Advanced Example 1\Append Ex-amplesUnited States Sales.xslx** and click **Open** on the file.

3. In the Navigator, choose tblSales from the spreadsheet and click OK.

4. Rename the Query to US Sales from tblSales.

5. Next, you need to add a new column named EnglishCountryRegionName to the U.S. Sales query and default its value to **United States**. To do this, click the Add Column tab and choose Custom Column from the General grouping, as shown in Figure 1-65. Configure the values as shown in Figure 1-65 and then click OK. See Listing 1-11 for the M code that will be generated from this step.

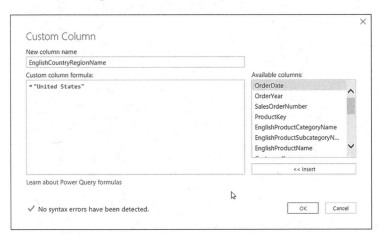

FIGURE 1-65 Custom Column dialog

LISTING 1-11 M code for the Custom column

```
= Table.AddColumn(#"Changed Type", "EnglishCountryRegionName ", each "United States")
```

6. Next change the data type from the **Any Type**, which is denoted with the ABC123 icon, to **Text**.

7. Our queries are now aligned, so now you can go ahead and append them. First, highlight the US Sales Query and from the Home tab, Choose Append from the Combine grouping. You can choose Append or Append Queries As New. Choose Append Queries As New to create a new query.

8. You should now see the Append dialog in Figure 1-65, which is where you choose what to append. Notice that you are only appending two files but using this method you can choose three or more. For this step, configure the values as shown in Figure 1-65. Once done, click **OK**.

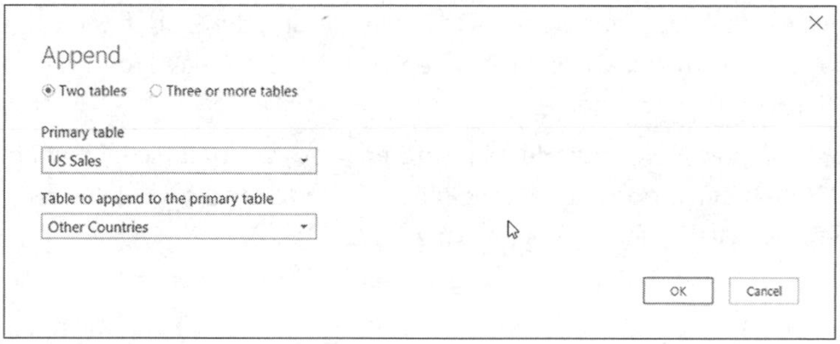

FIGURE 1-66 Append dialog

9. You will now have a new query named Append1, which is the default name given to the newly created query. Rename this query to Internet Sales All Countries. Notice that this query only has one entry in Applied Steps.

10. Now look at the M code for the Append, which is in Listing 1-12. Notice that this code resides in the first step named Source of the newly created query.

LISTING 1-12 M code for the Append as New Query function

```
= Table.Combine({#"US Sales", #"Other Countries"})
```

You have completed the steps to Append the data together that is the fact table in the star schema that you are populating. Now you need to bring in some other dimensions. The first ones to bring in are the Product, Product Subcategory, and Product Category files. Once you have these loaded, use the Merge function to bring them into one query.

To begin the process of merging data, perform the following steps:

1. If you are in the Query Editor, click **Home** > **New Query** > **New Source** > **File** > **Excel**.

2. When the Import File dialog box opens, browse to the location where you downloaded the Book Sample file and navigate to **\Chapter 1\Advanced Example 1\Merge Examples** then bring each of the files in one by one and choose the table object in each file. Repeat steps 1 and 2 until the Product, Product Subcategory, and Product Category Excel files have been imported.

3. Rename each of the queries as below:

   ▪ tblProducts should be renamed to Products

- tblProductSubcategory should be renamed to ProductSubcategory
- Table1 to ProductCategory

4. Now, you need to merge the queries so that all the values in the hierarchy are in the Product table. For the first merge, select the Product query and then choose **Home** tab, **Combine Group** > **Merge Queries**.

5. Configure the values as shown in the Merge dialog in Figure 1-67. The Products query should show up at the top because it was the query you selected when you executed the Merge command.

6. Next, choose what table you want to merge to it by choosing the ProductSubcategory table from the drop-down box. Once this has been selected, you need to tell Power Query which fields you want to merge.

7. In this example, you only join the ProductSubcategoryKey in each table by highlighting each column. Note that it is possible to use multiple fields to merge the columns. In that case, the order in which you choose columns matters.

8. Lastly, you need to choose a Join Kind. In this example, you choose Left Outer because you want all rows in the first query, regardless as to whether a match exists in the right-hand (bottom) query. However, even with this configuration, notice that you have an error at the bottom of the screen which says that you need to Select columns of the same type to continue. What happened? To find out, cancel out of this window for now so you can correct the issue.

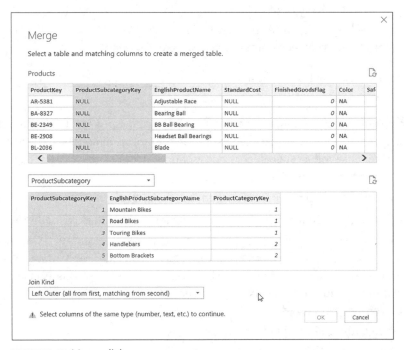

FIGURE 1-67 Merge dialog

9. Upon inspecting the queries, you'll notice that the ProductSubcategoryKey in the Product table has been defaulted to the Text data type by Power Query, and the ProductSubcategoryKey in the ProductSubcategory query value is an integer. To fix this make the following change:

    A. Make the ProductSubcategoryKey in the Product Query a Whole Number. When making this change, you might see the warning message in Figure 1-68. Power Query is asking if it should just replace the conversion it made with this one, or if you intended on creating a separate step in Query Settings. Select **Replace Current**.

FIGURE 1-68 Change Column Type Question dialog

10. We can now repeat the instructions in Step 4. At the bottom of Figure 1-67, you should now see the message in Figure 1-69. Once complete press OK.

FIGURE 1-69 Join Match Information

11. The next step is to finish the Merge process by selecting which columns from the Product Subcategory table to keep in the Product table. To do this, select in the Product query and move to the far-right side where you see the last column represented as a Table shown in Figure 1-70. Also, see the M code in Listing 1-13.

FIGURE 1-70 Screenshot showing the table expander

LISTING 1-13 M code for the Merge Function

```
= Table.NestedJoin(#"Changed
 Type",{"ProductSubcategoryKey"},ProductSubcategory,{"ProductSubcategoryKey"},
"ProductSubcategory",JoinKind.LeftOuter)
```

12. Click on the table expand icon highlighted in Figure 1-70 and then you are presented
    with the screen in Figure 1-71. Configure the values as shown. ProductSubcategorykey
    would be redundant to keep, so uncheck it. You need the Product Category key to per-
    form the next Merge. The resulting M code the table expanded is in Listing 1-14. More
    information on the configuration values is provided below.

    - **Expand** Use this if you want to bring in rows one for one according to the Join
      Type.

    - **Aggregate** Used to aggregate values before the merge.

    - **Use original column name as prefix** This prepends all new column names with
      the original table name.

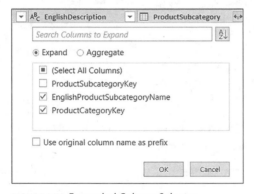

FIGURE 1-71 Expanded Column Selector

LISTING 1-14 M code for the Table Expand Function

```
= Table.ExpandTableColumn(#"Merged Queries", "ProductSubcategory",
 {"EnglishProductSubcategoryName", "ProductCategoryKey"},
 {"EnglishProductSubcategoryName", "ProductCategoryKey"})
```

13. Now that you have merged the two tables that you needed, you can now merge Prod-
    uct with Product Category. To do this, ensure that the Product query is highlighted and
    choose Merge.

14. Configure the Merge with the values in Figure 1-72 and then click OK.

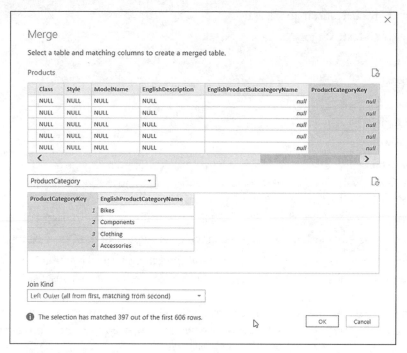

FIGURE 1-72 Merge dialog

15. Once complete, expand the new table out as shown in step 12, check the EnglishProductCategoryName, and uncheck the Use Original Column Name As Prefix option as in Figure 1-73. Click OK when complete.

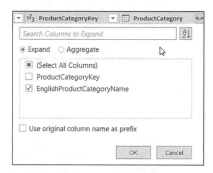

FIGURE 1-73 Expanded Column Selector

16. Now, you have all columns that you need in the Product table that enables a traditional Star Schema Product Dimension versus the snowflake that you started with. Remove columns that you do not need by using the Choose Column command. Keep the following columns and then put them in the order below using Move:

   ■ ProductKey
   ■ EnglishProductName

- EnglishProductSubcategoryName
- EnglishProductCategoryName
- Color
- ListPrice
- Size
- SizeRange
- Weight

Now that you have cleaned up the table, you have two tasks left to make the table consumer-ready. Replace the null values in EnglishProductSubcategoryName and the EnglishProductCategoryName columns with Text value values. Replace each with Undefined Subcategory and Undefined Category, respectively.

1. Ensure that the Products query is selected in the Queries pane of the Query Editor.

2. To replace the values, right-click on the EnglishProductSubcategoryName column and choose Replace Values from the context menu to open the Replace Values dialog in Figure 1-74. In this figure, you are replacing the null values in EnglishProductSubcategoryName with the text value Undefined Subcategory. This makes the end-user reporting easier to understand. Take note that you have two additional advanced options available that you can specify to use. Once done, click **OK**.

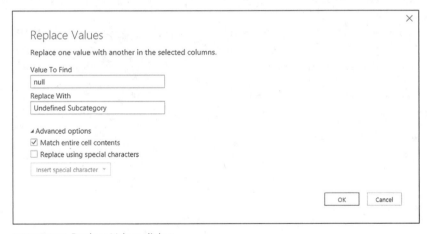

FIGURE 1-74 Replace Values dialog

LISTING 1-15 M code for the Replace Values Function

```
= Table.ReplaceValue(#"Reordered Columns",null,"Undefined
  Subcategory",Replacer.ReplaceValue,{"EnglishProductSubcategoryName"})
```

3. Repeat Step 2 for the EnglishProductCategoryName column and replace null with Undefined Category.

4. Now get rid of any duplicate rows in the Products query. To do this, click the ProductKey column then right-click it to get the context menu and choose Remove Duplicates.

5. You now have a well-formed product dimension for your users to consume. At this point it is worth looking at the Query Dependencies that are forming between the sources you have imported and merged together. In the **View** tab > **Dependencies** group > click **Query Dependencies** to see the screen in Figure 1-75. You can see the sources and how they feed into queries and then how the queries merge. You can also see the load state, and if you had any query metadata defined it would show up in the diagram as well. Click Close to close the diagram.

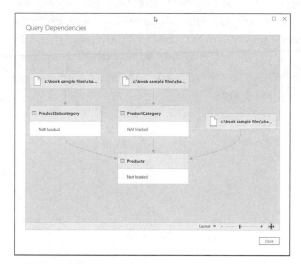

FIGURE 1-75 Query Dependencies

6. Try to delete a query that has a dependency to see what happens. Highlight the Product-Subcategory query, right-click, and select Delete from the context menu. You should see the dialog shown in Figure 1-76. Click Close, and you can continue to bring in additional queries for your model.

FIGURE 1-76 Delete Query warning

So far in this example, you have brought in Internet Sales data by combining and merging data from files and you have merged the product tables into one table. To help support our analysis, the business has asked you to also bring in Customer and Customer demographic information. Follow these steps to prepare the Customer query:

1. If you are in the Query Editor, click **Home** tab > **New Query** group > **New Source** > **File** > **Excel**.

2. When the Import Data dialog box opens, browse to the location where you downloaded the Book Sample file and navigate to **\Chapter 1\Advanced Example 1\Customers. xlsx** and click **Import**.

3. In the Navigator dialog, choose the tblCustomers object and then Click **OK**.

4. In the Query Editor, rename the newly imported query to Customers.

5. Now you want to bring in some additional Demographic information to the customer query from the AdventureWorks database. Connect to the SQL Server where your AdventureWorks2016 is located and configure the SQL Server Database connection as in Figure 1-77. Note that since we are writing a SQL query, we must supply a Database name. The SQL statement is shown in Listing 1-16. Once done Click OK.

6. Click OK on the next screen, which is a preview of the data that will be returned query. This will bring you back to the Query Editor.

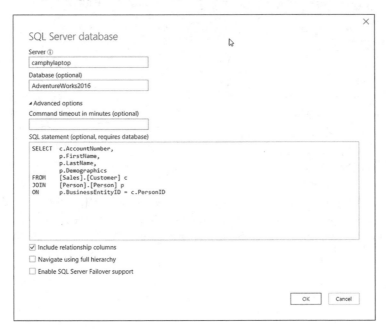

FIGURE 1-77 SQL Server Configuration dialog

LISTING 1-16 SQL Code to obtain the extended demographics information

```
SELECT    c.AccountNumber,
     p.FirstName,
     p.LastName,
     p.Demographics
FROM    [Sales].[Customer] c
```

```
JOIN    [Person].[Person] p
ON      p.BusinessEntityID = c.PersonIDRename the new query to CustomerDemographics
```

7. In the Data preview pane, highlight the demographics column in your new query. Notice that the data in the column is XML data. You want to parse this out by going to the **Transform** tab > **Text Column** group > Parse, and click the **XML** command. You can see that the XML is transformed into a table as in Figure 1-78. Also, the M code is shown in Listing 1-17.

FIGURE 1-78 XML Transformed to Table dialog

LISTING 1-17 SQL Code to obtain the extended demographics information

```
= Table.TransformColumns(Source,{{"Demographics", Xml.Tables}})
```

8. Click the Expand table icon in Figure 1-78 to display the attributes that are in the XML string. You might only see a few values in the dialog, so it might be necessary to click Load More to see all attributes.

9. In the dialog, choose the TotalPurchaseYTD column and do not check Use original column name as prefix. Click OK when you are done. Listing 1-18 shows the M code that is generated by this step.

LISTING 1-18 Table Expand XML code

```
= Table.ExpandTableColumn(#"Parsed XML", "Demographics", {"TotalPurchaseYTD"},
{"TotalPurchaseYTD"})
```

10. Change the data type to Currency.

11. Next, Merge this piece of data to the Customers query using the steps described earlier in the Merge section. Highlight on the Customers query and choose **Home** tab, **Combine** group, and click **Merge Queries**.

12. In the Merge dialog box, ensure that Customers is the top table and then choose CustomerDemographics as the second table. Choose Left Outer Join Between CustomerKey in the Customers Query and AccountKey in the CustomerDemographics Query. Click **OK**.

13. Once you do this, you may be presented with Figure 1-79, which is asking you to configure Privacy levels between the sources. For both, choose **Private** and Click **Save**.

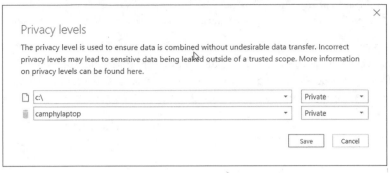

Privacy levels

The privacy level is used to ensure data is combined without undesirable data transfer. Incorrect privacy levels may lead to sensitive data being leaked outside of a trusted scope. More information on privacy levels can be found here.

| c:\ | Private |
| camphylaptop | Private |

Save   Cancel

FIGURE 1-79 Privacy level settings dialog

14. In the CustomerDemographics column at the end of the Customers query, expand the table and choose the TotalPurchaseYTD column, and deselect Use original column name as prefix. Click **OK** when you are done.

15. We now have the TotalPurchaseYTD demographic information in the Customers query.

The last table that you need to bring into the model is Sales Territories. As you can see, this table contains a hierarchy that is embedded into one field. Take this column and use the Split function to create fields for each level of the hierarchy, then capitalize the top level of the hierarchy per a business requirement.

1. If you are in the Query Editor, Click **Home** > **New Query** > **New Source** > **File** > **Excel**.

2. When the Import Data dialog box opens, browse to the location where you downloaded the Book Sample file and navigate to **\Chapter 1\Advanced Example 1\Sales Territories**. xlsx and click **Import**.

3. In the Navigator dialog, choose the tblSalesTerritories object and then Click **OK** to bring it into the Query Editor.

4. Rename the query to SalesTerritories.

5. Highlight on the SalesTerritoryRollup column and then in the Transform tab, Text Column grouping click Split Column by Delimiter. Note that you have the option to also Split by characters if your field had that requirement. If you use the Split function from the Transform tab, the original column is replaced when you are complete. Configure the following options and Click OK when don2e. Listing 1-19 contains the M code for the Split.

   - **Select Or Enter Delimiter** You have the option of choose common delimiters such as columns, tabs, and spaces or entering a Custom delimiter like the one in this example. Type the pipe symbol | as your custom delimiter.

   - **Split At** You can choose Left-Most Delimiter, Right-Most Delimiter, or Each Occurrence Of The Delimiter. Select Each Occurrence Of The Delimiter.

   - **Split Into** Your options are Columns or Rows; choose Columns.

- **Number of columns to split into** You can choose how many columns that you want your data Split into. In our example, type **3**.

- **Quote Character** Choose the quote character to detect. Leave the default setting.

- **Split using special characters** Available if your Split requires special characters.

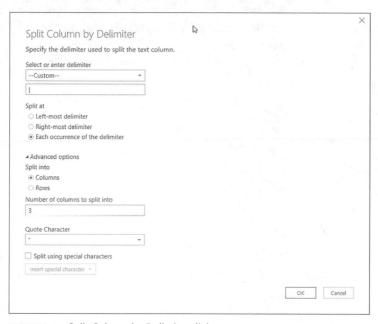

FIGURE 1-80 Split Column by Delimiter dialog

LISTING 1-19 Split M code

```
= Table.SplitColumn(#"Changed Type", "SalesTerritoryRollup",
 Splitter.SplitTextByDelimiter("|", QuoteStyle.Csv), {"SalesTerritoryRollup.1",
 "SalesTerritoryRollup.2", "SalesTerritoryRollup.3"})
```

6. You should now see **three** columns in the Data preview pane. Rename each as described below:

- **SalesTerritoryRollup.1** to Territory

- **SalesTerritoryRollup.2** to Country

- **SalesTerritoryRollup.3** to Continent

7. Now capitalize the Continent column. Highlight the Continent field, right-click, and choose **Transform** > **Uppercase** from the context menu. The M code for this step is shown in Listing 1-20.

LISTING 1-20 UPPERCASE transform M code

```
= Table.TransformColumns(#"Renamed Columns",{{"Continent", Text.Upper}})
```

Now that you have a model that is complete and ready for consumption, it is time for you to load the data into to the Data Model.

1. First you should categorize the objects in Queries pane. In this example, you create a group for queries that are eventually output to the Data Model, and one for objects that are used only in the Transformation process that will never be exposed to the end users. Create the Groups and move the objects to the Groups as shown and in Figure 1-81.

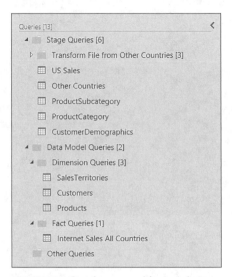

FIGURE 1-81 Queries pane with groupings

2. Once you have done this, close the Query Editor and then in Excel, ensure that the Queries and Connections pane is open as in Figure 1-82. On each of SalesTerritories > Customers > Products and Internet Sales All Countries, right-click and choose Load To. In the Import Data dialog box, check the Add This Data To The Data Model option. These tables are in the Excel Data Model, which is covered more in Skill 2.1 from Chapter 2.

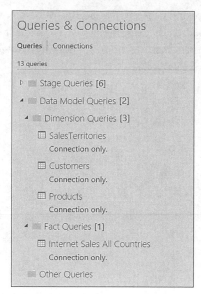

FIGURE 1-82 Queries & Connections

Some other items worth discussing that fall into the category of Query management are Data Source Settings, Manage Queries, and Recent Sources.

To Manage Data Source Settings, from the Query Editor go to the Home tab, Data source, and click Data Source Settings to open the dialog where you can choose **Manage Data Source Credentials** > **Privacy Levels** > and change the source as in Figure 1-83.

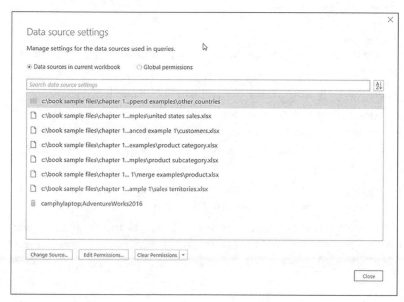

FIGURE 1-83 Data source settings

To change the source, highlight the first data source and click Change Source. When moving the source, you are presented with the same dialog box that you initially configured when connecting to your source. Remember that the structures after the initial configuration need to remain the same or your subsequent query steps will likely fail.

To manage Credentials and Privacy levels, Click **Edit Permissions** to be presented with the dialog shown in Figure 1-84.

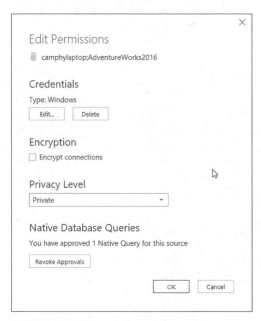

FIGURE 1-84 Edit Permissions dialog

To Manage queries, go to the **Query Editor** at **Home** > **Query** > **Manage**. You can perform the following three commands:

- **Delete**   Does as advertised and deletes the object if it has no dependencies.
- **Reference**   This option creates a new Query that references the query you want. The new query is created with a source step that calls the referenced query. This is useful when you have repetitive logic that needs to be applied to many queries that you want to write once and refer to many times.
- **Duplicate**   This option creates a distinct copy of the query you want to copy and after the duplication process it's completely disconnected from the original.

Recent Sources can be managed in the Query Editor as well. To do this, click the Home tab, New Query, and click on Recent Sources, which shows the connection information for sources that you have connected to. It can help speed up the process of connecting to data sources that you have already connected to.

Apply business rules

Now, let's examine some of the functions that are available for applying business rules to your data. Often in operational systems, data is entered without following appropriate business rules. It is then up to the data-shaping process to apply those business rules so analysis can be performed. This typically involves using functions within your data-shaping steps that enable you to provide more complex logic.

Columns from examples

Columns from examples is a user-friendly method for building new columns from existing ones. Power Query attempts to recognize the pattern that you are entering, trying to extract text according to your pattern. It is modeled after Flash Fill in Excel. Try to use this to extract the username from the part of the email address before the @ symbol:

1. Go to the Customers query and highlight on the EmailAddress column.

2. Then go to **Add Column** tab, **General** group, **Columns From Examples** > **From Selection**, as shown in Figure 1-85. The last column initially starts blank. In that column, you begin to type the pattern that you want to find in the Email Address column and the detection process begins. If you type jon24 in the first row and then press Enter, Power Query determines that the Text before delimiter function should be applied to the column. If this is what you need, Click **OK** to complete.

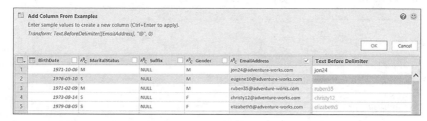

FIGURE 1-85 Add Column from example

Invoke custom function

To invoke a custom function, you first need to create one. You are going to create a function that takes the EngishCountryRegionName and passes out the ISO-ALPHA-3 value. Follow these steps to create the function and invoke it:

1. If you are in the Query Editor go to the **Home tab** > **New Query** > **New Source** > **Other Sources** > **Blank Query**. This creates a blank query in the Other Queries Group as shown in Figure 1-86.

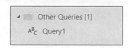

FIGURE 1-86 Screenshot of new Blank Query

2. Rename the new query from Query1 to ConvertCountryNameToISO-ALPHA-3.

3. With the query still selected in the Queries pane, go to the Home tab and click the Advanced Editor.

4. Using Widows File Explorer, navigate to where you downloaded the Book Sample files and **Open \Chapter 1\Function\ConvertCountryNameToISO-ALPHA-3.txt** using your favorite text editor.

5. In the Advanced Editor, delete any existing code, then cut and paste the code from the text file to the Advanced Editor.

6. With the **ConvertCountryNameToISO-ALPHA-3** function highlighted, test it by entering the parameter value of **Canada** in the **Input** text box. Click **Invoke** and the output should be **CAN**. Note that this is case-sensitive, so you need to handle this when invoking the function.

7. Now invoke the custom function by opening the **InternetSalesAllCountries** query and click **Add Column** tab > **General** group > **Invoke Custom Function**. Configure the dialog as shown in Figure 1-87 and below. Click **OK** and then verify that the new column is added.

   - **New column name**   EnglishCountryRegionISO3Code
   - **Function query**   ConvertCountryNameToISO-ALPHA-3
   - **Input (optional)**   EnglishCountryRegionName

FIGURE 1-87 Invoke Custom Function dialog

Conditional Column

A Conditional Column operates as an IF statement. A new column is created in the query based on one or more conditional expressions you define within the Add Conditional Column dialog box.

In this example, create a new column based on the customer's yearly income. Place them into four categories: student, low income, middle income, and high income. This information can be used to help target marketing promotions as well as with customer profiling.

Follow these steps:

1. Select the **YearlyIncome** column in the **Customer** query.

2. Select **Add Column** tab > **General** group > **Conditional Column**.

3. In the **Add Conditional Column** dialog box, enter **Income Category** as the **New Column Name** and configure the values as in Figure 1-88.

4. Click **OK** when complete.

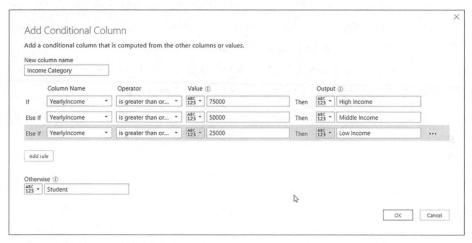

FIGURE 1-88 Add Conditional Column dialog

Index Column

An Index column can be added to a table for many purposes. There are three options for creating an Index column:

- **From 0**   Creates an index that starts at 0 and increments by 1
- **From 1**   Creates an index that starts at 1 and increments by 1
- **Custom**   Allows you to choose the start and increment values

Change data format to support visualization

One of the jobs of the person performing data shaping is to shape the data in a manner that makes building visualizations as easy as possible. The target state of any data set is that is to set it up so that consumers can simply drag and drop values from the Excel data model into PivotCharts or PivotTables for analysis. If users find themselves having to perform transformations when they are building visualizations, these situations are normally candidates for pushing back into the data-shaping layer, especially if they are often-used fields for display or filtering.

Group By

A common task for visualizations is to provide pre-aggregated data. In this example, you take the InternetSalesAllCountries and create a new query that Aggregates Sales Amount by Year and Country. Follow these steps to perform this:

1. Highlight the **Internet Sale All Countries** query.

2. Right-click on it and select **Reference** from the context menu. This allows you to take advantage of the effort put into creating **Internet Sales All Countries**.

3. A new query is created with a single step that refers to Internet Sales All Countries.

4. Rename the query **Internet Sales By Year And Country**.

5. From the Home tab go to **Transform** group and choose **Group By**.

6. Configure the **Group By** as in Figure 1-89 and then click **OK**.

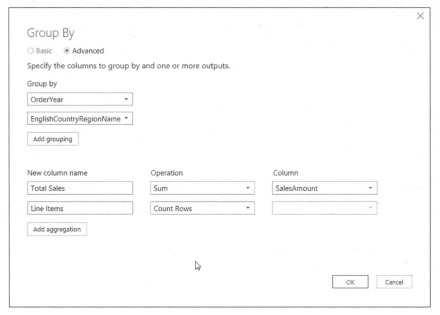

FIGURE 1-89 Group By dialog

Filter data

One of the often-overlooked simple performance tuning mechanisms in any data analysis tool is to only bring in the data that is necessary to support the analytics at hand. Ultimately you want to build flexible solutions that can handle the next question that is asked of it—building flexible and performant applications is your job as the person building these solutions for your organization.

Text Filters

If you have a text-based field highlighted, in the Data preview pane you can select the drop-down that presents you with the filtering criteria for the data type that has focus. Figure 1-90 has the drop-down on the field highlighted.

FIGURE 1-90 Filter selector location

FIGURE 1-91 Text Filters

Numeric Filters

If you have a numeric-based field highlighted, from the Data preview pane you can select the drop-down that presents you with the filtering criteria for the data type that has the focus.

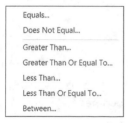

FIGURE 1-92 Numeric Filters

Date Filters

If you have a date-based field highlighted, from the Data preview pane you can select the drop-down that presents you with the filtering criteria for the data type that has focus. There are many available Date filters.

FIGURE 1-93 Date Filters

> ***NEED MORE REVIEW?* DATA TYPE FILTERS**
>
> For more review on the usage of data type filters, see *https://support.office.com/en-us/article/Filter-a-table-Power-Query-b5610630-f5bf-4ba4-9217-a628f9b89353*.

Parameters

One way to limit the data that is brought in for analysis is to take advantage of Parameters. In this example, you restrict the years that are brought into the Internet Sales All Countries query. Follow these steps to parameterize the value:

1. **Home** > **Parameters** > **Manage Parameters** > **New Parameter**.

2. Configure the values as in Figure 1-94 and then **Click OK**.

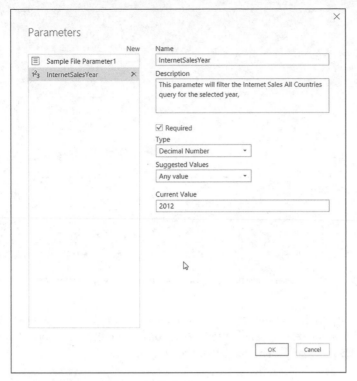

FIGURE 1-94 Manage Parameters dialog

3. You should now see a parameter in the Queries pane that has been created with the name InternetSalesYear and with "2012" in parentheses, which denotes the current parameter value.

FIGURE 1-95 Parameter with its current value

4. Now use the filter to restrict the OrderYear in Internet Sales All Countries. In the Data preview pane, click the drop-down box next to the OrderYear column title to view the context menu. Now choose **Number Filters** > **Equals** to get the Filter Rows dialog box shown in Figure 1-96. Choose Equals and ensure that you choose a parameter from the second drop-down box, then select the InternetSalesYear parameter. Click **OK** when done and observe that the Internet Sales query now only contains data for the year set in the parameter. The generated M code is shown in Listing 1-21.

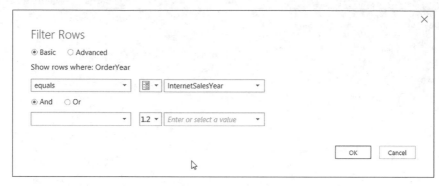

FIGURE 1-96 Filter Rows dialog

LISTING 1-21 Filter Rows with Parameter M code

```
= Table.SelectRows(#"Changed Type", each [OrderYear] = InternetSalesYear)
```

Now enhance the parameter by making the user choose from a list versus hardcoding values.

1. To make this modification, Click Manage Parameters and configure the Parameter values for InternetSalesYear as shown in Figure 1-97. Be sure that in the dialog box that you have the **InternetSalesYear** parameter highlighted on the left.

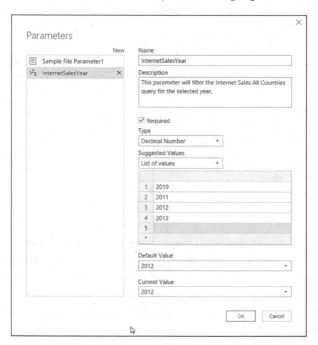

FIGURE 1-97 Manage Parameters dialog

2. Now the values for the parameter are restricted to the list of values you provided. To verify, observe the data in the **Internet Sales All Countries** query.

   Lastly, make one more change that drives the parameter values from a dynamic list rather than a hardcoded one as you just did.

1. First, you need to create a list of values by making a list. To do this, duplicate the **Internet Sales All Countries** query. Highlight the **Internet Sales All Countries** query, right-click on it and select **Duplicate** from the context menu.

2. Rename the query to **ListValidYears**.

3. Remove the **Filtered Rows** step from **Applied Steps** in the **Internet Sales All Countries** query.

4. In the **ListValidYears** query, highlight the **OrderYear** column.

5. Then in the **Transform** tab > **Any Column** group > choose **Convert To List**.

6. Now you have a new tools tab named **List Tools**. From here, select **Transform** > **Manage Items** > **Remove Duplicates**, which gives you a list of years that are valid for that dataset.

7. Open the **Manage Parameters** dialog and change the **Suggested Values** to **Query** and the Query drop-down to **ListValidYears**.

Format data

Data often needs to be formatted for final presentation. The format functions can be found in the both the **Transform** and **Add Columns** tabs, in the **From Text** grouping.

- **Lowercase**   Returns the lowercase of a text value.
- **Uppercase**   Returns the uppercase of a text value.
- **Capitalize Each Word**   Returns a text value with first letters of all words converted to uppercase.
- **Trim**   Removes any occurrence of spaces at the beginning or end of a string.
- **Clean**   Returns the original text value with non-printable characters removed.
- **Add Prefix**   Adds a prefix to the text you are working with.
- **Add Suffix**   Adds a suffix to the text you are working with.

Skill 1.3: Cleanse data

When performing analysis, it is important to first ensure that you are working with data that is fit for this purpose. This involves taking any necessary steps to improve the quality of data before using it. Data cleansing, as it is commonly known, is the process of detecting and correcting or removing data from a data set, before use, if it not fit for purpose. It is very common for data values to be missing, incomplete, or inaccurate.

It is often up to you as the analyst to make the determination as to when data does not fit your needs and to act. Fortunately, Power Query has a vast array of functions that allow you to clean data, manage incomplete data by replacing values, filling in missing values, keeping rows, removing rows and even invoking sophisticated functions that can be used to detect business rule violations within data fields.

In addition to managing data quality issues, Power Query can help to clean up data that is delivered to you in the form of reports that often need some cleanup prior to you getting at the data that is contained within them.

> **This section covers how to:**
> - Manage incomplete data
> - Handle data received as a report

Manage incomplete data

In this example, extract competitor sales data from a table in an Excel spreadsheet that has missing data and an incorrect header. You also need to replace from data in one of the cells with text that makes more sense for the users when they are performing analysis as someone clearly made some personal comments in one of the fields.

Follow these steps to cleanse this data:

1. From within in Excel, navigate to **Data > Get & Transform Data > Get Data > From File > From Workbook**.

2. In the Import File dialog box, navigate to **\Chapter 1\Excel\Manage incomplete data. xlsx** and click **Open**.

3. In the Navigator, choose **tblCompetitorSales** and then click **Edit**. When you move to the Query Editor, your Data preview pane should look like Figure 1-98. Notice that the header is not correct and that Power Query was not able to determine data types for two of the columns as denoted by the Any data type icon **ABC123**.

	ABC123 Column1	AB_C Column2	ABC123 Column3
1	OrderYear	EnglishCountryRegionName	Total Sales
2	2010	Australia (look bob)	899120.54
3	null	Canada (look bob)	221852.74
4	null	France (look bob)	37399.89
5	null	United Kingdom (look bob)	18176.5532
6	null	United States (look bob)	44501.6946
7	2011	Australia (look bob)	215353508.9
8	null	Canada (look bob)	57157179.84

FIGURE 1-98 Data preview pane

4. The first activity to perform is to Promote Headers since the items in **Row 1** appear to be your headers. To do this, go to the **Transform** tab > **Use First Row As Headers**.

5. Change the Data Type for **OrderYear** to **Whole Number** and **Total Sales** to **Currency**.

6. Next, it appears the **Year** columns should repeat itself until the data in the rows moves to the next year. To do this, ensure the **OrderYear** has focus and go to the **Transform** tab, **Any Column** group, **Fill Down**. Notice that there is also an option to **Fill Up** should the use case arise.

7. Now let's get rid of the portion of the text that says (look bob) in the **EnglishCountryRegionName** field. Go to the **Transform** tab > **Any Column** group > **Replace Values**. When the dialog box opens, ensure to **Value To Find** is "(look bob)" without the quotes and the **Replace With** is an empty string. (Do not put anything in the box.)

8. Now we should ensure that the **EnglishCountryRegionName** has no blank characters at the beginning or end of each value. Highlight the column and go to the **Transform** tab > **Text Column** group > **Format** > **Trim**.

9. And finally Rename the query from **tblCompetitorSales** to **CompetitorSales**.

10. Once you are done, be sure to review the M code generated by these steps.

Handle data received as a report

Often when you are asked to perform analysis, it can be hard to find a data source to support it that comes in the traditional rows and columns format. Sometimes the best way to get the data is to have someone just run a report for you and then to perform the work of cleaning things up so that you can get at the data it contains.

Unpivot data

In this example, take a report that has been made available to you and perform the steps to make the data ready for analysis.

Follow these steps to cleanse this data:

1. From Excel, navigate to **Home** > **Get Data** > **From File** > **From Workbook**.

2. In the Import File dialog box, navigate to **\Chapter 1\Advanced Example 3\Pivot Examples\Product Category Sales By Year and Month Pivot Report.xlsx** and click **Open**.

3. In the object **Navigator,** choose **Sheet 2** and then click **Edit**. When you move to the Query Editor, your Data preview pane should look like Figure 1-99.

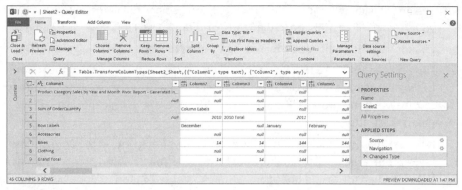

FIGURE 1-99 Data preview pane with initial data load

4. First, you need to remove the rows at the top of the report. To do this, go to the **Home** tab > **Reduce Rows** group > **Remove Top Rows.** When the Remove Top Rows dialog box opens, choose **2** as the number of rows.

5. Next, you need to Transpose the table. Click **Transform** tab > **Table** group > **Transpose.**

6. Now Remove the column named **Column1.**

7. Fill down **Column2 by** clicking the **Transform** tab > **Any Column** group > **Fill Down.**

8. Promote the first row to Headers since the items in Row 1 now appear to be your headers. To do this, choose the **Transform** tab > **Use First Row As Headers**.

9. Now, you need to remove the totals rows in **Column1** (notice that the Column1 name is now back, even though it is not the same column) by filtering. You can do this by manually selecting the values, but this would not be flexible going forward. To be more dynamic, you first need convert the data type of **Column1** to **Text** so that you can take advantage of a wider range of filtering options as the Any data type only has a few options for filtering.

10. You are now ready to filter the rows out. Right-click **Column1** and in the context menu, navigate to the **Text Filter** option, and in the sub-menu, choose **Does Not Contain**.

11. In the dialog box, type **Total**.

12. The goal of this step is to take the values in each of the categories and unpivot them into one row per Year, Month and Category. To do this, ensure that **Column1** and **Row Labels** are selected in the Data preview pane. Now select the **Transform** tab > **Any Column** group > **Unpivot Other Columns**.

13. Rename the columns and change the data types as below:

   - **Column1**   Name=Year and Data Type=Whole Number
   - **Row Labels**   Name=Months and Data Type=Text
   - **Attribute**   Name=Product Category, Data Type=Text
   - **Values**   Name=Sales, Data Type=Currency

14. Filter out the Grand Total column by clicking the drop-down box next to the **Product-Category** field name > select **Text Filters** > **Does Not Equal**. When the dialog box opens, type **Grand Total**.

15. Rename the query from **Sheet2** to **UnpivotExample**.

16. Save your work by going to **Home** tab > **Close** group > **Close & Load**.

17. In the Import Data dialog, choose to **Only Create the Connection** and check the **Add This Data To The Data Model** check box.

Pivot data

Now suppose that you want to Pivot a data set.

Follow these steps to Pivot your dataset:

1. In the Queries pane, click on the **UnpivotExample** query, then right-click and choose **Reference** from the context menu.

2. Rename the new query from **UnpivotExample (2)** to **PivotExample**.

3. The goal of this step is to move the Product Category values and move them into column headers with their associated values below. In the Data preview pane of the new query, highlight the **Product Category** field. Now click the **Transform** tab > **Any Column** group > **Pivot Column**.

4. In the dialog box that opens, choose **Sales** as the **Values Column** and select **Sum** as the Aggregate Value Function in the **Advanced** tab. Once you are done, Click **OK**.

5. In each of the three resulting columns, Replace the null with the number 0, since this is what this analysis requires.

1^2_3 Year	A^B_C Month	$ Bikes	$ Accessories	$ Clothing
10	2011	May	174	0	0
11	2011	November	208	0	0
12	2011	October	221	0	0
13	2011	September	185	0	0
14	2012	April	219	0	0
15	2012	August	294	0	0
16	2012	December	355	106	22
17	2012	February	260	0	0

FIGURE 1-100 Data preview Snippet from end of last exercise

Thought experiment

In this thought experiment, apply what you've learned in this chapter. Each Thought experiment is directly followed by a Thought experiment answer.

1. When loading data into your model you use the Query Editor and you select Load To. You are asked to select how you would like to view this data in your worksheet. Which selection will not load the data to a traditional Excel object?

A. Create Connection Only

B. Table

C. PivotTable Report

D. PivotChart

2. The marketing department has asked you to perform some analysis of 2017 sales. They have given you access to their Azure SQL Database which contains 1.2 million rows. What options do you have for importing this data into Excel knowing that they want to analyze all the data?

3. In which version of Excel was the Excel Data Model introduced? What was it originally called?

4. How many data models can a workbook have?

5. Name the four valid text file formats that you can find in Get & Transform.

6. If you want to be able to choose related tables when connecting to a SQL Server Database, what two things need to be in place for the related tables functionality work?

7. When you create a connection to an external data source such as an Analysis Services Database, where is connection information stored?

A. Office XML (.oml File)

B. Office Data Connection File (.odc)

C. ODATA File

D. ODBC

8. Which Data Source in Get & Transform Data allows you to connect to live data?

A. Analysis Service Tabular

B. Analysis Services Multi-Dimensional

C. Text Files

D. Web Page

9. When ingesting files using the From Folder or From SharePoint Folder, what characters must the files share?

10. What is Query Folding?

11. Which two ways can be used to reduce the number of rows in a data set?

A. Filter Functions

B. Remove Columns

C. Parameters

D. Extract

12. What is the difference between the Extract Power Query Function that exists on the Transform tab versus the Add Column tab?

Thought experiment answers

1. Answer **A**: Create Connection Only creates a connection to the source only. Data is not loaded to a Table, PivotTable Report, or PivotChart, but you do have the option of loading the data to the Excel Data Model.

2. The question said that the data is imported into Excel. Given this, the Excel Data Model is your only option as traditional Excel spreadsheets have a 1,048,576-row limit.

3. The Data Model was first introduced into Excel 2010 as PowerPivot. The two terms are still used interchangeably.

4. Each Excel workbook may only have one data model

5. Text, CSV, JSON, and XML.

6. First, the database must have referential integrity in place, and second you need to include relationship columns in the SQL Server Database connection configuration window.

7. Answer **B**: Office Data Connection File.

8. Answers **A** and **B**: Analysis Service Tabular and Dimensional.

9. The files all must share the same structure.

10. Query folding is when Power Query converts its transformations in the Native query language of the data source.

11. Answers **A** and **C**: Filter Functions and Parameters. Remove columns does not remove rows, and Extract is used to remove portions of text fields.

12. Like many functions, it is important to know the context in which you are using it. If you have chosen a column as the subject of an Extract, know that if you do this from the Add Column tab that a new column with the extracted value is created. If you do this from the Transform tab the column value is replaced with the newly extracted value.

Chapter summary

- A Data Model is used to integrate data from multiple sources into one or more tables inside an Excel workbook. Tables are then related so that Data Models can be used to provide tabular data that can be used by PivotTables, PivotCharts, and Power View reports.

- When importing data using a SQL database, you can optionally choose to write a native query instead of selecting object by object. This can be convenient when complex queries have already been written that you can reuse.

- When importing data from text files, Power Query tries to determine the File Locale, Delimiters also try to detect data types for each column.

- Excel can connect to the following Azure sources which commonly store data that can be used in Analysis, Azure SQL Server, SQL Data Warehouse, Data Lake Store, HDInsight, and BLOB and Table Storage.

- Privacy Levels are used to Isolate Data sets from each other.

- M is a functional case sensitive language that used to manage the data shaping process in Power Query. It is generated by the GUI are as you perform transformation and cleansing tasks. M code can be viewed in the Formula Bar or through the Advanced Editor.

- When creating Applied Steps, you can add step name of your choosing and a description through the Step Properties dialog.

- You can create columns from example tries to identify patterns in your data as supplied by you to accelerate the M code writing process.

- You can create custom functions in M and then call them row by row using the Invoke Custom Function call.

- Data for reporting can be formatted using Format functions such as Uppercase, Lowercase, Capitalize Each Word, Add Prefix/Suffix, Trim, and Clean.

- The Extract functions allow you to remove certain portions of text fields.

- If a column contains XML or JSON, you can use Parse XML or JSON to expand values.

- Query Dependencies is useful for viewing how your queries relate to each other. This is especially important as solutions grow.

- The Folder data source is useful way to combine one or many files from a directory if they all share the same structures.

- The Group By function can be used to aggregate data sets for use in the data shaping process or for consumption in the data model.

- Filters are used to remove entire rows that do not meet a specified criterion. Filters are specific to each data type in M. The most commonly used Filters are for Text, Number, and Date.

- Parameters are useful for enabling filtering of data in Power Query. Parameters can come from ad-hoc manual entry, a list of values as set-up in parameter management, or they can come from a query.

- Power Query has mechanisms to easily Pivot and Unpivot data sets.

CHAPTER 2

Model data

Data modeling is one of the most important, yet often overlooked, tasks that needs to be undertaken when building any analytical solution or using any tool. How a model is designed from the ground up is one of the largest contributing factors to driving usability and ultimately adoption from an end-user community. The more intuitive a model is, the greater the likelihood that the model will be used—and will be used correctly and predictably by your users. The focus of this chapter is to review the methods used to create a data model that not only performs well but is easy to understand and use from an end-user perspective. In this chapter, we look at creating an Excel data model and then iteratively enhancing the model to promote ease of self-service while considering how to make it perform.

Skills in this chapter:

- Skill 2.1: Create and optimize data models
- Skill 2.2: Create calculated columns, measures, and tables
- Skill 2.3: Create hierarchies
- Skill 2.4: Create performance KPIs

Skill 2.1: Create and optimize data models

In Chapter 1, "Consume and transform data by using Microsoft Excel," you reviewed how to load shaped and cleansed data to the data model. The discussion at that point revolved around how to take the work that you performed in the data-shaping process and make it available for end-user consumption. Recall that you can take data from the shaping process and import it into traditional Excel objects or the Excel data model. The focus of this skill is continuing the discussion of building and enhancing the data model so that it is production-ready. The act of performing the load is just the first step in this process. Once data is loaded, you need to determine how data is related and then create and manage those relationships. Managing relationships is an important part of modeling because it is the process that enables you to bring your data together in a meaningful manner. While doing this, you should always be planning to optimize your models for reporting, as most models tend to grow in breadth and depth over time. In practice, this is a highly iterative process, as you will cycle back and forth between the topics in the three chapters of this book as you continually refine models for end-user consumption.

This section covers how to:

- Understand the Excel data model
- Perform get & transform
- Manually enter data
- Create automatic relationships
- Create manual relationships
- Manage data relationships
- Optimize models for reporting

Understanding the Excel data model

Before you dive into the data model itself, it is a good idea to take a tour of the Power Pivot interface where you will spend the most time working with the data model. As a note, through-out this book and online you will hear the data model and Power Pivot used interchangeably. Figure 2-1 shows the Data View screen, which is the default screen you see when you navigate to the data model from within Excel. Each numbered callout bubble in the Figure maps to a description in the numbered list immediately below the Figure. When you get to the Skill on relationships, the Diagram View will be described as the main location to Manage Relationships in your model.

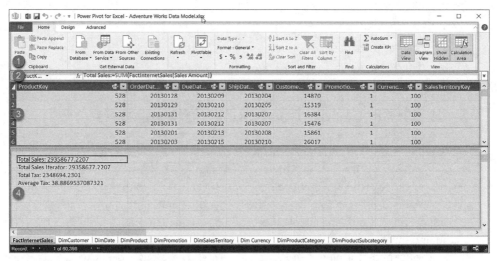

FIGURE 2-1 The Power Pivot Data View screen

1. **Ribbon** The ribbon is where you will find the many commands you will use to enhance the data model. This includes bringing data in, optimizing the model for reporting, adding DAX functions, managing hierarchies, and so on. Scroll through each of the tabs to look at the various functions that are available. Each of these will be covered in the remainder of this chapter and in Chapter 3 "Visualize data."

2. **Formula Bar**   The Formula Bar is used to add and manage DAX formulas for calculated columns and measures.

3. **Data View**   The Data View provides a preview of the data that is loaded into the data model. Column headers that have been brought from a source or through the Query Editor are colored green, and any new DAX-calculated columns that you create will have a black column header. The calculation area can be toggled on and off in the ribbon by navigating to **Home** tab, **View** group, and clicking either the **Data View** or **Diagram View** commands (only one of these two views can be open at a time).

4. **Calculation Area**   The Calculation Area is where measures—both explicit and implicit—are located. As you will see when you create a measure, you create it in the context of a table which is its home table, used mainly for organizing measures logically. In practice, you can create a measure in the calculation pane of any table; how it is calculated will not change. The Calculation Area can be toggled on and off in the ribbon by navigating to **Home** tab > **View** group >and clicking the **Calculation Area** to show or hide it, depending on its current visibility.

As was touched upon in Skill 1.1 "Import from data sources," the Excel data model first appeared in Excel 2010 as a separate add-in called Power Pivot. The data model could be used indirectly (and still can be) even though a user might not have enabled the add-in, as Excel attempts to nudge users toward more optimal storage means. You can see this behavior if you try to create a PivotTable using multiple Excel tables. Excel will notify you that to use multiple tables in your Analysis, a new PivotTable needs to be created using the data model.

With the advent of the data model, Excel now has two distinct places where data can be stored. It can either be stored in native Excel objects such as tables, ranges or sheets; or within the Excel data model. Traditional users of Excel will be very familiar with loading data in traditional objects, as this has been the sole way to store data for many years.

So, what is the data model from a technical perspective? Effectively, the data model is the Analysis Service tabular engine running inside of Excel, which is also referred to as the xVelocity Engine. It is also a distinct storage structure from Excel, and you need to keep that in mind when performing work.

Advantages of the data model

Knowing this is great, but it does not address some of the advantages of using the data model over traditional means. Some of the major advantages are:

- **Overcomes Excel's row limit**   Native Excel only allows for 1,048,576 rows of data. Most modern analysis goes well past this limit, and users typically had to aggregate data to fit under this limit. The side effect of this was that the manipulated data often became less useful as more and more questions were asked.

- **Data compression via columnar database structure**   Data is stored in columns versus rows as in a traditional database management system. Keep in mind that it is still displayed as rows and columns in the Data View. The advantage of columns-based storage is that in most analytic situations, users are interested in a few columns of data for reports. This storage method leads to highly compressed models and supports fast queries.

- **In memory**   The model is loaded and compressed into memory which enables very fast query response times over large data sets.
- **Promotes centralization of logic**   As you will see in the section on optimizing models for reporting in this chapter, the data model helps to promote centralization of business logic and provides a central means to optimize reporting that all downstream reports can share.

Composition of the data model

There are many other benefits of the data model that are described briefly below. Each of these benefits maps to a component of the data model, and with that, you need to understand what comprises the data model. A brief synopsis of the objects and each is discussed in detail through the remainder of this book.

- **Tables**   Data is stored in tables (do not confuse with Excel tables) within the model. These are columnar in nature and are loaded into memory.
- **Columns from source systems**   These are columns from source systems that have been brought in 1 for 1 or may have undergone shaping.
- **Calculated columns**   These are columns that have business logic built into them and are created using the DAX language. Keep in mind that these might have also gone through some steps that optimize the column for reporting, as will be discussed later in Skill 2.2 "Create calculated columns, measures, and tables."
- **Relationships**   These relate various tables together so that data can be retrieved from multiple tables when performing analytics. These are similar to VLOOKUPS, except that they are much more performant and flexible.
- **Measures**   These are aggregates of data that are defined via business logic. They are created using the DAX language. Keep in mind that these may have also gone through some steps that optimize the column for reporting, as will be discussed later in Skill 2.2.
- **Hierarchies**   These are structures that enable users to easily and consistently drill up and down within data structures.
- **KPIs**   Key performance indicators are visual measures of performance that are based on measures within the data model.
- **Perspectives**   Perspectives allow you to create custom views of data that you define for a user group or business scenario. This makes it easier to navigate large data sets as they can be sectioned to help provide focus.

Other data model facts

Below are a few other data model facts:

- **Power PivotTables are read-only**   Unlike Excel tables which are both read and write; Power Pivot data is not directly editable. If you need to edit data, you will either need to do this back at the source or have sources that you create to augment analysis that are under your control. You will see an example of this in the section titled "Manually Enter Data."

- **One data model per Excel workbook**   An Excel workbook can only have one data model.

- **A data model can contain one or many tables**   You are allowed more than two million tables, which should be more than enough for most needs.

Now that you have seen what the Excel data model is and why you would want to use it, you will now look at how to build out the components of a data model, populate the data model, and then consume it for reporting.

> **MORE INFO**   **DATA MODEL SPECIFICATION AND LIMITS**
>
> For more information regarding data model specifications and limits, read the following: *https://support.office.com/en-us/article/Data-Model-specification-and-limits-19aa79f8-e6e8-45a8-9be2-b58778fd68ef.*

Get & Transform

You spent the better part of Chapter 1 learning how to connect to various sources systems, choosing what data to extract, and then performing any necessary transformation and cleansing activities. Most of this was driven through the Get & Transform Data function. It is also possible to take data from external sources and load them into the data model using functionality within Power Pivot.

Loading data directly from Power Pivot using a new connection

There are several ways to get into the data model. With Excel open, you can go to the **Data** or **Power Pivot** tabs and follow one of these paths:

- **Data** tab > **Data Tools** group > **Manage Data Model**
- **Power Pivot** tab > **Data Model** group > **Manage**

Once you have followed one of these paths, you will be presented with a screen like the one in Figure 2-2.

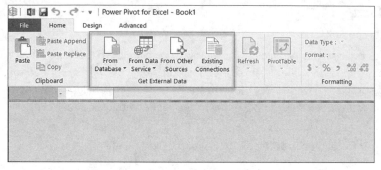

FIGURE 2-2 Power Pivot window highlighting the Import Data functions

You can see the following options as highlighted in Figure 2-2:

- From Database
- From Data Service
- From Other Sources
- Existing Connections

> **NOTE** **LOADING DATA VIA POWER PIVOT**
>
> Many of the import functions shown here have been replicated and enhanced in Get & Transform using the Query Editor, which has a much richer interface and capabilities. They are covered here because they potentially are subject to examination. For more information, see *https://support.office.com/en-us/article/Get-data-using-the-Power-Pivot-add-in-f0431904-aab1-49c3-b50c-c6f5d4517a66*.

Of the three options, the From Other Source covers all the available sources and presents them in one window as shown in Figure 2-3. You have the option to connect to data in one of these four categories:

- Relational databases
- Multidimensional sources
- Data feeds
- Text files

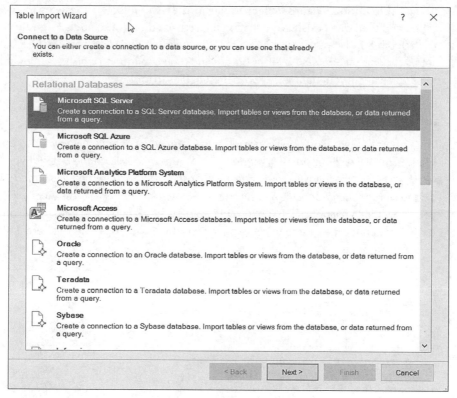

FIGURE 2-3 Table Import Wizard data source selection screen

In this example, you will Import from SQL Server database. You do this one table at a time so that you can see multiple ways to import data using SQL and how these impact connections.

1. Open a new workbook and then navigate to the data model.

2. Navigate to the **Home** tab > **Get External Data** group > **From Database** > **From Microsoft SQL Server** command as shown in Figure 2-3.

3. In the **Table Import Wizard–Connect To A Microsoft SQL Server Database** dialog box, configure the following and then click **Next** when complete.

   - **Friendly Connection Name**   Chapter 2 SQL Server Sample Connection.
   - **Server Name**   Your SQL Server Name.
   - **Log On To The Server**   Use the authentication method that your database uses.
   - **Database Name**   AdventureWorksDW2016.

4. In the **Table Import Wizard – Choose How To Import The Data** window, choose **Select From A List Of Tables And Views To Choose The Data To Import** and then click **Next**. Note that you can write a SQL Query should you have the expertise to do so by choosing **Write A Query That Will Specify The Data To Import**.

5. In the **Table Import Wizard–Select Tables And Views** window, choose the following tables and then click **Finish**. Note that on this screen you can also add a **Friendly Name** to each table you import and you also can filter columns and rows from the final data set by clicking the **Preview & Filter** button and then configuring which columns and rows you want in your data set. Choose these tables to import:

   ▪ **DimProduct**

   ▪ **FactInternetSales**

6. The Import process window will become active, and when complete you will see the **Table Import Wizard–Importing** window as in Figure 2-4. Click on the Details hyperlink which will show the following message: *Relationship: dbo.FactInternetSales[ProductKey] -> dbo.DimProduct[ProductKey] - Status: Success, Active - Status: Success, Active.* This lets you know that a relationship has been created between FactInternetSales and DimProduct and that it is active. More to come on this shortly. Click **Close** when you are done with this window.

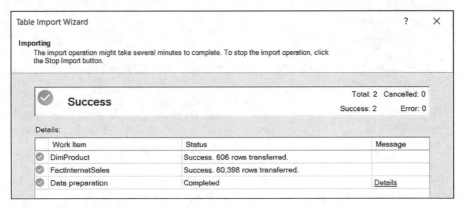

FIGURE 2-4 Import status window

7. Now navigate to **Home** tab > **View** group > **Diagram View** and in Figure 2-5, you will see the two imported tables and how they are related.

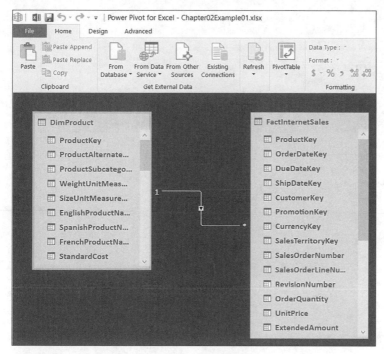

FIGURE 2-5 Diagram view for the two imported tables

8. **Save** this file with your book samples files as **\Chapter2\CH02Demo0102.xlsx** with your book sample files and keep it open for the next example.

Suppose that you now wanted to import the DimProductSubcategory and DimProductCategory tables because you realized that you forgot them in the previous step. You could repeat the same steps as before and only choose these two tables from the list of tables. If you did it this way, you would need to enter the same connection information again. The problem with this is that you now have multiple connections to the same database which becomes a maintenance challenge. If you use one connection and anything about that connection changes, you only need to change the configuration in one place.

In this example, you Import from SQL Server Database using an existing connection. We will bring in the DimProductSubcategory and DimProductCategory using the previous connection and file that by following these steps:

1. If not already done, open the **\Chapter2\CH02Demo0102.xlsx** you built in the previous example.

2. From within the data model, navigate to the **Home** tab > **Get External Data** > **Existing Connections**, and you will be presented with the **Existing Connections–Select An Existing Connection** dialog in Figure 2-6. You will notice that the Workbook has a connection to the database listed under **Workbook Connections**. Also, you have the **Power Pivot Data Connection** where you can not only edit the tables selected but the server connection information as well.

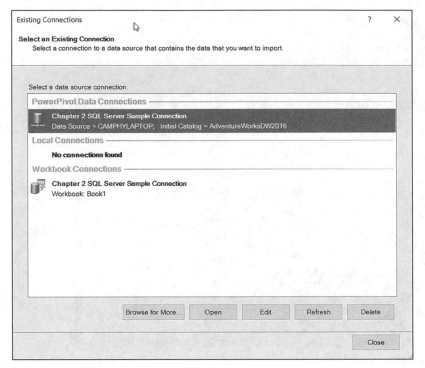

FIGURE 2-6 Existing Connections

3. With **Chapter 2 SQL Server Sample Connection** highlighted in the Power Pivot Data Connections section, you will notice the relevant options are:

   - **Refresh**   Click this to refresh all the data that is part of the connection.
   - **Edit**   This will allow you to edit the server connection details.
   - **Open**   You will be taken to the Table Import Wizard when you can add in and modify objects.
   - **Delete**   Delete the connection.

4. Click **Open**.

5. In the **Table Import Wizard – Choose How To Import The Data**, choose **Select** from a list of tables and views to choose the data to import and click **Next**.

6. In the **Table Import Wizard – Select Tables And Views** window, choose the **Dim-ProductSubcategory** and **DimProductCategory** tables and then click **Finish**. After the tables have been uploaded, click **Close**.

7. Now navigate to **Home** tab > **View** group > **Diagram View** and you will see that you have four tables in the model as in Figure 2-7.

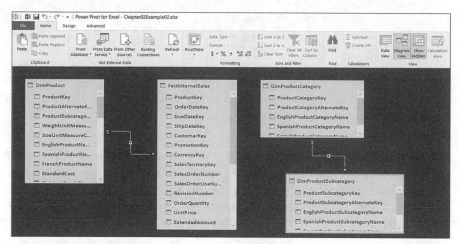

FIGURE 2-7 Data model with the four tables imported

8. **Save** your work and then close the workbook.

Manually enter data

As mentioned earlier, the data model is a read-only construct, unlike data that is stored in Excel objects. If you need to make your data editable, you will need to do that though Excel objects or back at the source.

Often you will be in situations in which there is no real source for data that you want to you in your analysis, so you will need to manually create one and perhaps maintain it in a spreadsheet. If the data is for the sole purpose of supporting analysis in your current workbook, you might want to look at storing the data in an Excel table inside the workbook that houses your data model.

In this example, you manually enter data into Excel tables and import them into the data model. Follow these steps to do this:

1. Open the **\Chapter2\CH02Demo03Start.xlsx** file, which is supplied in this book's sample files. Notice that on **Sheet1** of the workbook, there are two Excel tables named **Sales** and **SalesPerson**. Neither of these tables are in the data model. You can check this for yourself by navigating to the data model if you choose to do so.

2. Now let's add these tables to the data model. Highlight any **Cell** within the **Sales** Excel table and then click the **Power Pivot** tab, and from the **Tables** group, select **Add To Data Model**. After a moment, you will be taken to Power Pivot, and you will see that the Sales table has been added to the data model.

3. Do the same with the **SalesPerson** table. As a note, if these had not been set up as tables, you could have clicked **Add To Data Model**, and then you would have been prompted to **Choose A Range Of Data** so that you could create the table for Excel to add to the data model

4. The data model tables themselves are not editable, but in this scenario, you can edit the Excel tables. In the **SalesPerson** table, add a new row with the following values:

   - **SalesPersonID:** 3

   - **SalesPersonName:** Hernady, Robert

5. Go back into Power Pivot and click **Home** tab, **Refresh** to refresh the currently active table or **Refresh All** to refresh all tables.

6. Now that you have imported this data into the data model, let's look at the resultant connection information. In Excel, navigate to the **Data** tab, **Queries & Connections** group, and click **Queries & Connections** (see Figure 2-8). In this figure, notice that **ThisWorkbookDataModel** connection is created each time a data model is created. Also, you see the two workbook connections that you made from the Excel tables to the data model.

7. Now save the file using **Save As \Chapter2\CH02Demo03End.xlsx** and then close the workbook.

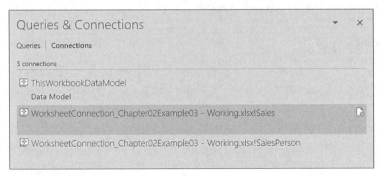

FIGURE 2-8 Queries & Connections pane

***NOTE* LINKED TABLES**

Linked tables in Power Pivot and the Excel data model have been replaced with refreshable tables. Previously, adding data to the data model using the above steps would create a linked table. Now Excel will create a refreshable table in the data model instead. Any existing linked tables in your model will be automatically converted to refreshable tables. For more information, see the following article at *https://support.office.com/en-us/article/Where-are-my-linked-tables-in-Power-Pivot-7356CF3C-1423-49FF-877E-6ABC6824D182.*

Manage data relationships

Moving from traditional Excel methods for data preparation and modeling to the new methods available in Power Query and the Excel data model requires some unlearning of traditional methods. In traditional means, data was often matched to a single object because PivotTables could only consume data from one table at a time. This often made the initial modeling process and subsequent analysis a challenge because users typically ended up with mixed grains of data in their tables. This can also be a dangerous situation for users to consume, especially if they are unaware of these mixed grains, which can lead to miscalculations.

Traditional integration

To overcome the limitation of PivotTables only being able to consume from one location, users were forced to bring all data, regardless of grain, into one data structure. The technique was to use VLOOKUP to bring columns one by one from a source table into a target data table. The challenges were:

- VLOOKUP can be cumbersome to use.
- VLOOKUP can be slow because they are recalculated as the workbook changes.
- They were only able to access one column from the referenced table, meaning that if you want multiple columns of data from a source that you would need two or more VLOOKUPs, thereby adding to the first challenge.

What are relationships?

A relationship is a connection between two tables on one column in each table of the data model. A relationship is used to traverse between tables as the user navigates data in the data model. Unlike a VLOOKUP, calculating how to move between tables is done only when needed, which means relationships perform better than VLOOKUPs.

Figure 2-9 shows the Diagram View within Power Pivot. The numbered callout bubbles correspond to the numbered list below. The main areas are:

1. **Ribbon**   Same as it was in Data View.
2. **Relationship window**   This is where you can view tables, columns, hierarchies, and the relationships between the tables. From a Relationship perspective, you can also perform several management tasks, such as inactivating, deleting, or editing a relationship on the diagram.
3. **Fit To Window and Zoom slider**   The **Fit To Window** button will take your model and size it to fit inside the current window. The **Zoom** slider enables you to zoom in and out of regions on your diagram.
4. **Switch View buttons**   These toggle buttons enable you to switch between **Data** and **Diagram** views like the buttons in the ribbon.

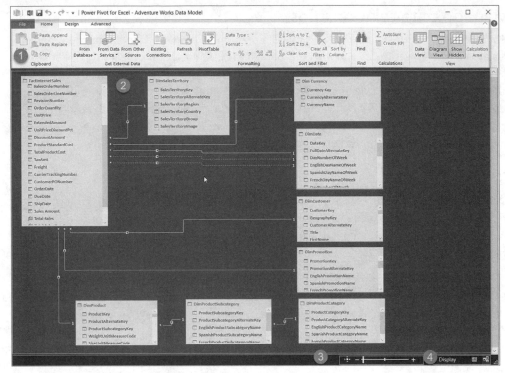

FIGURE 2-9 The Power Pivot Diagram View screen

There are two ways to create a relationship. Either the data model will automatically create the relationship for you, or you can manually create them on your own. Either way, care needs to be taken when specifying relationship because they are the glue of the data model. You will see how to create relationship both ways shortly.

One thing that you will notice when you begin to write DAX against the model is that unlike writing SQL where you specify joins at query time, you specify them when building the data model. This means that when you write DAX, the model already knows how to relate the tables, thus saving you a step when writing queries and formulas.

To dive deeper into relationships, open the **\Chapter2\Adventure Works Data Model. xlsx** file and navigate to the Diagram View in the data model, which should look like Figure 2-9, which has been rearranged for display purposes.

Focus in on the **DimProduct** and **FactInternetSales** tables and notice that there is a line between the tables which represents the relationship. Although not immediately apparent, there are five other attributes worth pointing out:

- **Related Tables** These are the tables that are involved in the relationship. In this case, it is DimProduct and FactInternetSales.

- **Related Columns** When you hover your mouse over the line, you will notice that the ProductKey column in both tables is highlighted. This is the column to which these two tables are related.

- **Cardinality** This shows that for every row found in one table, how many equivalent rows are in the other. You will see a 1 next to the DimProduct table and a * next to FactInternetSales. This means that an individual row in the product table has zero or many related rows in FactInternetSales. In other words, a product might not have sold at all (zero) or may have sold many times (many). As a note, Excel only supports one-to-many relationships.

- **Relationship Direction** This shows which way the filters flow when applied to a table. In this case, filters flow from the Dim table to the Fact table. As a note, Excel only supports filtering in one direction going from the one side to the many side.

- **Status** This shows whether the relationship is active. When there are multiple relationships between two tables, only one may be active. An Active relationship is indicated with a solid line, and inactive relationships are shown as a dashed line.

Double click or right-click on the line between **FactInternetSales** and **DimProduct** and choose Edit Relationship to be presented with the **Edit Relationship** dialog box in Figure 2-10. This shows us the relationship that was automatically created when you loaded the first two tables. The relationship has the following definition:

- **Source Table** This is the Fact table in the relationship with the FactInternetSales.

- **Foreign Key Column** This is the column in the Source Table that you will use to look up values from the Related Table. In this case, it is the ProductKey. Notice that this column is highlighted blue, which shows that this is the column that you want to use in the relationship.

- **Related Table** This is the table you will use to get values. In this case, the related table is DimProduct.

- **Related Column** This the Primary Key column of the Related Table. In this case, it is ProductKey. Notice that this column is highlighted blue, which shows that this is the column that you want to use in the relationship.

- **Status** It is marked as Active.

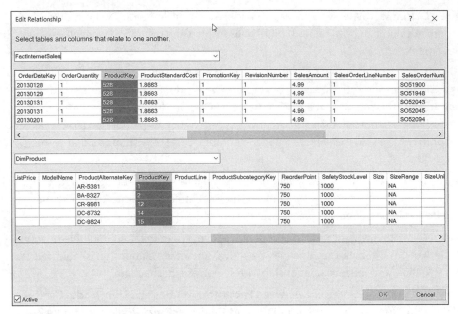

FIGURE 2-10 Edit Relationship dialog box

Requirements for a relationship

For a relationship to be created, several criteria must be met (see Table 2-1).

TABLE 2-1 Requirements for a relationship

Criteria	Description
Single Column	Only a single column in each table can be chosen. Composite relationships are not allowed. If you have a composite key relationship, you may need to look at combing those values into one field using concatenation.
Unique related column	The column that is the related column must contain unique values. A column cannot contain multiple blank, null, or empty strings.
Data type compatibility	The related columns must have compatible data types. Data types will be discussed in Section 2.2.
Cardinality	The cardinality of the relationship can only be 1:1 or 1:M (one-to-many). When you create the relationship, the engine will inspect the column values in each to verify whether this criterion can be met.

Unsupported in a table relationship

The following types of relationships are unsupported in the data model:

- **Many to many**   A data model does not support many to many relationships between tables.

- **Composite Keys**   Relationships between two tables need to be on single columns in each table. Unlike SQL tables that can contain a multi-part key, this is not allowed in a data model.

- **Self-Joins**   Relationships from a table to itself are not allowed. This type of situation commonly arises when modeling Employee Hierarchies in SQL databases.

EXAM TIP

Watch for these types of questions on the exam. Often an invalid relationship will be presented, and you be asked what is wrong with what is being presented. Being able to visually detect these attributes quickly is invaluable.

Multiple relationship between tables

Multiple relationships between two tables are allowed in a data model. However, no more than one relationship can be active at any given time. Any other relationships are marked as Inactive, but they may be specified in queries and formulas. An example of this in the Adventure Works model lies in the existence of multiple date fields in the Internet Sales Fact table (see Figure 2-11). You will notice that FactInternetSales contains an OrderDateKey, ShippedDateKey, and DueDateKey, which are all dates that relate to the DateKey in DimDate. If you imported DimDate and FactInternetSales together, you will notice that three relationships are created, but only one is active. In the supplied Adventure Works Data Model.xlsx the active relationship is between OrderDateKey and DateKey.

In this example, you will create multiple relationships between tables.

1. In a new blank workbook, follow steps 1, 2, 3, and 4 from the Import from SQL Server database example to establish the connection the SQL Server database.

2. In the **Table Import Wizard–Select Tables And Views** window, choose the following tables and then click **Finish**.

    - **DimDate**

    - **FactInternetSales**

3. One the Import is complete, click **Close** and open Diagram View in Power Pivot. You should see a screen like Figure 2-11. In this example, the relationship between Due-DateKey is active.

4. **Save** the workbook as **\Chapter2\CH02Demo04.xlsx**.

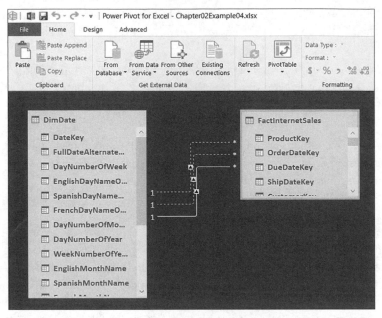

FIGURE 2-11 Multiple relationships between two tables

> **NOTE   QUERYING ACROSS TABLES**
>
> When you query across tables in a data model, the Active relationship is what is used when you utilize the RELATED and RELATEDTABLE functions. To force DAX to use an Inactive relationship, you will need to use the USERELATIONSHIP function.

Create automatic relationships

When importing data using Power Pivot, as described earlier in this chapter, relationships are automatically created if there is supporting metadata in the source systems. In these examples, Primary Key and Foreign Key relationships existed, which formed the basis for creating the relationship. In Figure 2-4, you can see that the last step that was performed when importing the data was that it did a data preparation step to create the relationships.

When importing data using the Query Editor, relationships can also be created automatically by using metadata from the underlying system, such as referential integrity from a database management system. (See "Skill 1.1: Import from data sources" in Chapter 1.) The following building blocks need to be in place to enable the automatic creation of relationships:

1.   The first building block is for source system referential integrity to be in place. Without this, the data model does not have enough information to create the relationship with the necessary degree of accuracy.

2.   Second is that you configure the Import process to include relationship columns on the initial import. Recall that when you imported data from Databases that you were

asked via checkbox if you wanted to include relationship columns. Enabling this did two things. It enabled you to choose related tables in the Database Object navigator and it set up the ability to automatically create updated relationships on load, which is the next building block.

3. Third is that you have the Query Options properly configured in the Query Editor. In the **Query Editor**, select the **File** tab and choose **Options And Settings**, **Query Options**. In the **Current Workbook** section, select **Data Load**. You will be presented with the screen in Figure 2-12. In the relationships section, you have two configurable options:

- **Create Relationships Between Tables When Adding To The Data Model For The First Time** Before loading data to the data model, it finds existing relationships between tables, such as Foreign Key relationships and then imports them with the data. This setting is turned on by default.

- **Update Relationships When Refreshing Queries Loaded To The Data Model** This option exists only if Create Relationships between tables has been selected. This will check the current relationship status in the sources system each time a data load is performed. For example, if you had a relationship between the Currency ID fields in the Internet Sales Fact and Currency Dimension in the AdvenureWorks2016DW database (which was picked up on the first load and then the Primary-Foreign Key relationship was removed from the system), this relationship would be dropped by the data model in a subsequent data load. Be aware that this may add new relationships and remove manually created ones on each load. This is turned off by default.

FIGURE 2-12 Current workbook data load query options

Create manual relationships

The preferred way to create relationships is to manually create them. This allows you, as the developer, to verify whether the relationship that is going to be created is correct. There are plenty of real-world examples in which there are two columns, in two different tables, with the same names and data types but with different underlying meanings that should not be related together automatically. The exception to this is when relationships are being created automatically using existing metadata from a source system such as SQL Server. There are a few ways that relationships can be created manually.

In this example, you have two tables that have been imported into the data model but do not yet have a relationship established. You will use drag and drop and the Manage Relationships window to create them manually.

1. Open the **\Chapter2\CH02Demo03End.xlsx** file you saved earlier.

2. Open the data model and navigate to the **Diagram View**. You should see two tables, one named **Sales** and the other **SalesPerson** with no relationships.

3. To create a relationship via drag and drop, click and highlight on the **SalesPersonID** in the **SalesPerson** table and then drag it on top of the **SalesPersonID** column in the **Sales** table. The relationship is established per Figure 2-13. Notice that both fields are highlighted in each table, signifying the related columns. And finally, the relationship is one-to-many from SalesPerson to Sales, as indicated by the * on the line next to the **Sales** table and the **1** on the line next to the **SalesPerson** table.

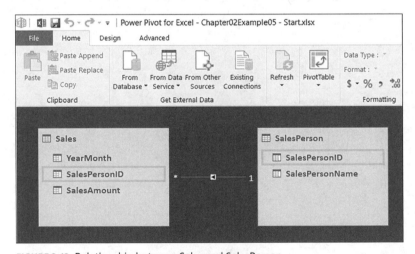

FIGURE 2-13 Relationship between Sales and SalesPerson

4. Now delete the relationship by right-clicking on the line between the tables and selecting **Delete** from the context menu. On the subsequent dialog box, click **Delete From Model**.

5. Now re-create the relationship using Manage Relationships. **Highlight** on the **Sales** table in the **Diagram View** and then navigate to **Design** tab, **Relationships** group, **Manage Relationships**. When the **Manage Relationships** window opens, click **Create**.

6. Notice that the Sales table you had highlighted is the top table in the list. Highlight on the **SalesPersonID** column in the **Sales** table. In the drop-down box for the lower table, select **SalesPerson** and then ensure that the **SalesPersonID** column is highlighted in that table as well. The relationship is marked as **Active,** and even if you uncheck the box, it will be created as active since it is the only relationship between the tables. When done, click **OK** and then **Close**.

7. **Save As \Chapter2\CH02Demo05End.xlsx** and keep it open for the next example.

One of the first things you should do shortly after loading tables is to check to see if the correct relationships are in place. This is especially true if you are about to do any reporting off the model. What would happen if you forgot to do this? This example demonstrates what happens when you encounter a situation where a relationship is missing.

1. If not already done, open the **\Chapter2\CH02Demo05End.xlsx** from the previous example and navigate to the data model.

2. Once again, **Delete** the relationship because you will build a PivotTable using these tables with no relationships between them.

3. Create a PivotTable using the data model by navigating to the **Home** tab and selecting **PivotTable** from within the Power Pivot window. When the **Create PivotTable** dialog box comes up and asks you where you want to place the PivotTable, choose **New Worksheet** and then click **OK**.

4. In the PivotTable, drag these fields to the following locations in the **PivotTable Fields** pane:

    - **Columns: YearMonth** from the **Sales** table
    - **Rows: SalesPersonName** from the **SalesPerson** table
    - **Values: SalesAmount** from the **Sales** table

5. When you are done with this, your screen should look like Figure 2-14. Notice the repeating values in the Pivot and the warning in the **PivotTable Fields** list. The Pivot has detected that something is wrong. To fix this error, you can either click **Auto-Detect** or the **Create** button to manually perform the action. When you click **Auto-Detect**, the **Auto-Detect Relationship** process will create the relationship, and then you will notice that the pivot reports the data as it should be reported. This process used the column names and Data Types to help it create the relationship. Click **Close** when finished.

6. Save as **\Chapter2\CH02Demo06End.xlsx** and keep it open for the next example.

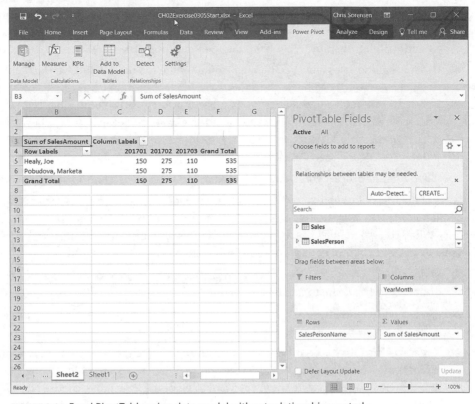

FIGURE 2-14 Excel PivotTable using data model without relationship created

> **MORE INFO** **RELATIONSHIPS BETWEEN TABLES IN A DATA MODEL**
>
> For more information and examples around creating relationships between tables in a data model, consult the following site:
>
> *https://support.office.com/en-us/article/relationships-between-tables-in-a-data-model-533dc2b6-9288-4363-9538-8ea6e469112b.*

Optimize models for reporting

Optimizing for reporting should always be kept in mind when developing a data model. There are many things that you, as a developer, can do to keep things optimized so that your model performs and users stay happy. One of the great things about the data model is that when the below techniques are used, these configurations are stored centrally and are reused. This becomes very useful when you move into reporting, which is the topic of Chapter 3. The time and effort put into optimization will pay dividends because many of these tasks will only need to be done once, centrally.

There are two components of optimization that you typically need to be concerned with. The first is the performance and the second is usability by end-users. You will find that these often overlap because when you make a model more compact and focused for users, performance can benefit.

Also keep in mind that In Office 365, both SharePoint Online and Excel Web App restrict the size of an Excel file to 10 MB. It is quite easy for data models that contain millions of rows to get to this 10 MB limit quickly.

Here are some of the things that you can do to optimize your model from a performance perspective:

- **Keep models compact and focused**   Bring in only the tables, columns, and rows that will be necessary when performing the analysis. Early in a development cycle, you might end up bringing in more data than needed, but as clarity transpires around what will be used, begin to remove unnecessary rows and columns. This not only helps with performance but keeps the models digestible to end users that may be consuming your models.

- **Bin data where possible**   Columns with more unique values than others require more memory to be stored. For example, a column that only has values of Male and Female will take up less space than one that contains phone numbers.

- **Choose an appropriate data type**   If you have a Datetime database column that you import but you never need the time components for it, remove the time component.

- **DAX Columns**   It is advantageous to use DAX measures instead of calculated columns where possible. Measures are defined once in the model and are evaluated only when used.

- **Workbook Size Optimizer**   The workbook size optimizer analyzes the makeup of data model within your workbook to see if the data in it can take less space and if possible, enables better compression. The workbook size optimizer can be found at *https://www. microsoft.com/en-us/download/details.aspx?id=38793*.

> *MORE INFO*   **CHECKLIST FOR MEMORY OPTIMIZATIONS IN POWER PIVOT AND TABULAR**
>
> The following article from SQLBI provides more details as to specific tasks that can be undertaken to help with optimizing the memory usage in your data models: *https://www.sqlbi. com/articles/checklist-for-memory-optimizations-in-Power Pivot-and-tabular-models/*.

Making a model easy to use for your end users should always be top of mind when designing models for consumption. The following sections outline some of the things that you can do to optimize your model from a usability perspective.

Hide tables and columns

Only show columns and tables that are necessary for your users to use for reporting. Unnecessary information clutters a model and makes it hard for a user to navigate and find the information that they need.

To hide an entire table from client reporting tools, you can right-click the table name in either the Diagram or Data View and then choose **Hide From Client Tools**. Once you do this, the table name will remain in both interfaces but will be unavailable. As the developer, you can continue to work with the table normally, as this change only affects visibility to client tools such as PivotTable and PivotCharts.

To hide a single column, you can right-click a column name in either the **Diagram View** or **Data View** and then choose **Hide From Client Tools**. The same rules apply to hiding both tables and columns.

Intuitive naming conventions and descriptions

A model that has easy-to-understand naming conventions is worth its weight in gold. Choose names for tables and columns that have meaning to end users and that are clear.

In addition to naming conventions, both tables and columns have description properties that can be filled out in cases where further descriptions are necessary. To do this, in the data model, ensure that **Data View** is open and then right-click on any **Column Name** in a table or a **Table** tab and choose **Description** from the context menu.

Synonyms

Synonyms are useful when an entity in an organization might be referred to by multiple terms. For example, when something is sold in a retail setting, sales might refer to that metric as sales, whereas finance might call it earned revenue. In a transaction table, you might call it sales on the physical columns, but you would like the physical column to also go by a synonym.

To do this, in the data model, open the Synonyms pane by clicking the **Advanced** tab, **Language** group, **Synonyms**. The Diagram View appears, and on the right side of the page, you will have the Synonyms pane. In the Diagram View, choose the table to which you want to apply a synonym. You will then be provided a list of column names, including the table name itself in which you can provide a comma-separated list of synonyms for the physical table or column name.

Perspectives

As mentioned earlier, Perspectives allow you to create custom views of data that you define for a user group or business scenario. This makes it easier to navigate large data sets because they can be sectioned to help provide focus. With Perspectives, you can include any combination of tables, columns, measures, and KPIs.

To create a Perspective, open the **Advanced** tab and navigate to **Perspectives** > **Create And Manage**. From here you can add, delete, and rename the perspective and then add the tables, columns, measures, and KPIs that are required.

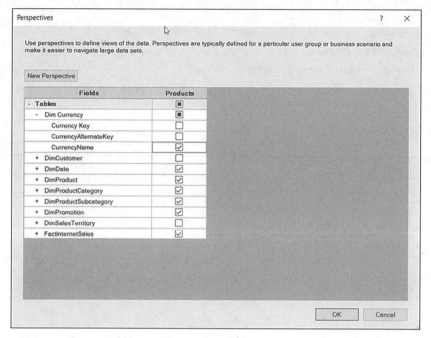

FIGURE 2-15 Create and Manage Perspective window

Sort By column

Sort By columns are used to provide sorting information to a column based on another column's value. The classic example for this is when you use month names on a visual or within a PivotTable, their values display in alphabetic order. Figure 2-16 shows the default behavior of the EnglishMonthName column when brought onto the Rows of a new PivotTable. In other words, they sort using a string sort.

FIGURE 2-16 The English month name displayed as rows in a PivotTable using default data-type sorting

To solve the problem, you can assign the values from another column to use for sorting. In this case, you will use the MonthNumberOfYear column.

1. Open **\Chapter2\CH02Demo07Start.xlsx**. You should see the PivotTable as represented in Figure 2-16.

2. Navigate to the data model and within Data View, open the **DimDate** table.

3. Select the **EnglishMonthName** column and navigate to **Home** tab, choose the **Sort And Filter** group, and select **Sort By Column**.

4. In the dialog box, choose to sort **EnglishMonthName** by **MonthNumberOfYear**. Click **OK** when done.

5. Once you do this, navigate back to the PivotTable. You will notice that the values in Figure 2-16 will now have the desired sort order.

6. Close the file without saving.

When choosing a column to do your sorting on, it is important to ensure that the values in the Sort By column are unique for each value that you want to sort. For example, if your table was similar to Table 2-2 and you tried to do the same sort as described above, the sort would not work and you would get the following error message: *"Cannot sort EnglishMonthName by MonthNumberOfYear because at least one value in EnglishMonthName has multiple distinct values in MonthNumberOfYear."* This happens because the value of January has a month number value of 1 and 2 when it should only have one value.

TABLE 2-2 Sample of Data Table data with values that will fail the sort

EnglishMonthName	MonthNumberOfYear
January	1
January	2
February	2
February	2

> **NOTE** **SORTING BY A COLUMN FROM ANOTHER TABLE**
>
> You can only use a column from the same table to define a different sort order. To sort by a column from a different table, first, you need to add the column from the other table into the selected table. To add a column from another table, add a calculated column using the RELATED DAX function.

Formatting columns

Some of the things that you can do for your columns are to format them so that they have consistent display and behaviors when used in reporting. Formatting options can be found in the data model's **Home** tab > **Formatting** group. Here are some of the things that you can do to format columns. They are described here, and in Chapter 3, Skill 3.1. We will use these as we work with the data model in a reporting scenario.

- **Data Type**   The first thing that you need to take care of when data lands in a data model is to choose the correct data type. This is important as the data type not only has storage implications but also affects the range of DAX functions that you can use on the column and which formats, summarizations and categorizations are available to be applied to the column.

- **Formats**   Formats are used to further style your data at display time. Each of the different data types have a range of formats that can be applied.

- **Summarization methods**   With numeric-based columns, you can designate a summarization method. This is used to determine how a column should be displayed when it is brought onto a reporting canvas. For example, a key column should be set to Do not summarize since it makes no sense to perform summarizations where a column such as sales might require a default summarization of Sum. This formatting method is in the **Advanced** tab, **Summarize By**.

- **Categorization**   Categorization is used to provide extra information about the column of data to a reporting tool. It can be found in the **Advanced** tab > **Reporting Properties** group > **Data Category**. For example, a column might contain a Country value, which to the data model is merely a string of text. You add a categorization to the column so that when used in a reporting tool, the tool knows that the column has special meaning. In this case, if you were mapping data, the categorization can help place values on a map with more accuracy. Note that Data Types and Categorization are two distinct attributes of a column. The following is a list of categorizations that you can apply to your data:

  - Address
  - City
  - Company
  - Continent
  - Country/region
  - County
  - Date
  - Image
  - Image URL
  - Latitude
  - Longitude
  - Organization
  - Place
  - Postal Code

- Product
- State or Province
- Web URL
- Custom Category

Date tables

Having a Date table is important to almost every kind of analytic you might develop. It is very rare to write a report that does not need a time perspective. And as you will see shortly, the time intelligence functions in DAX rely on the existence of a well-formed date table to function properly.

Depending on where you are getting your data, a date table may or may not exist at source for you to import and use. The Adventure Works Database that you have been using for demonstrations already has a date table that has been built for use with the fact tables in the model.

Look at the Adventure Works date table, and you will notice that it has an array of fields to represent the various ways that users may want to use dates for labels on reports, filters, or hierarchies. If you know that users will want to do such things, it is advisable to add columns to the data table to enable this.

The purpose of this example is to augment the Date table by adding an extra column to the date dimensions using DAX and then to mark it as a Date table.

1. Open **Adventure Works Data Model.xslx**, navigate to the data model and open the **DimDate** table.

2. Notice the field named **EnglishDayNameOfWeek**, which is the full spelling of the day of the week. Suppose that a user wants the abbreviation for Month name and not just the full name. You would simply add the column to the table using DAX. Add a calculated column named **EnglishDayNameOfWeekAbbr** with the following formula:

   ```
   = FORMAT(DimDate[FullDateAlternateKey], "DDD")
   ```

3. Now you have a new column that users can simply drag and drop onto a report.

4. Next, it is important to Mark the DimDate table as a Date table so that when you go to use it with the DAX time intelligence functions that this functions properly. In **Diagram View** of your model, highlight on **DimDate**.

5. In the **Design** tab, navigate to **Calendars** group, **Mark As Date Table** which will open the **Mark As Date Table** dialog as in Figure 2-17. Notice that the first field that qualifies as the unique identifier of the table has been selected, and it is of the Date Data type. Click **OK** to accept this setting.

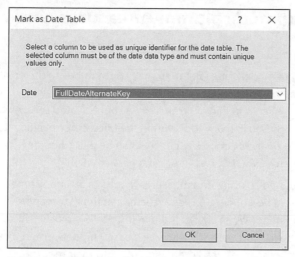

FIGURE 2-17 Mark as Date Table dialog box

6. Note now that you can now change the settings by navigating to the **Design** tab > **Calendars** group > **Mark as Date Table** > **Date Table Settings**.

7. You can now **Save** and **Close** your file.

Now suppose that you have a model such as the one above, but it does not contain a date table. This is a very common scenario when performing analytics and not using a source that has been dimensionally modeled. In this case, you can create your own Date table directly within Excel. In this example, you add a date table to the data model and mark it as date table.

1. Open **\Chapter2\CH02Demo09start.xlsx** and navigate to the data model.

2. In the **Design** tab > **Calendars** group > **Date Table** > click **New**.

3. A new Date table named **Calendar** has been added to the model. What is interesting about this table is that it has already been Marked as the Date table. The second thing to note is how the date range was created. The creation process finds the earliest and latest dates that exist anywhere in data model and then it creates a continuous range of dates from the first date of the earliest year to last date in the last year (for example, January 1 – December 31).

4. **Close** the workbook without saving.

MORE INFORMATION   **MORE ON GENERATING DATE DIMENSION TABLES**

For more details and examples of alternate ways of creating date tables in the data model, see "Automatically Generating Date Dimension Tables in Excel 2016 Power Pivot." Chris Webb is an excellent source of information around Analysis Services, MDX, DAX, Power Pivot, Power Query and Power BI. *https://blog.crossjoin.co.uk/2015/06/26/automatically-generating-date-dimension-tables-in-Excel-2016-power-pivot/.*

Skill 2.2: Create calculated columns, measures, and tables

You can take analytics using the data model quite far, but to really push things to the next level, it is important to get to know Data Analysis Expressions (DAX). Picking up the basics of DAX is straightforward to start and then, of course, can get much more sophisticated should your models need it. The language itself is used in many tools within the Microsoft Analytics stack. You can write DAX queries to query Analysis Services cubes that can be placed inside of the Excel data model or in other tools such as SQL Server Reporting Services (SSRS).

You will see how to create calculated columns and measures that have business logic wrapped into them so that your users do not need to keep re-creating logic over and over. This promotes reusability and consistency when analytics are being performed, which is a big benefit. The notion here is as you build more robust, self-service based models, you typically want to supply your users with metrics that they can drag and drop into their reports and be maintained in one place.

DAX itself is a functional language that is meant to resemble Excel formulas. The premise is that DAX is aimed at making things easier for those familiar with Excel to pick the concepts up quickly. One big difference is that Excel formulas operate on cells and DAX operates on rows, columns, and tables, not individual cells. This also improves maintainability when done properly. It is beyond the scope of this book to cover every DAX function, but this skill will introduce you to some of the more common functions and will provide a solid foundation from which to build.

This section covers how to:

- Create DAX formulas
- Create DAX queries
- Create Excel formulas

Create DAX formulas

DAX formulas are created within the data model to either help with creating additional columns to tables through the use of Calculated Columns or by adding Measures that serve to aggregate data. This section will walk through the major building blocks and functions that are used when building DAX expressions. Many of the formulas that you will use in this section will apply when you get into the section on DAX queries. This section will cover some of the most important functions and skills needed to pass the exam. There are more than 200 functions in DAX. It is beyond the scope of this book to cover all 200 functions.

DAX Basics

Before you jump into some of the deeper waters in the DAX space, we will do a review of basic syntax. This includes knowing how to write a valid formula that is free of syntax issues and uses proper data types and operators.

> **MORE INFO   DAX BASICS AND SYNTAX**
>
> If you need a deeper dive into DAX syntax, you might want to look at *https://msdn.microsoft.com/en-us/library/ee634217*.aspx. If you need a quick start, the following link has a great introduction: *https://support.office.com/en-us/article/QuickStart-Learn-DAX-Basics-in-30-Minutes-51744643-c2a5-436a-bdf6-c895762bec1a*.

Calculated columns

To start breaking syntax down, let's look at a calculated column. A calculated column is added to a table in the data model by writing an expression. They take up storage space in the model and are generally used for report labels (columns or rows) or as filters and slicers, as you will see in Chapter 3. For example, they are also useful as values if you need to display an actual calculated value in a table. Calculated columns are evaluated on a row-by-row basis, and their values are refreshed every time your data set is refreshed or when a value depends on change. The syntax in Figure 2-18 is used to create a column named "Sales Amount" in the FactInternetSales table in the Adventure Works Data Model.xlsx file.

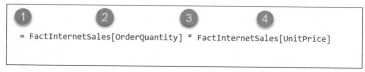

FIGURE 2-18 Sales Amount calculated column formula

The parts of the expression are listed below, and the number match to the callout bubble in Figure 2-18.

1. The equal sign (=) denotes the beginning of the formula.

2. FactInternetSales[OrderQuantity] is a column from FactInternetSales table in the model. Strictly speaking, you can omit the table name in a calculated column, but we include it here for completeness.

3. The * is an operator that performs multiplications.

4. FactInternetSales[UnitPrice] is a column from FactInternetSales table in the model. Once again, you can omit the table name in a calculated column, but we include it here for completeness.

Notice that unlike Excel where you reference cells by coordinates, DAX expressions use column names in much the same manner as you refer to values in Excel Tables.

To add a calculated column, you can either:

- Navigate to the **Design** tab and in the **Columns** group, click **Add**. This will add a column to the end of the table that has focus in Data View.

- Go to the far right of the table you want to add the column to and then click the **Add Column** text in the table.

- Right-click in the header row of the table and choose **Insert Column** from the context menu.

- To give the column a name, you can double-click on the name and edit it or right-click the name and choose **Rename Column** from the context menu.

Measures

Measures are used to aggregate information that you want to display in a PivotTable or PivotChart. They typically use aggregations such as SUM, AVGERAGE, or COUNT and are written using DAX. A measure is attached to a Home Table but can be stored with any table in the model. For housekeeping purposes, they are generally placed in Calculation area of the table that makes the most logical sense.

Another feature of a measure is that its value is calculated when used, which is unlike a calculated column that is computed and stored when created. Also, its value is influenced by the current Evaluation context which will be explained shortly. Figure 2-19 shows the components of creating a measure.

FIGURE 2-19 Total Sales Measure formula

The parts of the expression are:

1. Measure name, which is Total Sales.

2. The measure name is followed by a colon and an equals sign; the equals sign assigns the expression value to the measure name.

3. SUM is the aggregation function that is being applied to the column.

4. The FactInternetSales[Sales Amount] column in the FactInternetSales table that is being aggregated.

Measures are created in the formula bar shown in Section 1 of Figure 2-20, and they are kept in the Calculation pane, which is shown in Section 2. The value of the measure with no filter context applied is shown in Section 3.

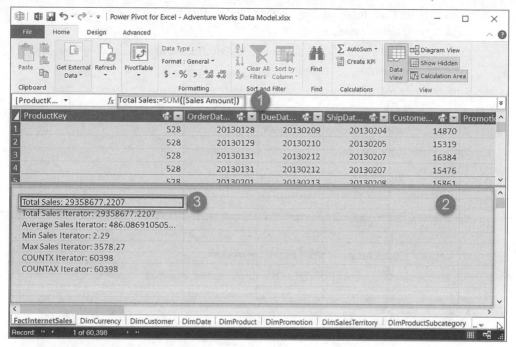

FIGURE 2-20 Creating a measure in the Data View

The parts of Figure 2-20 are:

1. The Formula bar with the DAX measure expression.

2. The Calculation Area where measures reside. In this screen capture, the **Total Sales Measures Home** table is **FactInternetSales**.

3. The measure name, formula, and value with the current filter context, which does not exist in this screen capture.

> **NOTE   MEASURE NAME UNIQUENESS**
>
> A measure name must be unique across the entire collection of names used for either calculated columns or measures. For example, if you attempt to create a measure named CommuteDistance and CommuteDistance was a column in DimCustomer, it will not be created. You will get an error message stating that a measure or column with the name CommuteDistance already exists and that you should choose a different name. Two columns can have the same name if they reside in different tables.

Explicit Measures can be created in the data model using the Calculation Area and from within Excel itself. From Excel, navigate to **Power Pivot** tab and the **Calculations** group, then select, **New Measure,** or if you have the PivotTable Fields pane open in Excel, you can right-click on any table and choose **Add Measure** from the context menu. These options all create explicit measures that are stored back in the data model. With that, let's demonstrate the notion of Explicit and Implicit measures.

1. Open the Excel workbook named **\Chapter2\CH02Demo10start.xlsx** and navigate to the data model.

2. With the data model open, navigate to **Home** tab and choose **PivotTable**.

3. When prompted in the **Create PivotTable** dialog, choose **Existing Worksheet** and choose a location within that worksheet.

4. In the **PivotTable Fields**, drag the following values to these locations:

   - **Rows** **CurrencyName** from **DimCurrency**.

   - **Columns** FiscalYear from **DimDate**.

   - **Values** TotalSales from **FactInternetSales**. Note that in the PivotTable Fields pane, it will have a function symbol next to it.

   - **Values** **Sales Amount** from **FactInternetSales**.

5. You should end up with a PivotTable that looks like Figure 2-21.

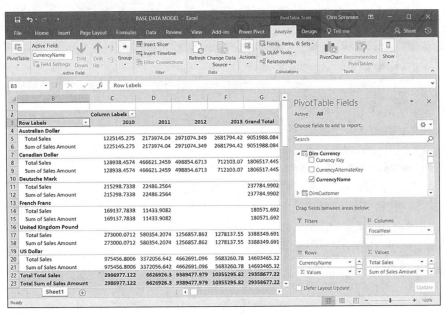

FIGURE 2-21 PivotTable containing an Implicit and Explicit Measure

6. Notice that you have two values in the Values area and they both give the same result. Total Sales is what is known as an Explicit measure, and Sum of Sales Amount is known as an Implicit Measure. More to come on these at the end of the example.

7. Now navigate back to the data model and select the **Advanced** tab and choose **Show Implicit Measures**. With the **FactInternetSales** table highlighted, scroll to find the

Sales Amount column. Notice that a value has been added to the Calculation Area under this column; the value also appears if you hover over the blue double arrow icon as shown in Figure 2-22. If you hover over the icon, the following message will be displayed: "*This measure was automatically generated by adding a field to the Values area of the Fields list in Excel.*" This field is read-only and will automatically be deleted if you delete the column.

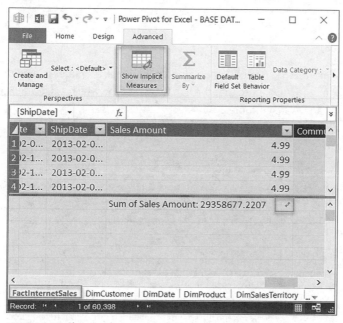

FIGURE 2-22 Showing how an Implicit measure is shown in the Data View of the data model

8.   **Save** this workbook as **\Chapter2\CH02Demo10end.xlsx** because it will be used as the starting point for the next example.

One of the best features of the data model is that Explicit measures are a part of the data model and are reusable, which promotes code centralization and consistency across your model. This is especially important as the complexity of business rules and resulting DAX code increases. You can write it once and use it many times. When you write DAX on your own to create a measure, it is known as an Explicit measure.

An Implicit measure is only usable in the context of the PivotTable in which it was created. Also, they are limited to the following standard aggregation (SUM, COUNT, MIN, MAX, DISTINCTCOUNT, or AVGERAGE), and must use the data format that is defined for that aggregation.

EXAM TIP

Be prepared for a few questions that test your ability to recognize valid syntax. These are a favorite type of question on any technical exam. With these types of questions, it is best to go slow and eliminate wrong answers first, then inspect the ones that look the most correct to find the one that is the right answer. Be sure to spend some time learning how to quickly recognize valid and invalid syntax. If you can get good at this technique, these questions become easy points.

Data Types

Data types within the data model are strongly typed, and unlike Excel, all values in a column will adhere to the same data type. Also, note that the variant data type which exists in Excel does not exist as a data type in DAX (see Table 2-3).

TABLE 2-3 DAX Data Types

Data type in Power Pivot UI	Data type in DAX	Description
Whole Number	A 64-bit (eight-bytes) integer value	Numbers that have no decimal places. Integers can be positive or negative numbers but must be whole numbers between -9,223,372,036,854,775,808 (-2^63) and 9,223,372,036,854,775,807 (2^63-1).
Decimal Number	A 64-bit (eight-bytes) real number	Real numbers are numbers that can have decimal places. Real numbers cover a wide range of values: Negative values from -1.79E +308 through -2.23E -308 Zero Positive values from 2.23E -308 through 1.79E + 308 However, the number of significant digits is limited to 15 decimal digits.
TRUE/FALSE	Boolean	Either a True or False value.
Text	String	A Unicode character data string. Can be strings, numbers, or dates represented in a text format. Maximum string length is 268,435,456 Unicode characters (256 mega characters) or 536,870,912 bytes.
Date	Date/time	Dates and times in an accepted date-time representation. Valid dates are all dates after January 1, 1900.
Currency	Currency	Currency data type allows values between -922,337,203,685,477.5808 to 922,337,203,685,477.5807 with four decimal digits of fixed precision.
N/A	Blank	A blank is a data type in DAX that represents and replaces SQL nulls. You can create a blank by using the BLANK function and test for blanks by using the logical function, ISBLANK.

Operators

Table 2-4 lists the operators that are available in DAX.

TABLE 2-4 DAX Operators

Operator Type	Symbol and Use
Parenthesis operator	() precedence order and grouping of arguments
Arithmetic operators	+ (addition) - (subtraction) * (multiplication) / (division) ^ (exponentiation)
Comparison operators	= (equal to) > (greater than) < (less than) >= (greater than or equal to) <= (less than or equal to) <> (not equal to)
Text concatenation operator	& (concatenation)
Logic operators	&& (and) || (or)

Evaluations Contexts

Evaluation contexts are one of the most important concepts to understand when it comes to building out DAX formulas for use within reporting solutions. To understand the end-results of reports that are built up using DAX, time needs to be spent on building up your understanding around this topic.

There are two evaluation contexts that are present when the evaluation of a DAX expression occurs. These are the Row and Filter contexts.

The Row Context exists when you:

- Create calculated columns.
- Iterate over a table row-by-row to calculate input values for aggregations.

In Figure 2-23, you can see that the result of the Calculated Column named Sales Amount as FactInternetSales[OrderQuantity] * FactInternetSales[UnitPrice], which is calculated for each row. Logically DAX is using the context of each row to determine the values for each input as it goes row-by-row through the table and computes a value for Sales Amount. You will come back to the second use of the Row context after Filter contexts are introduced.

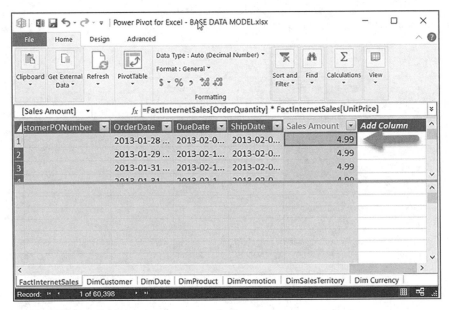

FIGURE 2-23 Data Grid showing the row context

The Filter Context exists when you use measures in reporting solutions and the filters that surround the measures are considered when calculating a value that will be displayed. You will look at both via example. You will first use the Sales Amount Calculated Column as a base to a Measure which you will put into a PivotTable.

1. With the **\Chapter2\ CH02Demo10end.xlsx** that you saved from the previous demo open, remove all values in the PivotTable Field list except for the **Total Sales** measure. You should end up with the result seen in Figure 2-24. The value of Total Sales is the sum of Sales Amount across the entire data set. In other words, no filters have been applied.

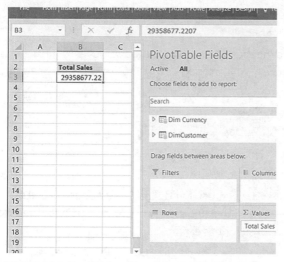

FIGURE 2-24 PivotTable with nothing in the Filter Context

2. Drag the following fields into the **PivotTable Fields** list and observe the results, which are shown in Figure 2-25. Move the following fields to the locations shown here:

- **Columns   FiscalYear** from **DimDate**
- **Rows   CurrencyName** from **DimCurrency**
- **Filters   MaritalStatus** from **DimCustomer** and set its value to **S** for single

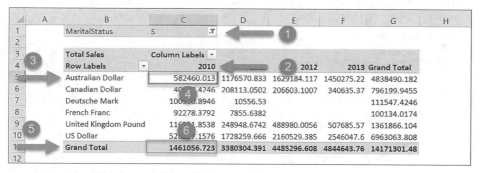

	A	B	C	D	E	F	G	H
1		MaritalStatus	S					
2								
3		Total Sales	Column Labels					
4		Row Labels	2010		2012	2013	Grand Total	
5		Australian Dollar	582460.013	1176570.833	1629184.117	1450275.22	4838490.182	
6		Canadian Dollar	40.4246	208113.0502	206603.1007	340635.37	796199.9455	
7		Deutsche Mark	100.8946	10556.53			111547.4246	
8		French Franc	92278.3792	7855.6382			100134.0174	
9		United Kingdom Pound	116.8538	248948.6742	488980.0056	507685.57	1361866.104	
10		US Dollar	52.1576	1728259.666	2160529.385	2546047.6	6963063.808	
11		Grand Total	1461056.723	3380304.391	4485296.608	4844643.76	14171301.48	
12								

FIGURE 2-25 PivotTable for explaining Filter Context

You will notice that there are three inputs into the Filter context that come from the values on rows, columns, and filters. You can think of each cell in the PivotTable that has a numeric value (from Total Sales) as having its value influenced by the three filters.

For example, the highlight value of 582460.013 (callout bubble 4) can be thought of as being calculated like this:

1. The SUM of Sales Amount - The Measure
2. WHERE Currency Name = Australian Dollar - callout bubble 3

3. AND Fiscal Year = 2010 - callout bubble 2

4. AND Marital Status = S - callout bubble 1

The value of each cell is calculated independently using the logic above. To further illustrate, here is how the value for callout bubble 6, which has a value of 1461056.723, has been calculated:

1. The SUM of Sales Amount - The Measure

2. WHERE Currency Name = All Currencies - callout bubble 5

3. AND Fiscal Year = 2010 - callout bubble 2

4. AND Marital Status = S - callout bubble 1

Disregard the fact that you do not know whether you can really add up these dollar amounts unless they have all been converted to a single currency such as USD. Assume that adding up different currencies makes sense for this example.

Finally, in the section on iterators, you will look at the Row Context that is created when you use Iterators to create measures.

Aggregate Functions

Aggregating data is far and away the most common operation in analytics. The most commonly used Aggregate functions are SUM, AVERAGE, MIN, and MAX. They can operate on Dates or Numeric. You have already seen the SUM aggregate function in action in the section on measures. The SUM function sums up all the numbers in the column that is passed in. The following examples can be found in the file named \Chapter2\CH02FunctionDemos.xlsx.

TABLE 2-5 Aggregate Functions

Function	Description	Example	Data Type of input
SUM(column)	Returns the sums of the column's values	SUM Order QTY := SUM(Aggregation[Order QTY])	Numeric or date
AVERAGE(column)	Returns the arithmetic mean of the column's values	AVERAGE Order QTY := AVERAGE(Aggregation[Order QTY])	Numeric or date
MIN(column)	Returns minimum value of the column's values	MIN Order QTY := MIN(Aggregation[Order QTY])	Numeric or date
MAX(column)	Returns maximum value of the column's values	MAX ORDER DATE := MAX(Aggregation[Order Date])	Numeric or date
MIN(expr1, expr2)	Returns minimum value of the column's values	MIN TWO EXPR := MIN(1,2)	Numeric or date
MAX(expr1, expr2)	Returns maximum value of the column's values	MAX TWO EXPR := MAX(-1, Blank())	Numeric or date

Order Date	Shipped Date	Order QTY	Sales Amount
2015-01-01 12:00:00 AM	2015-01-02 12:00:00 AM	5	100
2015-01-02 12:00:00 AM	2015-01-10 12:00:00 AM	10	500
2015-01-02 12:00:00 AM	2015-01-08 12:00:00 AM	2	700
2015-01-02 12:00:00 AM	2015-01-08 12:00:00 AM		

MAX ORDER DATE: 2015-01-02 12:00:00 AM   SUM Order QTY: 17   MIN TWO EXPR: 1
MIN ORDER DATE: 2015-01-01 12:00:00 AM   AVERAGE Order QTY: 5.666...   MAX TWO EXPR: (blank)
    MIN Order QTY: 2
    MAX Order QTY: 10

FIGURE 2-26 Results of the functions from Table 2-5

> **NOTE** **DAX FUNCTION REFERENCE**
>
> All the function definitions in this section have been sourced from the Microsoft DAX Function Reference which is located at *https://msdn.microsoft.com/en-us/library/ee634396.aspx*.

Counting Functions

Sometimes you want to perform counts on the rows in a table. There are several counting functions that can be used. The following examples can be found in the file named **\Chapter2\ CH02FunctionDemos.xlsx**.

TABLE 2-6 Counting Functions

Function	Description	Example	Data Type of input
COUNT(column)	Counts the number of values in a column	COUNT Order Date := COUNT(Aggregation[Order Date])	Column that is numeric, text, or date
COUNTA(column)	Counts the number of values in a column	COUNTA Order Date: = COUNTA(Aggregation[Order Date])	Column of any type
COUNTBLANK(column)	Counts the number of blank values in a column	COUNTBLANK Order Qty := COUNTBLANK(Aggregation[Order QTY])	Column of any type
COUNTROWS(table)	Counts the number of rows in a table	COUNTROWS Aggregation := COUNTROWS(Aggregation)	Table
DISTINCTCOUNT(column)	Counts the number of distinct values in a column	DISTINCTCOUNT Order Qty := DISTINCTCOUNT(Aggregation[Order QTY])	Column of any type

Order Date	Shipped Date	Order QTY	Sales Amount
2015-01-01 12:00:00 AM	2015-01-02 12:00:00 AM	5	100
2015-01-02 12:00:00 AM	2015-01-10 12:00:00 AM	10	500
2015-01-02 12:00:00 AM	2015-01-08 12:00:00 AM	2	700
2015-01-02 12:00:00 AM	2015-01-08 12:00:00 AM		

COUNT Order Date: 4   COUNT Order Qty: 3
COUNTA Order Date: 4   COUNTA Order Qty: 3
COUNTBLANK Order Date: (blank)   COUNTBLANK Order Qty: 1
COUNTROWS Aggregation: 4   DISTINCTCOUNT Order Qty: 4
DISTINCTCOUNT Order Date: 2

FIGURE 2-27 Results of the functions from Table 2-6

Iterators

You may have noticed that you created a calculated column and then used that value inside a Measure. This is all well and good, but what if you did not need that calculated column for filtering or for use as values for rows or columns? It is highly likely that this is the case and, as was mentioned when talking about optimization, you should avoid the situation where a calculated column is created and is never used in the filter contexts described above.

For this, you can take advantage of iterators to create a Row Context and then calculate the Measure value for which you are looking. As an example, the Total Sales Iterator function in Table 2-7 iterates over each row FactInternetSales and multiplies the Order Quantity and Unit Price for each Row Context and sums those values up over the entire table. This eliminates the need for the calculated column named Sales Amount that was created earlier. The examples in this section use the **\Chapter2\Adventure Works Data Model.xlsx** file.

TABLE 2-7 Iterator Functions

Function	Description	Example
SUMX(table, expression)	Returns the sum of an expression evaluated for each row in a table.	Total Sales Iterator := SUMX(FactInternetSales, FactInternetSales[OrderQuantity] * FactInternetSales[UnitPrice])
AVERAGEX(table, expression)	Calculates the average (arithmetic mean) of a set of expressions evaluated over a table.	Average Sales Iterator := AVERAGEX(FactInternetSales, FactInternetSales[OrderQuantity] * FactInternetSales[UnitPrice])
MINX(table, expression)	Returns the smallest numeric value that results from evaluating an expression for each row of a table.	Min Sales Iterator := MINX(FactInternetSales, FactInternetSales[OrderQuantity] * FactInternetSales[UnitPrice])
MAXX(table, expression)	Evaluates an expression for each row of a table and returns the largest numeric value.	Max Sales Iterator := MAXX(FactInternetSales, FactInternetSales[OrderQuantity] * FactInternetSales[UnitPrice])
COUNTX(table, expression)	Counts the number of rows that contain a number, date, text, or an expression that evaluates to a number when evaluating an expression over a table	COUNTX Iterator := COUNTX(FactInternetSales, FactInternetSales[OrderQuantity] * FactInternetSales[UnitPrice])
COUNTAX(table, expression)	The COUNTAX function counts non-blank results when evaluating the result of an expression over a table. That is, it works just like the COUNTA function, but is used to iterate through the rows in a table and count rows where the specified expressions result in a nonblank result.	COUNTAX Iterator := COUNTAX(FactInternetSales, FactInternetSales[OrderQuantity] * FactInternetSales[UnitPrice])

> ***MORE INFO*** **EVALUATION CONTEXTS**
>
> For more information regarding evaluation context, see the sample chapter excerpt from "The Definitive Guide to DAX, The: Business intelligence with Microsoft Excel, SQL Server Analysis Services, and Power BI." This book is a must-have reference for users of DAX. *https://www.microsoftpressstore.com/articles/article.aspx?p=2449191.*

Logical Functions

Logical functions are used to build conditions in an expression. They are typically used to create more complex DAX formulas. The following examples can be found in the file named **\Chapter2\CH02FunctionDemos.xlsx**.

TABLE 2-8 Logical Functions

Function	Description	Example
TRUE( )	Returns the value of TRUE	Order Date gt Shipped Date = IF(Aggregation[Order Date] > Aggregation[Shipped Date], TRUE(), FALSE())
FALSE( )	Returns the value of FALSE	Order Date gt Shipped Date = IF(Aggregation[Order Date] > Aggregation[Shipped Date], TRUE(), FALSE())
AND(expr 1, expr 2)	Returns TRUE if both expressions are TRUE, otherwise it returns FALSE	Expensive Per Unit Price = AND(Aggregation[Order QTY] < 3, Aggregation[Sales Amount] >100)
OR(expr 1, expr 2)	Returns TRUE if one of the expressions is TRUE, otherwise it returns FALSE	Valid Order = IF(OR(ISBLANK(Aggregation[Order QTY]), Aggregation[Order QTY] < 0), FALSE(), TRUE())
NOT(expr)	Negates the value of the expression. TRUE returns FALSE. FALSE returns TRUE and BLANK( ) returns TRUE	Invalid Order = NOT(Aggregation[Valid Order])
IF(logical test, value if true, value if false)	Evaluates a logical test and if the result is TRUE, then argument 2 is returned else argument 3	See above examples
IFERROR(values to test, return value if error exists)	Evaluates argument 1 and if it returns an error then argument 2 is returned	IFERROR(2 / BLANK(), 0) will return 0 IFERROR(1/1, 0) will return 1

Order Date	Shipped Date	Order Date gt Shipped Date	Order QTY	Sales Amount	Valid Order	Invalid Order	Expensive Per Unit Price
2015-01-01 12:00:00 AM	2015-01-02 12:00:00 AM	FALSE	5	100	TRUE	FALSE	FALSE
2015-01-01 12:00:00 AM	2015-01-10 12:00:00 AM	FALSE	10	500	TRUE	FALSE	FALSE
2015-01-02 12:00:00 AM	2015-01-08 12:00:00 AM	FALSE	2	700	TRUE	FALSE	TRUE
2015-01-02 12:00:00 AM	2015-01-08 12:00:00 AM	FALSE	-1	-100	FALSE	TRUE	FALSE
2015-01-07 12:00:00 AM	2015-01-06 12:00:00 AM	TRUE			FALSE	TRUE	FALSE

FIGURE 2-28 Results of the functions from Table 2-8

The SWITCH statement deserves greater explanation. A SWITCH statement is generally a more elegant and clean way to write a complex IF statement. There are two types of SWITCH statements; the first is known as a simple SWITCH, and the other is a searched SWITCH. The simple SWITCH first evaluates an expression and then looks to find the first value that matches, and then that matching result is returned. In DAX the searched SWITCH is mimicked by making the expression of a simple SWITCH, a TRUE or FALSE. Then the flow will search through all the values to find the first matching one. When using TRUE or FALSE, you can build more complex expressions which make for a very powerful and easier to read statement than an equivalent IF statement.

LISTING 2-1 DAX Switch Statement

```
--SIMPLE SWITCH
Month Full Text =
SWITCH (
    [Month Number],
    1, "January", 2, "February", 3, "March",
    4, "April", 5, "May", 6, "June",
    7, "July", 8, "August", 9, "September",
    10, "October", 11, "November", 12, "December"
     "Unknown month number"
)
--SEARCHED SWITCH
Color Name =
SWITCH (
    TRUE (),
    [Color Code] = "r", "Red",
    Aggregation[Color Code] = "g", "Green",
    Aggregation[Color Code] = "b", "Blue",
    "Unknown"
)
```

> **MORE INFO**   **LOGICAL FUNCTIONS**
>
> For more information and examples on the Logical Functions reference, see: *https://msdn. microsoft.com/en-us/library/ee634365.aspx.*

Date and Time Functions

Data and Time functions are used to create calculations based on dates and time. They use the datetime data type and depending on the function can take values from a column as an argument.

The CALENDAR and CALENDARAUTO functions are used to return a table with a single column of contiguous dates named Date. The range of dates is determined by the inputs to the function. CALENDAR takes two parameters. The first is a start date and the second is the end date. CALENDARAUTO uses the smallest and largest dates in the data model as a basis for determining its start and end dates. It also takes on optional fiscal year-end parameter, which is a value between 1 and 12 (see Table 2-9). The following examples can be found in the file named **\Chapter2\CH02FunctionDemos.xlsx**.

TABLE 2-9 Date and Time Functions

Function	Description	Example
DATE(year, month, day)	Returns a date constructed from the inputs of the Datetime type	DATE Demo = DATE(DateFunctions[Year] ,DateFunctions[Month], DateFunctions[Day])
TIME(hour, minute, second)	Returns a time component constructed from the inputs of the Datetime type	TIME Demo = TIME(DateFunctions[Hour], DateFunctions[Minute], DateFunctions[Second])
NOW( )	Returns current date and time	NOW Demo = NOW( )
TODAY( )	Returns date with no time component (defaults to 12AM)	TODAY Demo = TODAY( )

Year	Month	Day	Hour	Minute	Second	DATE Demo	TIME Demo	NOW Demo	TODAY Demo
2017	12	10	11	12	30	2017-12-10 12:00:00 AM	1899-12-30 11:12:30 AM	2018-01-28 6:15:26 PM	2018-01-28 12:00:00 AM
2018	1	2	16	55	21	2018-01-02 12:00:00 AM	1899-12-30 4:55:21 PM	2018-01-28 6:15:26 PM	2018-01-28 12:00:00 AM
2018	1	28	9	21	59	2018-01-28 12:00:00 AM	1899-12-30 9:21:59 AM	2018-01-28 6:15:26 PM	2018-01-28 12:00:00 AM

FIGURE 2-29 Results of the functions from Table 2-9

TABLE 2-10 Date and Time Functions

Function	Description	Example
DATEDIFF(start date, end date, interval)	Returns a number that corresponds to the interval you wish to measure between a start- and end-date datetime value. The interval can be Years, Quarters, Months, Weeks, Days, Hours, Minutes, or Seconds.	DATEDIFF Demo = DATEDIFF(DateFunctions2[Start Date], DateFunctions2[End Date], DAY)
EDATE(date value, months value)	Returns a date that is indicated by the number of months before or after the date value.	EDATE Demo = EDATE(DateFunctions2[Start Date], 1)
EOMONTH(date value, months value)	Returns a date at the end of the month that is indicated by the number of months before or after the date value.	EOMONTH Demo = =EOMONTH(DateFunctions2[Start Date], 0)

Start Date	End Date	DATEDIFF Demo	EDATE Demo	EOMONTH Demo
2015-01-01 12:00:00 AM	2015-01-02 12:00:00 AM	1	2015-02-01 12:00:00 AM	2015-01-31 12:00:00 AM
2015-01-02 12:00:00 AM	2016-01-10 12:00:00 AM	373	2015-02-02 12:00:00 AM	2015-01-31 12:00:00 AM
2015-02-02 12:00:00 AM	2015-05-08 12:00:00 AM	95	2015-03-02 12:00:00 AM	2015-02-28 12:00:00 AM
2015-07-02 12:00:00 AM	2015-12-08 12:00:00 AM	159	2015-08-02 12:00:00 AM	2015-07-31 12:00:00 AM

FIGURE 2-30 Results of the functions from Table 2-10

There are several functions that parse out a specified part of a datetime. Each of these functions takes a datetime value and returns an integer. The functions are YEAR, MONTH, DAY, HOUR, MINUTE, SECOND, WEEKDAY, and WEEKNUM.

And finally, there are two functions that take a text representation of a date or time and converts it to datetime data type. These are DATEVALUE and TIMEVALUE.

> **MORE INFO   DATE AND TIME FUNCTIONS**
>
> For more information and examples on the Date and Time Functions reference, see: *https://msdn.microsoft.com/en-us/library/ee634786.aspx*.

Text Functions

With the text functions in DAX, you can do such things as return parts of a string, look for text within a string, or concatenate string values. The following examples can be found in the file named **\Chapter2\CH02FunctionDemos.xlsx**.

TABLE 2-11 Text Functions

Function	Description	Example
CONCATENATE(value1, value 2)	Returns a number that corresponds to the interval you wish to measure between a start- and end-date datetime value. The interval can be Years, Quarters, Months, Weeks, Days, Hours, Minutes, or Seconds.	CONCATENATE Demo = CONCATENATE(TextFunctions[First Name], TextFunctions[Last Name])
CONCATENATEX(table, expression, delimiter)	Returns a date that is the indicated by the number of months before or after the date value.	CONCATENATEX Demo := CONCATENATEX(TextFunctions, [First Name], ", ")

First Name	Last Name	CONCATENATE Demo
Flemming	Pedersen	FlemmingPedersen
Adam	Harmetz	AdamHarmetz
Jean-Christophe	Pitie	Jean-ChristophePitie

CONCATENATEX Demo: Flemming, Adam, Jean-Christophe

FIGURE 2-31 Results of the functions from Table 2-11

TABLE 2-12 Text Functions

Function	Description	Example
FIND(text to find, text to search, [Start Position], [Value if not found])	Returns the numeric position of the first occurrence of the text to find in the text to search from left to right. Search is case-sensitive.	FIND Demo = FIND("m", TextFunctions[First Name], 1, BLANK())
SEARCH(text to find, text to search, [Start Position], [Value if not found])	Returns the numeric position of the first occurrence of the text to find in the text to search from left to right. Search is case-insensitive.	SEARCH Demo = FIND("M", TextFunctions[First Name], 1, BLANK())
REPLACE(original text, start position, length, replacement text)	Returns a newly formed string with the replaced text.	REPLACE DEMO = REPLACE(TextFunctions[First Name], 1, 2, "Mr.")
SUBSTITUTE(original text, text to replace, replacement text, instance occurrence to replace)	Returns a newly formed string with the replaced text.	SUBSTITUTE Demo= SUBSTITUTE(TextFunctions[First Name], "-", " ",1)
EXACT(value 1, value 2)	Compares two text strings and returns TRUE if they are the same, including case.	EXACT Demo = EXACT(TextFunctions[First Name], "Adam")
VALUE(text value)	Converts the text value to a number	VALUE Demo = VALUE("1")

First Name	Last Name	FIND Demo	SEARCH Demo	REPLACE Demo	SUBSTITUTE Demo	EXACT Demo
Flemming	Pedersen	4	4	Mr.emming	Flemming	FALSE
Adam	Harmetz	4	4	Mr.am	Adam	TRUE
Jean-Christophe	Pitie			Mr.an-Christophe	Jean Christophe	FALSE

FIGURE 2-32 Results of the functions from Table 2-12

TABLE 2-13 Text Functions

Function	Description	Example
LEN(value to measure)	Returns the length of the string.	=LEN(TextFunctions[First Name])
TRIM(value to trim)	Returns a string with leading and trailing whitespace removed.	=TRIM(TextFunctions[First Name])
LEFT(value, number of characters to take)	Returns the left number of characters specified.	=LEFT(TextFunctions[First Name], 5)
RIGHT(value, number of characters to take)	Returns the right number of characters specified.	=RIGHT(TextFunctions[First Name], 3)
MID(value, start positions, number of characters to take)	Returns the characters from the starting position for the number of characters specified.	=MID(TextFunctions[First Name], 2,2)

First Name	Last Name	LEN Demo	TRIM Demo	LEFT Demo	RIGHT Demo	MID Demo
Flemming	Pedersen	10	Flemming	Fle	ing	F
Adam	Harmetz	4	Adam	Adam	dam	da
Jean-Christophe	Pitie	15	Jean-Christophe	Jean-	phe	ea

FIGURE 2-33 Results of the functions from Table 2-13

MORE INFO **TEXT FUNCTIONS**

For more information and examples on the Text Functions reference, see: *https://msdn. microsoft.com/en-us/library/ee634938.aspx.*

Information Functions

These functions look at the table or column that is passed in as an argument to and tells you whether the value matches the expected type. The examples in this section use the **\Chapter2\ Adventure Works Data Model.xlsx** file.

TABLE 2-14 Information Functions

Function	Description	Example
CONTAINS(table, columnName, value[, columnName, value]...)	Returns true if the table that is passed in contains the values listed.	Contains Name := CONTAINS(DimCustomer, [LastName], "Suarez") * This was created as a measure in FactInternetSales
LOOKUPVALUE(result columnName, search columnName, search value[, search column-Name>, search value...)	Returns the result column name to the originating table where the value of the search column name matches the search value from the originating table.	=LOOKUPVALUE (DimCustomer[FirstName], DimCustomer[CustomerKey], [CustomerKey]) * This was created as a calculated column named Customer First Name in FactInternetSales

Other Information Functions

- ISBLANK
- ISERROR
- ISEVEN
- ISLOGICAL
- ISNONTEXT
- ISNUMBER
- ISONORAFTER
- ISTEXT

MORE INFO **INFORMATION FUNCTIONS**

For more information and examples on the Information Functions reference, see: *https:// msdn.microsoft.com/en-us/library/ee634552.aspx.*

Filter Functions

The following group of functions is primarily used in the process of filtering data. You will look at CALCULATE, FILTER, ALL, and USERELATIONSHIP functions, which are some of the most commonly used filtering functions.

The CALCULATE function is likely the most widely used function in DAX. It is used to modify the context in which your data is filtered, and it evaluates an expression in the context that you specify by using filters. In Listing 2-2, you are calculating the Total Sales by using the overriding the context to be the United States only.

LISTING 2-2 CALCULATE Function

```
//
US Sales :=
CALCULATE (
    [Total Sales],
    DimSalesTerritory[SalesTerritoryCountry] = "United States"
)
```

Figure 2-34 shows the U.S. sales measure as using the Total Sales measure and then modifying the Filter Context the Year and Country on the columns and rows. The U.S. Filter in Calculate overrides the Country Filter context on the rows and accepts the Year filter on the columns to produce the PivotTable values. To verify, you will notice that the values with a Row Table of Total Sales and U.S. sales both report the same values.

Row Labels	Column Labels 2010	2011	2012	2013	Grand Total
Australia					
Total Sales	1288137.418	2178638.451	3041367.016	2552857.7	9061000.584
US Sales	1085715.552	2146168.281	2839388.068	3318517.61	9389789.511
Canada					
Total Sales	143251.5374	625180.6523	535958.3824	673454.29	1977844.862
US Sales	1085715.552	2146168.281	2839388.068	3318517.61	9389789.511
France					
Total Sales	177171.702	520523.5656	1024692.387	921630.06	2644017.714
US Sales	1085715.552	2146168.281	2839388.068	3318517.61	9389789.511
Germany					
Total Sales	237784.9902	523412.41	1057435.598	1075679.34	2894312.338
US Sales	1085715.552	2146168.281	2839388.068	3318517.61	9389789.511
NA					
Total Sales					
US Sales	1085715.552	2146168.281	2839388.068	3318517.61	9389789.511
United Kingdom					
Total Sales	290891.4212	592285.9522	1306168.298	1202366.54	3391712.211
US Sales	1085715.552	2146168.281	2839388.068	3318517.61	9389789.511
United States					
Total Sales	1085715.552	2146168.281	2839388.068	3318517.61	9389789.511
US Sales	1085715.552	2146168.281	2839388.068	3318517.61	9389789.511
Total Total Sales	3222952.62	6586209.312	9805009.748	9744505.54	29358677.22
Total US Sales	1085715.552	2146168.281	2839388.068	3318517.61	9389789.511

FIGURE 2-34 PivotTable showing the US Sales and the Total Sales Measures side by side

The FILTER Function is used to restrict the rows in the table that you are working with, and it is used in conjunction with other functions that require a table as an argument. In Listing 2-3, you FILTER the Product Table to products that have a list price of greater than $10. This measure is influenced by the context that surrounds it.

The second measure named **Products over 10 ALL** in Listing 2-3 uses the ALL function to remove the context that might be influencing what values are seen in Dim Product. This explains why the value of 380 repeats for each row as the Grand Total amount is not influenced by the filtering context.

Also, notice that a (blank) is inserted as the last product category, and this is due to the fact you are using the EnglishProductCategoryName from the DimProductCategory. In this data structure, there are Products that have no Subcategories and hence no Categories, so a blank is inserted into the result set.

LISTING 2-3 The FILTER Function

```
//
Products over 10 :=
COUNTROWS ( FILTER ( DimProduct, DimProduct[ListPrice] > 10 ) )
//
Products over 10  ALL :=
COUNTROWS ( FILTER ( ALL ( DimProduct ), DimProduct[ListPrice] > 10 ) )
```

Row Labels	Products over 10	Products over 10 ALL
Accessories	27	380
Bikes	125	380
Clothing	41	380
Components	187	380
(blank)		380
Grand Total	380	380

FIGURE 2-35 Pivot to show measures side by side within filter context

As mentioned earlier in the Chapter when establishing relationships, you were made of aware of the fact that you can have multiple relationships between two tables, but only one of them can be active at a time. To take advantage of the inactive paths, you need to use the USEREALTIONSHIP function.

In the Adventure Works Data Model.xlsx, the DimDate table has three relationships between it and FactInternetSales. They are:

- OrderDateKey to DateKey: Active
- ShippedDateKey to DateKey: Inactive
- DueDateKey to DateKey: Inactive

The first measure in Listing 2-4 counts the number of order in FactInternetSales. The second measure Counts the number Orders Shipped using the inactive path. Figure 2-36 shows the result of comparing these values in a PivotTable.

LISTING 2-4 The USERELATIONSHIP Function

```
//COUNT OF THE NUMBER OF ORDERS
Count of Orders :=
COUNTROWS ( FactInternetSales )

//COUNT OF ORDERS SHIPPED. THIS USES THE INACTIVE SHIPPED DATE RELATIONSHIP
COUNT OF ORDERS SHIPPED :=
CALCULATE (
    [COUNT OF ORDERS],
    USERELATIONSHIP ( DIMDATE[DATEKEY], FACTINTERNETSALES[SHIPDATEKEY] )
)
```

Row Labels	Count of Orders	Count of Orders Shipped
⊟ 2010	14	
December	14	
⊟ 2011	2216	2178
January	144	123
February	144	144
March	150	150
April	157	155
May	174	176
June	230	214
July	188	198
August	193	187
September	185	199
October	221	192
November	208	233
December	222	207
⊟ 2012	3397	3220

FIGURE 2-36 Pivot showing a calculation using an inactive relationship

Additional Filter Functions:

- ADDMISSINGITEMS
- ALLEXCEPT
- ALLNOBLANKROW
- ALLSELECTED
- CALCULATETABLE
- CROSSFILTER
- DISTINCT
- EARLIER
- EARLIEST
- FILTERS
- HASONEFILTER
- HASONEVALUE
- ISCROSSFILTERED
- ISFILTERED
- KEEPFILTERS
- RELATEDTABLE
- SELECTEDVALUE

MORE INFO **FILTER FUNCTIONS**

For more information and examples on the Filter Functions reference, see: *https://msdn.microsoft.com/en-us/library/ee634807.aspx.*

Time Intelligence Functions

Time Intelligence functions are used to create references to data across time periods. They use built-in intelligence that relies on calendars and dates. When used in combination with aggregations or calculations, you can build sophisticated comparison across time periods. For many of these functions to work properly, it is important that you have a table marked as a Data Table in the model. Some of the more commonly used data functions are shown in the next two listings.

The TOTALMTD, TOTALQTD, and TOTALYTD functions calculate running totals for the time from referenced below. The TOTALYTD function in Listing 2-5.

LISTING 2-5 The TOTALYTD Function

```
//
Total Sales YTD:=TOTALYTD (
    SUM ( FactInternetSales[Sales Amount] ),
    DimDate[FullDateAlternateKey]
)
```

The SAMEPERIODLASTYEAR function returns a set of dates from the previous year so that you can calculate the previous year amounts for comparative purposes.

LISTING 2-6 The SAMEPERIODLASTYEAR Function

```
//
Total Sales PY:=CALCULATE (
    SUM ( FactInternetSales[Sales Amount] ),
    SAMEPERIODLASTYEAR ( DimDate[FullDateAlternateKey] )
)
```

To see the behavior of the TOTALYTD and SAMEPERIODLASTYEAR, you can open the Adventure Works Data Model.xlsx spreadsheet and go to the TimeIntelligence tab to see the PivotTable behind Figure 2-37.

The Total Sales Column uses the Total Sales measure from earlier. Notice that it keeps track of totals by each month and then the year. The Total Sales YTD keeps a running Total Sales measure over the time frame. And finally, observe how the Total Sales PY repeats the Total Sales measures for the previous year.

The Time Intelligence Functions are very powerful and make doing periodic analysis possible in only a few lines of code.

Row Labels	Total Sales	Total Sales YTD	Total Sales PY
⊞ 2010	**43421.0364**	**43421.0364**	
⊟ 2011	**7075525.929**	**7075525.929**	**43421.0364**
January	469823.9148	469823.9148	
February	466334.903	936158.8178	
March	485198.6594	1421357.477	
April	502073.8458	1923431.323	
May	561681.4758	2485112.799	
June	737839.8214	3222952.62	
July	596746.5568	3819699.177	
August	614557.935	4434257.112	
September	603083.4976	5037340.61	
October	708208.0032	5745548.613	
November	660545.8132	6406094.426	
December	669431.5031	7075525.929	43421.0364
⊟ 2012	**5842485.195**	**5842485.195**	**7075525.929**
January	495364.1261	495364.1261	469823.9148
February	506994.1876	1002358.314	466334.903
March	373483.0054	1375841.319	485198.6594
April	400335.6145	1776176.934	502073.8458
May	358877.8907	2135054.824	561681.4758
June	555160.1428	2690214.967	737839.8214
July	444558.2281	3134773.195	596746.5568
August	523917.3815	3658690.577	614557.935
September	486177.4502	4144868.027	603083.4976
October	535159.4846	4680027.512	708208.0032
November	537955.517	5217983.029	660545.8132
December	624502.1667	5842485.195	669431.5031
⊟ 2013	**16351550.34**	**16351550.34**	**5842485.195**

FIGURE 2-37 Pivot showing Time Intelligence Function results

> **MORE INFO** **TIME INTELLIGENCE FUNCTIONS**
>
> For more information and examples on the Time Intelligence Functions reference, see the following two articles: *https://msdn.microsoft.com/en-us/library/ee634763.aspx* and *https:// support.office.com/en-us/article/time-intelligence-in-power-pivot-in-Excel-016acf7b-9ded-411e-ba6c-ed8b8c368011*.

Statistical, Math, and Trig Functions

Statistical, Math, and Trig Functions are used to provide various operations when working with numeric data. The following examples in Listing 2-7 and can be found in the file named **\Chapter2\CH02FunctionDemos.xlsx**. The outputs of these functions are shown in Figure 2-38.

LISTING 2-7 The Statistical, Math, and Trig Function

```
=ABS(Numbers[Numbers])
=CEILING(Numbers[Numbers], 1)
=FLOOR(Numbers[Numbers], 1)
=ROUND(Numbers[Numbers], 2)
=ROUNDUP(Numbers[Numbers], 2)
=ROUNDDOWN([Numbers], 2)
=TRUNC(Numbers[Numbers], 1)
=EVEN(Numbers[Numbers])
=ODD(Numbers[Numbers])
```

Numbers	ABS	CEILING	FLOOR	ROUND	ROUNDUP	ROUNDDOWN	TRUNC	EVEN	ODD
1.5432	1.5432	2	1	1.54	1.55	1.54	1.5	2	3
2.4534	2.4534	3	2	2.45	2.46	2.45	2.4	4	3
6.897665	6.897665	7	6	6.9	6.9	6.89	6.8	8	7
59.7652	59.7652	60	59	59.77	59.77	59.76	59.7	60	61
0	0	0	0	0	0	0	0	0	1
-7.256	7.256	-7	-8	-7.26	-7.26	-7.25	-7.2	-8	-9
-7.679	7.679	-7	-8	-7.68	-7.68	-7.67	-7.6	-8	-9

FIGURE 2-38 Results of the functions from Listing 2-7

> **MORE INFO**   **STATISTICAL, MATH, AND TRIG FUNCTIONS**
>
> For more information and examples on the Math and Trig Functions reference, see: *https://msdn.microsoft.com/en-us/library/ee634241.aspx*. For more information and examples on the Statistical Functions reference, see: *https://msdn.microsoft.com/en-us/library/ee634822.aspx*.

Parent and Child Functions

There are several Parent and Child Functions that are presented here that are used to flatten out and work with hierarchy data. They will be discussed in detail in Skill 2.3 when you learn about resolving hierarchy issues. They are listed here for completeness:

- PATH
- PATHCONTAINS
- PATHITEM
- PATHITEMREVERSE
- PATHLENGTH

> **MORE INFO**   **PARENT AND CHILD FUNCTIONS**
>
> For more information and examples of the Parent and Child Functions reference, see: *https://msdn.microsoft.com/en-us/library/mt150102.aspx*.

Other Functions

The following functions perform actions that do not fit into any of the above categories of functions as previously discussed:

- EXCEPT
- GROUPBY
- INTERSECT
- UNION
- NATURALINNERJOIN
- NATURALLEFTOUTERJOIN
- ISEMPTY
- SUMMARIZECOLUMNS
- VAR

> **MORE INFO**   **ADDITIONAL DAX RESOURCES**
>
> This section of the book is meant as an overview of the functions that are available in the DAX to prepare you for the exam. For a more in-depth dive into DAX, any of these three groups are considered gurus in the space and all have books that should be on your book-shelf. Marco Russo and Alberto Ferrari of *https://www.sqlbi.com/*; Rob Collie of *https://Power Pivotpro.com/*; and Matt Allington of *https://Exceleratorbi.com.au/*.

Create DAX queries

The exam will test your ability to write basic DAX queries. DAX queries are very useful for help-ing you retrieve data from Analysis Services Tabular Models into your data models. You have already seen a few places in this book in which you have imported data from these sources, but have gone directly to tables themselves to retrieve them in their entirety. Now you will see how to write your own queries so that you can build more custom solutions for retrieving data based on unique needs.

> **NOTE**   **ADVENTUREWORKS TABULAR SAMPLE DATABASE**
>
> The examples in this section require you to have the same AdventureWorks tabular models installed that you needed in Chapter 1. If you did not install these at that point but want to use them now, please refer to the instructions at the beginning of Chapter 1, Skill 1.1.

DAX query structure

The structure of a DAX query is straightforward but does differ from what you may have seen in T-SQL or MDX. The examples walk through the progressions of building a more complex DAX query in a manner like how one would learn when building T-SQL statements. Listing 2-8 contain the most basic form of DAX query; it simply retrieves all the columns and rows of data from the table.

If the table name contains any spaces or reserved words, it would need to be surrounded by quotes. If not, the quotes are not necessary. The statements in the EVALUATE could also be surrounded by brackets.

LISTING 2-8 DAX Query

```
EVALUATE
'Internet Sales'

--OR the following is valid as well

EVALUATE (
'Internet Sales'
)
```

To run the first queries in this section, you will use the Get External Data functions from within Power Pivot. This is initially the most convenient way to write initial DAX queries, and it allows you to easily go back and modify them. You will be connecting into an Analysis Services Tabular Model for this, but you could also connect to a Power Pivot Workbooks so long as it resides in SharePoint.

Additionally, as you move through the Table Import Wizard, you will notice that the last screen asks you to write an MDX statement. In this case, a DAX query is what you will use since you are connecting to a Tabular Model. In this example, you use EVALUATE to execute your first DAX query.

1. Create a new Excel workbook and then from the Power Pivot window navigate to **Home**, **From Database**, **From Analysis Services Or PowerPivot**.

2. In the **Table Import Wizard–Connect to a Microsoft SQL Server Analysis Service Database** screen, configure the following and when complete click **Next**.

    - **Friendly Connection Name**   Adventure Works Internet Sales Model Connection
    - **Log Onto The Server**   Windows Authentication
    - **Server Or File Name**   Your Server Name
    - **Database Name**   Adventure Works Internet Sales

3. In the **Table Import Wizard–Specify An MDX query** window, configure the following and then click **Finish**.

    - **Friendly Query Name**   Type Internet Sales. This will translate to the name of the table in the data model, so choosing an appropriate name at this point is wise.
    - **MDX Statement**   Use one of the two blocks of code in Listing 2-8.

4. You should now see one table in your data model named **Internet Sales**, which is a one for one copy of the Internet Sales Table in the Adventure Works Internet Sales database. **Save** your work as **\Chapter2\CH02DAXQueries.xlsx** and leave Excel open because the following examples will continue to build in the same location.

Next, you will look a syntax around ordering your data set should you want to override the default sorting. The ORDER BY clause is an optional clause that contains an expression you would like to sort your result set on, and it is listed in order of precedence or how you want the sort to occur. Any expression that can be evaluated at the Row level is valid. The default sort order is ascending, or if you wish to be explicit, you can specify ASC. To sort a column in descending order, use DESC.

Another optional clause that can be used with ORDER BY is START AT. The START AT clause is part of the ORDER BY clause and cannot be used outside of it. It defines the values at which the query results will start. In this example, you use the ORDER BY and START AT clauses.

5. Open the workbook that you previously saved as **\Chapter2\CH02DAXQueries.xlsx**.

6. With Power Pivot open, select **Design** > **Table Properties**. This will open the **Edit Table Properties** dialog, which has the DAX query for the **Internet Sales** table.

7. In the **MDX statement** text box, type the syntax from Listing 2-9. Click **Save** when complete and this will order the Internet Sales table by the Sales Order number in ascending order. Note that the ASC keyword is optional and only there for clarity.

LISTING 2-9 DAX with ORDER BY

```
EVALUATE (
'Internet Sales'
)
ORDER BY
'Internet Sales'[Sales Order Number] ASC
```

8. Next, you will modify the above statement so that the sorting starts at a certain point in the data set using START AT. Open the **Table Properties** again and modify the query to match Listing 2-10. Once complete, click **Save**.

LISTING 2-10 DAX with ORDER BY and START AT

```
EVALUATE (
'Internet Sales'
)
ORDER BY
'Internet Sales'[Sales Order Number] ASC
START AT
"SO75122"
```

9. You will now notice that as in Figure 2-39, only five rows are in the Internet Sales table since the START AT clause has a value near the end of the data set.

10. **Save** the **\Chapter2\CH02DAXQueries.xlsx** Excel workbook.

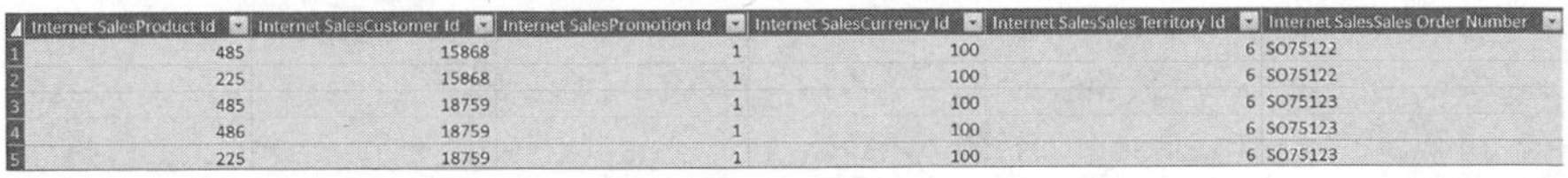

	Internet SalesProduct Id	Internet SalesCustomer Id	Internet SalesPromotion Id	Internet SalesCurrency Id	Internet SalesSales Territory Id	Internet SalesSales Order Number
1	485	15868	1	100	6	SO75122
2	225	15868	1	100	6	SO75122
3	485	18759	1	100	6	SO75123
4	486	18759	1	100	6	SO75123
5	225	18759	1	100	6	SO75123

FIGURE 2-39 Results of the functions from Listing 2-10

Now you will look at the SUMMARIZE function as used in a couple of different scenarios. As you may have noticed, DAX has no simple way to perform projection, which means only choosing certain columns from a table. The previous examples using EVALUATE simply chose all the columns in the table. This is unlike a SQL select clause where you only add items in the select list that you want to be displayed in your result set. To facilitate this in DAX, you will use the SUMMARIZE function. The first demo will mimic only selecting columns with no intent on performing aggregations. The second will use SUMMARIZE in a more traditional way in which it is used to aggregate data.

In this example, you use the SUMMARIZE for column projection. This example works as it takes advantage of the uniqueness of Sales Order Number and Sales Order Line Number. It effectively functions by aggregating individual rows, which is just like returning the underlying detail's rows.

1. Open the workbook that you previously saved as **\Chapter2\CH02DAXQueries.xlsx**.
2. With Power Pivot open, choose **Design**, **Table Properties**. This will open the **Edit Table Properties** dialog, which has the DAX query for the **Internet Sales** table.
3. In the **MDX statement** text box, type the syntax from Listing 2-11. This will summarize the Internet Sales table and will only return the columns listed.

LISTING 2-11 DAX SUMMARIZE function

```
EVALUATE
SUMMARIZE (
'Internet Sales',
'Internet Sales'[Sales Order Number],
'Internet Sales'[Sales Order Line Number],
'Internet Sales'[Total Product Cost]
)
```

4. Once you are done, click **Save** and then look at the Internet Sales table to verify that it has been built according to your criteria as shown in Figure 2-40.

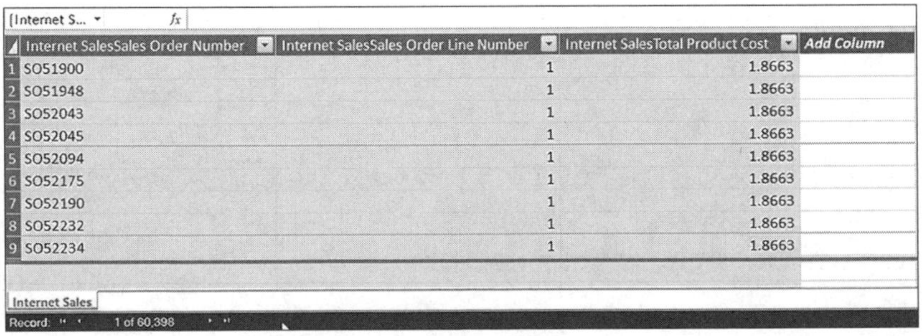

	Internet SalesSales Order Number	Internet SalesSales Order Line Number	Internet SalesTotal Product Cost	Add Column
1	SO51900	1	1.8663	
2	SO51948	1	1.8663	
3	SO52043	1	1.8663	
4	SO52045	1	1.8663	
5	SO52094	1	1.8663	
6	SO52175	1	1.8663	
7	SO52190	1	1.8663	
8	SO52232	1	1.8663	
9	SO52234	1	1.8663	

FIGURE 2-40 Results of the functions from Listing 2-11

> **MORE INFO** **TECHNIQUES FOR PROJECTION IN DAX**
>
> If you are interested in other means for performing projection, see the article from SQLBI:
> *https://www.sqlbi.com/articles/from-sql-to-dax-projection*.

In this example, you will perform a more traditional aggregation using SUMMARIZE for aggregation and FORMAT to style values. Here you will aggregate Total Product Cost and Order Quantity from the Internet Sales table, and you will group them by Calendar Year and Product Category Name from their respective dimension tables. Take note that in this demo, you are aggregating columns as opposed to using the Measures that have been created in the model. In the next demo, you use the Measures to take note to compare the differences.

Also, you will notice the use of the FORMAT function, which has the following syntax: FORMAT(<value>, <format_string>).

> **MORE INFO** **FORMAT**
>
> The FORMAT function is a straightforward function implement, and it has quite a bit of flexibility. For more information on how to use the FORMAT function, please refer to the article at *https://msdn.microsoft.com/en-us/library/ee634924.aspx*.

1. Open the workbook that you previously saved as **\Chapter2\CH02DAXQueries.xlsx**.

2. With Power Pivot open, choose **Design** > **Table Properties**. This will open the **Edit Table Properties** dialog, which has the DAX query for the **Internet Sales** table.

3. In the **MDX statement** text box, type in the syntax from Listing 2-12. This will summarize the Internet Sales table and will only return the columns listed. Notice that you also ordered the table in the same way it was returned, as can be seen in Figure 2-41. Also, Sales Amount has been formatted according to the provided format mask, and it has been stored as a Text Data Type.

LISTING 2-12 DAX SUMMARIZE Function performing aggregation

```
EVALUATE
    SUMMARIZE (
    'Internet Sales',
    'Date'[Calendar Year],
    'Product Category'[Product Category Name],
    "Sales Amount", FORMAT(SUM('Internet Sales'[Sales Amount]), "#,##0.00#"),
    "Order Quantity", SUM('Internet Sales'[Order Quantity])
)
ORDER BY
    'Date'[Calendar Year],
    'Product Category'[Product Category Name]
```

4. Once you are done, click **Save** and then look at the Internet Sales table to verify that it has been built according to your criteria.

DateCalendar Year	Product CategoryProduct Category Name	Sales Amount	Order Quantity
1	2010 Bikes	43,421.036	14
2	2011 Bikes	7,075,525.929	2216
3	2012 Accessories	2,147.08	106
4	2012 Bikes	5,839,695.325	3269
5	2012 Clothing	642.79	22
6	2013 Accessories	668,241.53	34409
7	2013 Bikes	15,359,502.36	9706
8	2013 Clothing	323,806.45	8686
9	2014 Accessories	30,371.35	1577
10	2014 Clothing	15,323.37	393

FIGURE 2-41 Results of the functions from Listing 2-12

What if you now want to include subtotals for each of the above groupings? This is where you can take advantage of the ROLLUP function. For an example of how this works, see Listing 2-13. After you execute the query in Power Pivot, you should see the results as in Figure 2-42.

LISTING 2-13 DAX SUMMARIZE with the ROLLUP option

```
EVALUATE
    SUMMARIZE(
        'Internet Sales',
            ROLLUP (
                'Date'[Calendar Year],
                'Product Category'[Product Category Name]
            ),
            "Total Sales",
                [Internet Total Sales],
            "Order Quantity",
                [Internet Total Units]
    )
ORDER BY
    'Date'[Calendar Year],
    'Product Category'[Product Category Name]
```

DateCalendar Year	Product CategoryProduct Category Name	Order Quantity	Total Sales	Add Column
1			60398	29358677.2207
2	2010		14	43421.0364
3	2010 Bikes		14	43421.0364
4	2011		2216	7075525.9291
5	2011 Bikes		2216	7075525.9291
6	2012		3397	5842485.1952
7	2012 Accessories		106	2147.08
8	2012 Bikes		3269	5839695.3252
9	2012 Clothing		22	642.79
10	2013		52801	16351550.34
11	2013 Accessories		34409	668241.53
12	2013 Bikes		9706	15359502.36
13	2013 Clothing		8686	323806.45
14	2014		1970	45694.72
15	2014 Accessories		1577	30371.35
16	2014 Clothing		393	15323.37

FIGURE 2-42 Results of the functions from Listing 2-13

A useful feature when writing DAX queries is to be able to create measures that only last the duration of the actual query. You might use this when debugging or trying to understand a model that someone has already created that you are consuming in your data model. Or perhaps you are experimenting with a measure that you are not sure you want someone to add to a tabular model yet. The example focuses on using Query Scoped Measures.

5. Open the workbook that you previously saved as **\Chapter2\CH02DAXQueries.xlsx**.

6. With Power Pivot open, choose **Design** > **Table Properties**. This will open the **Edit Table Properties** dialog, which has the DAX query for the **Internet Sales** table.

7. In the window, type in the syntax from Listing 2-14. This will take the Internet Sales and will only return the columns listed. Notice that the table has been ordered in the same way it was returned.

LISTING 2-14 Query Scoped Measure

```
DEFINE
    MEASURE 'Internet Sales'[Total Sales] =
        SUM ( 'Internet Sales'[Sales Amount] )
EVALUATE
SUMMARIZE (
    'Internet Sales',
    'Product'[Color],
    "Total Sales",
        'Internet Sales'[Total Sales]
)
ORDER BY 'Product'[Color]
```

CALCULATE is the same function that you looked at in the DAX Functions Section. It simply evaluates an expression in a context that is modified by a filter specified in the function. In Listing 2-15, you modify the current context by removing all filters by applying the ALL Function so that all the denominator for Sales Proportion can be calculated properly.

LISTING 2-15 CALCULATE and ALL Functions

```
DEFINE
    MEASURE 'Internet Sales'[Sales by Color] =
        SUM ( 'Internet Sales'[Sales Amount] )
    MEASURE 'Internet Sales'[All Sales] =
        CALCULATE ( SUM ( 'Internet Sales'[Sales Amount] ), ALL ( 'Internet Sales' ) )
    MEASURE 'Internet Sales'[Sales Proportion] =
        DIVIDE('Internet Sales'[Sales by Color], 'Internet Sales'[All Sales], 0)
EVALUATE
SUMMARIZE (
    'Internet Sales',
```

```
    'Product'[Color],
    "Total Sales by Color", 'Internet Sales'[Sales by Color],
    "Total Sales overall", 'Internet Sales'[All Sales],
    "Proportion", 'Internet Sales'[Sales Proportion]
)
ORDER BY 'Product'[Color]
```

It is also possible to apply the FILTER function similarly to what was done in the Section on creating DAX formulas. In Listing 2-16 you first filter the Internet Sales table to the products that are red. This then produces a table that is then fed into the SUMMARIZE function. Also, notice that you needed to take advantage of the RELATED function to enable the filtering to succeed.

LISTING 2-16 FILTER Function

```
DEFINE
    MEASURE 'Internet Sales'[Total Sales] =
        SUM ( 'Internet Sales'[Sales Amount] )
EVALUATE
SUMMARIZE (
    FILTER('Internet Sales', RELATED('Product'[Color]) = "Red"),
    'Product'[Color],
    "Total Sales",
        'Internet Sales'[Total Sales]
)
ORDER BY 'Product'[Color]
```

At this point, you have kept the FILTER criteria straightforward. It is possible to use Logic Functions to build up more complex filtering criteria. In Listing 2-17, you do so by layering in an OR statement so that you can bring in both red and blue products.

LISTING 2-17 FILTER with OR Logic

```
DEFINE
    MEASURE 'Internet Sales'[Total Sales] =
        SUM ( 'Internet Sales'[Sales Amount] )
EVALUATE
SUMMARIZE (
    FILTER (
        'Internet Sales',
        OR (
            RELATED ( 'Product'[Color] ) = "Red",
            RELATED ( 'Product'[Color] ) = "Blue"
        )
    ),
    'Product'[Color],
    "Total Sales", 'Internet Sales'[Total Sales]
)
ORDER BY 'Product'[Color]
```

If you have written SQL statements in the past, you will be familiar with the HAVING clause, which is used to filter data out of your result set after aggregations have occurred. DAX allows you to perform the functional equivalent by filtering your SUMMARIZE using a Measure value.

Notice that filtering of the rows that go into the SUMMARIZE is done using the FILTER clause. This happens before you aggregate your data into a Measure. Once your query has the rows that are needed for aggregations, the aggregation can be performed. Once this step is done, you can filter on the Measure.

LISTING 2-18 FILTER with by Measure

```
DEFINE
    MEASURE 'Internet Sales'[Total Sales] =
        SUM ( 'Internet Sales'[Sales Amount] )
EVALUATE
FILTER(
SUMMARIZE (
    'Internet Sales',
    'Product'[Color],
    "Total Sales", 'Internet Sales'[Total Sales]
), [Total Sales] > 2500000
)
ORDER BY 'Product'[Color]
```

> **MORE INFO**   **CREATING A DAX QUERY IN EXCEL**
>
> For more information on how to create a DAX query in Excel using another method, consult the following article: *https://www.sqlbi.com/articles/import-data-from-tabular-model-in-Excel-using-a-dax-query/.*

Create Excel formulas

Consuming data via PivotTables is a common and robust way for users to interact with data in the Excel data model and well as cubes in SQL Server Analysis services. More will be said about using PivotTables to navigate to the data model in Chapter 3, but as you may already know, they offer second-to-none flexibility for slicing and dicing information. However, this flexibility comes at a cost and has some limitations when results need to be displayed in certain ways.

The following are scenarios where the presentation to end-users begins to fall short when using PivotTables to display metrics in a manner as shown in Figure 2-43. If you wish to look at the finished product and its supporting objects, please refer to **\Chapter2\CH02CubeFunctionsEnd.xlsx**.

1. If a user wanted to build a dashboard for consumers that would remain static in shape and size, a PivotTable will fall short. PivotTables are dynamic by nature, and the simple nature of resizing makes consuming data from them a challenge, and additional members would affect the cell references needed to build reports and dashboards.

2. There are native Excel formatting options that are available when data is formatted in the manner below that are not easily replicated, or even possible, when using a Pivot-Table alone. The columns that are conditionally formatted and the Growth columns are not possible with a PivotTable alone.

	2010	2011	2012	2013	Growth 2010 to 2011	Growth 2011 to 2012	Growth 2012 to 2013
Accessories			$294,907.67	$405,852.29			38%
Bike Racks			$16,560.00	$22,800.00			38%
Bike Stands			$18,921.00	$20,670.00			9%
Bottles and Cages			$23,449.03	$33,349.16			42%
Cleaners			$3,052.80	$4,165.80			36%
Fenders			$19,496.26	$27,123.32			39%
Helmets			$93,003.42	$132,332.18			42%
Hydration Packs			$16,771.95	$23,535.72			40%
Tires and Tubes			$103,653.21	$141,876.11			37%
Bikes	$3,222,952.62	$6,586,209.31	$9,371,244.74	$9,137,737.98	104%	42%	-2%
Mountain Bikes	$568,998.32	$1,581,503.13	$3,995,042.02	$3,807,216.10	178%	153%	-5%
Road Bikes	$2,653,954.30	$5,004,706.18	$3,954,426.52	$2,907,497.03	89%	-21%	-26%
Touring Bikes			$1,421,776.20	$2,423,024.85			70%
Clothing			$138,857.34	$200,915.27			45%
Caps			$7,992.11	$11,695.99			46%
Gloves			$14,228.69	$20,792.01			46%
Jerseys			$70,740.39	$102,210.29			44%
Shorts			$30,585.63	$40,734.18			33%
Socks			$2,229.52	$2,876.80			29%
Vests			$13,081.00	$22,606.00			73%
Grand Total	$3,222,952.62	$6,586,209.31	$9,805,009.75	$9,744,505.54	104%	49%	-1%

FIGURE 2-43 Dashboard supported by CUBE Functions and native Excel formatting

Seven Cube Functions were introduced in Excel 2007 and were used to interact with SQL Server Analysis Services sources. This was extended to include the ability for the functions to interact with not only Analysis Services but the Excel data model as well. As you will see, these functions can be used to help us get around some of the shortcomings that were listed above. The seven cube functions are listed in Table 2-15, and further information can be found in the more information section below.

TABLE 2-15 The Seven Cube Functions available in Excel

Cube Function Name	Description
CUBEMEMBER function	Returns a member or tuple from the cube. Use to validate that the member or tuple exists in the cube.
CUBEVALUE function	Returns an aggregated value from the cube.
CUBEMEMBERPROPERTY function	Returns the value of a member property from the cube. Use to validate that a member name exists within the cube and to return the specified property for this member.
CUBESET function	Defines a calculated set of members or tuples by sending a set expression to the cube on the server, which creates the set and then returns that set to Microsoft Excel.
CUBESETCOUNT function	Returns the number of items in a set.
CUBERANKEDMEMBER function	Returns the nth, or ranked, member in a set. Use to return one or more elements in a set, such as the top sales performer or the top 10 students.
CUBEKPIMEMBER function	Returns a key performance indicator (KPI) property and displays the KPI name in the cell. A KPI is a quantifiable measurement, such as monthly gross profit or quarterly employee turnover, that is used to monitor an organization's performance.

Cube functions can be written as a query, cell by cell, against an MDX or Tabular source. Optionally, as a starting point, a PivotTable can be converted entirely to Cube Functions all in one action, as will demonstrated next. The most basic way to start using Cube Functions is to first create a PivotTable and then convert it in one step. In this example, we build a dashboard using data sourced from Cube Functions.

1. Open the file named **\Chapter2\CH02CubeFunctionsStart.xlsx** and navigate to the data model.

2. Choose **Home** > **PivotTable**. When the **Create PivotTable** dialog box opens, choose **Existing worksheet 'Sheet1'!B2**. You can really put this anywhere you like, but as to keep the explanations below aligned to the right cells in your work, use the reference as above.

3. Build out the PivotTable as follows by dragging the following fields into the specified location in the **PivotTable Fields** pane:

   - **Columns   FiscalYear** from **DimDate**
   - **Rows   H_Product** from to **DimProduct**
   - **Values   SalesAmount** from **FactInternetSales**

4. Now in the PivotTable, expand each of the Product Categories so that you see the Sub-categories as shown in Figure 2-43.

5. With your cursor anywhere in the PivotTable, navigate to **PivotTable Tools** > **Analyze** tab > **Calculations** group > **OLAP Tools** > **Convert to Formulas**.

6. You will notice that the PivotTable has disappeared and that each of the cells has been replaced with Cube Function, as can be seen in the formula bar. Move around what was this PivotTable and explore the functions in the formula bar.

7. To complete the rest of the demo, look at **\Chapter2\CH02CubeFunctionsEnd.xlsx** to see how the growth columns and conditional formatting were added on, as these are now standard Excel functions that you would be expected to know.

Now, look at the two functions that are used in this table which are CUBEMEMBER and CUBEVALUE. First look at the cells that make up the rows and columns and insect the Excel formulas in each. These are from the dimension tables named DimDate and DimProduct, and you can see that their members are retrieved using CUBEMEMBER. Then to get the numeric values or aggregates, the CUBEVALUE function is used along with the member coordinates from the 3 CUBEMEMBER to retrieve an aggregate from the cube. Navigate to the cells in the range C4 to G24 to see this function in use.

To further break this down, let's look at how the value of $16,560 in cell E5 is retrieved for Bike Racks in the Year 2012. Listing 2-19 shows the four formulas that are used together to retrieve the value.

- The B2 CUBEMEMBER formula is used to retrieve the cube coordinates for Sum Sales, which is the measure that you want displayed.

- The B5 CUBEMEMBER formula is used to retrieve the cube coordinates Bike Racks in the Product Hierarchy in DimProduct.

- The E3 CUBEMEMBER formula is used to retrieve the cube coordinates for 2012 in Dim-Date.

- The E5 CUBEVALUE formula uses the three above CUBEMEMBER coordinates to retrieve the Aggregate value of $16,560.

LISTING 2-19 Cube Member Functions

```
Cell B2 =CUBEMEMBER("ThisWorkbookDataModel","[Measures].[Sum of SalesAmount]")

Cell B5 =CUBEMEMBER("ThisWorkbookDataModel","[DimProduct].[H_Product].
[ProductSubcategory].&[Bike Racks]")

Cell E3 =CUBEMEMBER("ThisWorkbookDataModel","[DimDate].[FiscalYear].&[2012]")

Cell E5 =CUBEVALUE("ThisWorkbookDataModel",$B$2,$B5,E$3)
```

> **MORE INFO**   **CUBE FUNCTIONS**
>
> Cube functions are very useful for building many different types of reporting solutions for users within the context of Excel. Some good online references are: *https://Power Pivot-pro.com/2010/06/using-Excel-cube-functions-with-Power Pivot/*, *https://channel9.msdn. com/Events/TechEd/NewZealand/2013/DBI304*, and *https://dataonwheels.wordpress. com/2015/01/27/Excel-bi-tip-18-using-cube-functions-to-break-out-of-pivot-tables/.*

Skill 2.3: Create Hierarchies

Hierarchies offer a very convenient way for users to drill up and down within data sets in a pre-defined manner with ease. They are in use in almost every reporting situation in business, and creating them makes for a more consistent and simple-to-use reporting environment for end-users.

In this section, you will see that Hierarchies are created and managed from within the Diagram View in Power Pivot. Once created, they become a new object in the data model. Creating them is a straightforward task, so you will do some examples to support your knowledge in this space. You will see Hierarchies in action when you move into Chapter 3 where the focus is around consuming the data models for reporting purposes.

> **This section covers how to:**
> - Create date hierarchies
> - Create business hierarchies
> - Resolve hierarchy issues

Create date hierarchies

Likely the most common hierarchy you will see business is the date hierarchy. It is considered a natural hierarchy in that it is commonly agreed upon how the parent-child relationships should roll up. Not many would dispute that, from a calendar year point of view, January 1, 2018 should roll up into January and this should then roll into 2018. Another example of a natural hierarchy is Geography. Once again, not many could argue about how a City such as Seattle rolls into a State named Washington which rolls into a Country named the United States which rolls into a Continent named North America.

Hierarchies are great in that they offer a convenient way for users of your data to drill from Year to Quarter to Month to Day (or however you choose), using a seamless drill path. Common date hierarchies include Calendar, Fiscal, and Semester, and each can be defined in a model if needed.

In this example, you will create a simple date hierarchy that will allow users to roll data from Day to Month to Quarter to Year.

1. Open **\Chapter2\CH02HierarchiesDemo.xlsx** and navigate to the data model.
2. Switch to **Diagram View** and then highlight the **DimDate** table.
3. To create the hierarchy, you can either click on the yellow folder icon in the upper-right corner of the table as shown in Figure 2-44, or you can choose a field that you want in your hierarchy and then right-click on it and choose **Create Hierarchy** from the context menu.

FIGURE 2-44 Create Hierarchy button in Diagram View

4. Once you have completed Step 3, a new entry will appear at the bottom of the table as shown in Figure 2-45.

FIGURE 2-45 Renaming the Hierarchy in Diagram View

5. Name this Hierarchy **H_Calendar** and then **drag** the following columns on top of the new name to create the hierarchy.

- **CalendarYear**
- **CalendarQuarter**
- **EnglishMonthName**
- **FullDateAlternateKey**

6. Once you are complete, it should look like Figure 2-46. The order in which you do this is significant, although it can be reordered using drag and drop or by right-clicking any other nodes and choosing to move them up or down in the hierarchy.

FIGURE 2-46 The complete Date Hierarchy

7. Looking at this now, it would probably be nice to give the Hierarchy levels more meaningful names for your users; the source column names are in brackets and can be either hidden or displayed by right-clicking on a level. The name that will be used in reporting tools is to the left of the source name. Let's Rename the display columns as follows:

- **CalendarYear** to **Calendar Year**
- **CalendarQuarter** to **Calendar Quarter**
- **EnglishMonthName** to **Month Name**
- **FullDateAlternateKey** to **Date**

8. To test this out, from within the data model, navigate to **Home** > **PivotTable** and Create a PivotTable in a new worksheet. As in Figure 2-47, with the PivotTable field pane shown, expand the **DimDate** table, then drag **H_Calendar** to the **Rows** area and the remainder of the fields to the locations below. Now, expand 2012 and Quarter 1.

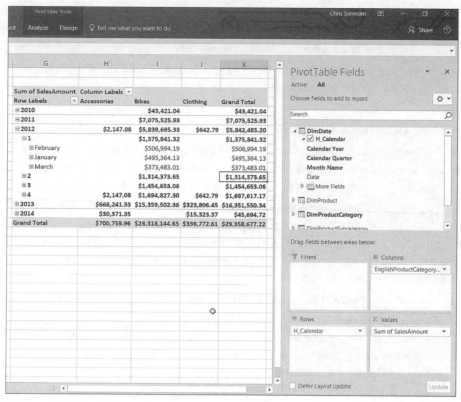

Sum of SalesAmount	Column Labels			
Row Labels	Accessories	Bikes	Clothing	Grand Total
⊞ 2010		$43,421.04		$43,421.04
⊞ 2011		$7,075,525.93		$7,075,525.93
⊟ 2012	$2,147.08	$5,839,695.33	$642.79	$5,842,485.20
⊟ 1		$1,375,841.32		$1,375,841.32
⊞ February		$506,994.19		$506,994.19
⊞ January		$495,364.13		$495,364.13
⊞ March		$373,483.01		$373,483.01
⊞ 2		$1,314,373.65		$1,314,373.65
⊞ 3		$1,454,653.06		$1,454,653.06
⊞ 4	$2,147.08	$1,694,827.30	$642.79	$1,697,617.17
⊞ 2013	$668,241.53	$15,359,502.36	$323,806.45	$16,351,550.34
⊞ 2014	$30,371.35		$15,323.37	$45,694.72
Grand Total	$700,759.96	$28,318,144.65	$339,772.61	$29,358,677.22

FIGURE 2-47 Using the Date Hierarchy in a PivotTable

9. Notice that you can drill down into the hierarchy, but if you look closer, the sorting of the months is incorrect. To fix this, go back to the data model and navigate to **DimDate** in the **Data View**. Now find the **EnglishMonthName** and highlight it.

10. Choose **Home** > **Sort And Filter** > **Sort By Column** and choose **MonthNumberOfYear** as the By Column as in Figure 2-48. Click **OK** when you are done.

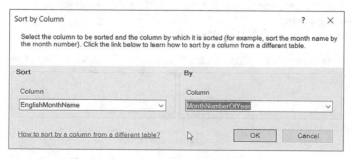

FIGURE 2-48 The Sort by Column dialog box

11. If you now navigate back to the PivotTable, the values should be sorted properly. This is a great feature of the data model in that the sorting property of this text label is now stored in the data model so that it can be reused.

12. Click **Save** to save this file, but keep it open because you will use it in the next demo on creating a business hierarchy.

Create business hierarchies

Business Hierarchies are maintained by individual businesses and are typically unique. For example, most businesses have a way of splitting up how they view Geography over and above what would be considered a Natural Hierarchy. Also, these hierarchies tend to change over time as businesses change. Once a business territory grows, it might need to be split in two.

In this example, you will create a business hierarchy on the product. What is interesting about this one is that you will need to get fields from multiple tables, since all fields for a hierarchy must be in the same table. You will use the RELATED relational function in DAX to bring the columns from the other tables.

1. Open **\Chapter2\CH02HierarchiesDemo.xlsx** and navigate to the data model.

2. The hierarchy that you want to create is the Product hierarchy. It should roll up from Product to Product Subcategory to Product Category. What you want to do is something like what you did in the previous example. Notice that each of the fields is in different tables. This is the first thing that you need to fix.

3. In the **Product** table, you need to create two calculated columns. The first column should be named **ProductSubcategory** and the second is **ProductCategory,** and both should have the definitions as in Listing 2-20.

LISTING 2-20 Bringing columns into the product table to support the hierarchy

```
--Bring the EnglishProductSubcategoryName from ProductSubcategory into a column named
 ProductSubcategory
=
IF (
    ISBLANK ( RELATED ( DimProductSubcategory[EnglishProductSubcategoryName] ) ),
    "No Product Subcategory Defined",
    RELATED ( DimProductSubcategory[EnglishProductSubcategoryName] )
)
--Bring the EnglishProductCategoryName from ProductCategory into a column named
 ProductCategory
=
IF (
    ISBLANK ( RELATED ( DimProductCategory[EnglishProductCategoryName] ) ),
    "No Product Category Defined",
    RELATED ( DimProductCategory[EnglishProductCategoryName] )
)
```

4. Once these columns are in the Product table, you can begin to create the hierarchy. Name this Hierarchy **H_Product** and then drag the following columns on top of the new name to create the hierarchy.

- **ProductCategory**
- **ProductSubcategory**
- **EnglishProductName**

5. When complete the hierarchy should look like Figure 2-49.

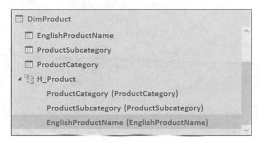

FIGURE 2-49 Product hierarchy

6. Now that you have done this, there is little point to exposing the ProductCategory and ProductSubcategory tables from data model to reporting tools. To hide the tables from the client tools so that they cannot be used in reporting scenarios, right-click on **ProductCategory** tables and choose **Hide From Client Tools** from the context menu. Do the same for **ProductSubcategory**.

Additional notes on managing hierarchies

The following are some additional notes to keep in mind when creating and managing hierarchies:

- A table can have multiple hierarchies defined in it.
- An individual column may be used in multiple hierarchies.
- An individual column can only be used once in a single hierarchy.
- You can use a hidden column when creating a hierarchy.
- You can use multi-select to bring columns into a hierarchy. When doing so, the engine assesses the cardinality of each column to determine how the parent-child relationships need to be defined.
- Any changes to Hierarchies will be reflected in downstream PivotTables and PivotCharts. Be aware that making changes to Hierarchies that are heavily used can have negative side-effects.
- You can move the levels of the Hierarchy around after it has been created.
- Additional levels can be added after initial creation.
- A hierarchy can be renamed.
- A hierarchy can be deleted.

Resolve hierarchy issues

One of the challenges with hierarchies is that a very common pattern that exists in organizations that is not something DAX handles easily. The pattern is known as Parent-Child relationship where the data is managed in a self-relating relationship such as the one in Figure 2-50.

Employee	Manager
Abercrombie, Kim	
Hanif, Kerim	Abercrombie, Kim
Patel, Sanjay	Abercrombie, Kim
Oberleitner, Gerwald	Patel, Sanjay
Parker, Darren	Patel, Sanjay
Nkya, Elly	Hanif, Kerim
Halmaert, Franck	Nkya, Elly
Nixon, Toby	Nkya, Elly

FIGURE 2-50 Sample Data for Parent-Child Hierarchy

DAX provides a set of functions that can help you flatten the hierarchy out into a structure much like you built in Demo 2-18. To achieve that result, you step through several functions one-by-one in the files named **\Chapter2\CH02RaggedHierarchiesDemo.xlsx**.

Notice that the table in Figure 2-50 has been loaded into the data model and that several Calculated Columns have been added to demonstrate breaking the source data down using DAX. Listing 2-21 shows all the Calculated Columns that were added the OrgChart table in the data model to flatten the data out. The results of these columns are shown in Figure 2-51.

LISTING 2-21 Calculated Columns used to flatten Parent-Child Hierarchy

```
//Calculated Column Named PATH which is used to build out the full path from Child to
 parent
=PATH ( OrgChart[Employee], OrgChart[Manager])

//Calculated Column Names LEVEL show the level of the hierarchy that the PATH value
 represents
=PATHLENGTH ( OrgChart[PATH])

//Calculated Column Named LEVEL 1. PATHITEM shows the element of the path for the passes
 in level
= PATHITEM ( OrgChart[Path], 1 )

//Calculated Column Named LEVEL 2
= PATHITEM ( OrgChart[Path], 2 )

//Calculated Column Named LEVEL 3
= PATHITEM ( OrgChart[Path], 3 )

//Calculated Column Named LEVEL 4
= PATHITEM ( OrgChart[Path], 4 )
```

Employee	Manager	PATH	LEVEL	LEVEL 1	LEVEL 2	LEVEL 3	LEVEL 4
Abercrombie, Kim		Abercrombie, Kim	1	Abercrombie, Kim			
Hanif, Kerim	Abercrombie, Kim	Abercrombie, Kim|Hanif, Kerim	2	Abercrombie, Kim	Hanif, Kerim		
Patel, Sanjay	Abercrombie, Kim	Abercrombie, Kim|Patel, Sanjay	2	Abercrombie, Kim	Patel, Sanjay		
Oberleitner, Gerwald	Patel, Sanjay	Abercrombie, Kim|Patel, Sanjay|Oberleitner, Gerwald	3	Abercrombie, Kim	Patel, Sanjay	Oberleitner, Gerwald	
Parker, Darren	Patel, Sanjay	Abercrombie, Kim|Patel, Sanjay|Parker, Darren	3	Abercrombie, Kim	Patel, Sanjay	Parker, Darren	
Nkya, Elly	Hanif, Kerim	Abercrombie, Kim|Hanif, Kerim|Nkya, Elly	3	Abercrombie, Kim	Hanif, Kerim	Nkya, Elly	
Halmaert, Franck	Nkya, Elly	Abercrombie, Kim|Hanif, Kerim|Nkya, Elly|Halmaert, Franck	4	Abercrombie, Kim	Hanif, Kerim	Nkya, Elly	Halmaert, Franck
Nixon, Toby	Nkya, Elly	Abercrombie, Kim|Hanif, Kerim|Nkya, Elly|Nixon, Toby	4	Abercrombie, Kim	Hanif, Kerim	Nkya, Elly	Nixon, Toby

FIGURE 2-51 Parent-Child Function Results

DAX also has two other functions that are useful when working with Parent-Child Hierarchies. Listing 2-22 shows the PATHCONTAINS and PATHITEMREVERSE functions, and their results are shown in Figure 2-52.

LISTING 2-22 Additional Parent-Child Functions

```
//Calculated Column Named PATHCONTAINS Sanjay Patel. PATHCONTAINS returns TRUE if the
 string to find is in the PATH, otherwise FALSE is returned.
=PATHCONTAINS([PATH], "Patel, Sanjay")

//Calculated Column Named REV LEVEL 1 -  PATHITEMREVERSE returns the path in REVERSE
 order
=PATHITEMREVERSE(OrgChart[PATH], 1)

//Calculated Column Named REV LEVEL 2- see above
= PATHITEMREVERSE( OrgChart[Path], 2 )

//Calculated Column Named REV LEVEL 3- see above
= PATHITEMREVERSE( OrgChart[Path], 3 )

//Calculated Column Named REV LEVEL 4- see above
= PATHITEMREVERSE( OrgChart[Path], 4 )
```

Employee	Manager	PATH	PATHCONTAINS Sanjay Patel	REV LEVEL 1	REV LEVEL 2	REV LEVEL 3	REV LEVEL 4
Abercrombie, Kim		Abercrombie, Kim	FALSE	Abercrombie, Kim			
Hanif, Kerim	Abercrombie, Kim	Abercrombie, Kim|Hanif, Kerim	FALSE	Hanif, Kerim	Abercrombie, Kim		
Patel, Sanjay	Abercrombie, Kim	Abercrombie, Kim|Patel, Sanjay	TRUE	Patel, Sanjay	Abercrombie, Kim		
Oberleitner, Gerwald	Patel, Sanjay	Abercrombie, Kim|Patel, Sanjay|Oberleitner, Gerwald	TRUE	Oberleitner, Ger...	Patel, Sanjay	Abercrombie, Kim	
Parker, Darren	Patel, Sanjay	Abercrombie, Kim|Patel, Sanjay|Parker, Darren	TRUE	Parker, Darren	Patel, Sanjay	Abercrombie, Kim	
Nkya, Elly	Hanif, Kerim	Abercrombie, Kim|Hanif, Kerim|Nkya, Elly	FALSE	Nkya, Elly	Hanif, Kerim	Abercrombie, Kim	
Halmaert, Franck	Nkya, Elly	Abercrombie, Kim|Hanif, Kerim|Nkya, Elly|Halmaert, Franck	FALSE	Halmaert, Franck	Nkya, Elly	Hanif, Kerim	Abercrombie, Kim
Nixon, Toby	Nkya, Elly	Abercrombie, Kim|Hanif, Kerim|Nkya, Elly|Nixon, Toby	FALSE	Nixon, Toby	Nkya, Elly	Hanif, Kerim	Abercrombie, Kim

FIGURE 2-52 Parent-Child Function Results

> ***MORE INFO*** **PARENT-CHILD HIERARCHIES**
>
> **For a complete discussion on how to handle Parent-Child hierarchies in DAX, refer to *https://msdn.microsoft.com/en-us/library/gg492192.aspx*. Also, Marco Russo discusses the topic in depth at *https://www.daxpatterns.com/parent-child-hierarchies/*.**

Skill 2.4: Create Performance KPIs

When a user performs analysis, it is often important to not only look at an absolute number such as actual value of Sales, for example, but to compare its status against some type of trend to see how well the actual number is performing against a set target. This forms a base to help users more easily spot trends in their data that they should potentially do something about. This is where Key Performance Indicators (KPIs) are useful. The KPI gauges performance of a value as defined by a base measure against some form of target value. In this section, you will create the actual value and target value, then will compare the two to indicate a status. This continues the topic of enhancing your data model so that it is more complete and user-friendly.

> **This section covers how to:**
> - Calculate the actual value
> - Calculate the target value
> - Calculate actual-to-target values

Calculate the actual value

The first thing to do is to create some measures in the model that will be used in the KPI calculations. As mentioned in the opening of the section, you want to compare this year's sales to the prior period so that you can determine growth, which will serve as the actual value in the KPI.

> **NOTE CREATING KPIS**
>
> KPIs can only be created on explicitly created measures in a data model. If you had previously created an implicit measure via a PivotTable, it would not be available.

In this example, you create three measures that will be used to support calculating the actual value for the KPI that you wish to create.

1. Open **\Chapter2\CH02KPIStart.xlsx** and navigate to the **data model**. Ensure that you are in **Data View** and that you have the **FactInternetSales** table is open.

2. Now create the following measures in the Calculations Area and format them as prescribed in Table 2-16.

TABLE 2-16 Measures to support the KPIs

Measure Name	Calculation	Format
Sales	Sales:=SUM(FactInternetSales[SalesAmount])	$ English (United States)
SalesPY	SalesPY:=CALCULATE([Sales], SAMEPERIODLASTYEAR(DimDate[FullDateAlternateKey]))	$ English (United States)
SalesGrowth	SalesGrowth:=DIVIDE(([Sales] - [SalesPY]) , [SalesPY], 0)	Percentage

Calculate the target value

1. In the continuation of the first example around creating the actual value, you now set the target values to support KPI calculations. In this example, you will use an absolute value as opposed to creating a measure that provides the target values. In real business scenarios, both occur frequently. The measure may be more useful in situations where targets differ between different planning objectives, as opposed to the blanket values you apply to the entire KPI as in this demo.

2. Now you are ready to create a KPI based on the SalesGrowth measure that you created. To do this, right-click on the **SalesGrowth** measure that you created in the Calculation Area and choose **Create KPI** from the context menu. Alternatively, you could highlight the measure and then choose **Home**, **Calculations**, **Create KPI**. You will be presented with the Key Performance Indicator (KPI) dialog as shown in Figure 2-53. Configure the values as follows:

   - **Define Target Value**   Choose Absolute values since you are using a percentage as the base. Type 0 as the value.

   - **Define Status Thresholds**   Choose -0.05 and 0.05 as the tolerances.

   - **Icon Style**   Choose one of your liking. In this example, the default is chosen.

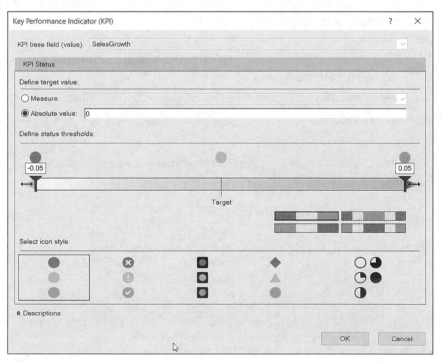

FIGURE 2-53 KPI Settings

3. Notice that you can also provide descriptions by clicking Descriptions, which is shown on the bottom left of Figure 2-53.

- KPI Description
- Value Description
- Status Description
- Target Description

4. Once you have made the above configurations, click **OK**.

5. You will then notice that the SalesGrowth measure has a KPI icon next to it as shown in Figure 2-54.

Sales: $29,358,677.22
SalesPY: $29,312,982.50
SalesGrowth: 0.16%

FIGURE 2-54 Measure as displayed in Calculation Pane

Calculate actual-to-target values

Now you need to consume the models that you just set up. To do this, you will build a Pivot-Table to enable us to visually display the data. In this example, you create a visual to compare the values.

1. From Power Pivot navigate to **Home** > **PivotTables** and when the dialog appears, choose to add the Pivot to a new worksheet.

2. In the **PivotTable Fields** list, drag the following objects to these locations:

- **Filter   H_Product**
- **Rows   H_Calendar**
- **Values   Sales** > **SalesPY** > **SalesGrowth Status** and **Sales Growth**

3. Once you are complete, you should have a visual that looks like Figure 2-55.

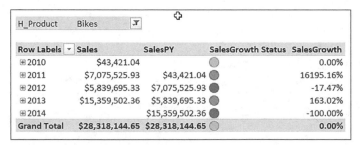

H_Product	Bikes			
Row Labels	Sales	SalesPY	SalesGrowth Status	SalesGrowth
⊞ 2010	$43,421.04		○	0.00%
⊞ 2011	$7,075,525.93	$43,421.04	●	16195.16%
⊞ 2012	$5,839,695.33	$7,075,525.93	●	-17.47%
⊞ 2013	$15,359,502.36	$5,839,695.33	●	163.02%
⊞ 2014		$15,359,502.36	●	-100.00%
Grand Total	**$28,318,144.65**	**$28,318,144.65**	○	0.00%

FIGURE 2-55 Pivot with all the measures displayed plus the KPI status

Thought experiments

In this thought experiment, you will test your knowledge pertaining to the data model. As practice for the exam, first, eliminate answers that you know are incorrect. This will help you narrow your choices.

1. Which of these objects is not part of the Excel data model?

    A. Measures

    B. Tables

    C. Relationships

    D. Power Query

2. What property do you need to enable in the data model so that you can edit data in the data model?

    A. Enable Write Mode on

    B. Updateable on

    C. Enable Fast Load

    D. The data model is read-only and therefore, you cannot edit data directly in the data model.

3. What might be a reason you would load data from SQL Server Analysis services into a data model?

4. Will the relationship between these two tables be created if you join on Customer ID? Why or why not? Assume that this data has been loaded into the data model but is being presented here as Excel tables so that you can observe the data in both.

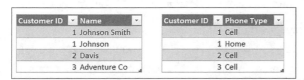

FIGURE 2-56   Sample Data to support question 4

5. Two tables are being pulled from a SQL database using the Table Import Wizard from within Power Pivot, and no underlying relationships exist in the database between the two tables. What options do you have for creating relationships?

6. Discuss the two sides of data model optimization and explain why you need to engage in an Optimization mindset.

7. What is the correct way to build a DAX Measure named "Total Sales" in the FactInternetSales table, which is meant to calculate the SUM of Sales Amount on the table in Figure 2-57? Choose all that are correct.

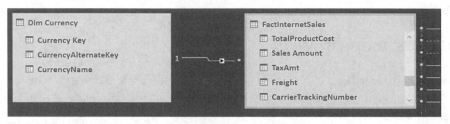

FIGURE 2-57 Relationship between Dim Currency and Fact Internet Sales

  A. Total Sales = SUM(Sales Amount)

  B. Total Sales := SUM(Sales Amount)

  C. Total Sales := SUM([Sales Amount])

  D. Total Sales := SUM(FactInternetSales[Sales Amount])

8. What is the result of the conversion when you write a calculated column by writing the following formula: = "8" + "7"?

  A. 87

  B. 15

  C. "8+7"

  D. An error message

9. The following two measures have been created and saved to the data model with a home table of FactInternetSales:

```
Total Sales := SUM(FactInternetSales[Sales Amount])
Total Tax := SUM(FactInternetSales[TaxAmt])
```

- You want to create a measure with the following name and definition in DimCustomers:

```
Total Sales := SUM(FactInternetSales[Sales Amount])
```

- What happens when you save the measure?

10. Which functions in DAX return a one-column table that contains the distinct values from the specified table or column? In other words, duplicate values are removed and only unique values are returned. Choose all that are correct.

  A. DISTINCT

  B. HASONEFILTER

  C. VALUES

  D. HASONEVALUE

11. Which DAX function can you use to evaluate the year-to-date value of an expression in the current context?

   A. RUNNINGTOTALYTD

   B. TOTALYTD

   C. SUMTYD

   D. ENDOFYEAR

12. When comparing the rows in two tables, which DAX function can be used to return the rows in one table that do not appear in another table? Choose all answers that are correct.

   A. INTERSECT

   B. NATURALINNERJOIN

   C. EXCEPT

   D. EXCLUDE

13. What is the return data type for the following format string?

   `FORMAT(SUM('Internet Sales'[Sales Amount]), "#,##0.00#")`

   A. Whole Number

   B. Decimal Number

   C. Text

   D. Currency

14. Which statement about Hierarchies is false?

   A. A table can have multiple hierarchies defined on it.

   B. An individual column may be used in multiple hierarchies.

   C. An individual column that can only be used once is a single hierarchy.

   D. You cannot use a hidden column when creating a hierarchy.

15. When creating a KPI, you need to set a Target value. What are the valid target values sources?

   A. Explicit Measure

   B. Excel Table

   C. Absolute value

   D. Implicit Measure

Thought experiment answers

1. Answer **D**: Power Query is a tool within Excel for loading data. All of the other objects are part of the data model.

2. Answer **D:** The data model is read-only. If you need to modify data in the data model it will need to be done back at the source or in some location other than the data model.

3. Using Integration With Analysis Services, you can query the data directly in the model without the need to bring it into Excel. Should you want to combine data from other sources with the data from the model, you will either need to get the owner of the Analysis Services source to bring the data into that model or you can do the same in the data model. Generally, the first step in this process is for the Excel developer to bring the data into the model to test it out and prove its value. Once this is done, you will make a choice in the future to continue to manage this process in Excel or to pass it over to the cube owner so that integration can be managed there. This is a typical iterative process and highlights the power of the data model.

4. The relationship as specified in the question will not be created. The data model will generate the following error. This is an example of a Many-to-Many relationship, which is not a valid relationship type.

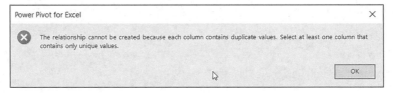

FIGURE 2-58 Error Message from question 4

5. In this example, you have a few options. If you want this handled automatically, you could first create the relationships directly in the database so that when the data is imported, the relationships will come along with it. This assumes that you have the permissions to do so. If you do not have this ability, you can create the relationships manually in the data model once the tables are loaded in the model.

6. When you optimize and model you are doing two things. The first is making the model perform promptly, which is what most people think of when you say the word "optimization." The second is making the model optimized from an end-user self-service perspective. These are things like using friendly column and table names; removing unneeded columns and tables so that the users can focus on what is important; building hierarchies and KPIs; and adding DAX calculated columns and measures that ease reporting and make it more consistent.

7. Answers **C and D**: Answer A has two flaws. Because you are creating a measure, you need to end the measure name with a colon. Additionally, Sales Amount needs to be

wrapped in square brackets. Only answer B has the square brackets flaw. Both C and D are syntactically correct.

8. **Answer B:** The addition operator will have the string value of 8 and 7 converted to decimal numbers.

9. It will not be created, and you will get an error message stating that a measure or column with the name Total Sales already exists and that you should choose a different name.

10. **Answers A and C:** The HASONEFILTER function returns TRUE when the number of directly filtered values on provide column is one; otherwise it returns FALSE. The HASONEVALUE function Returns TRUE when the context for providing the column has been filtered down to one distinct value only. Otherwise, it returns FALSE.

11. **Answer B:** RUNNINGTOTALYTD and SUMYTD are not valid functions. ENDOFYEAR returns the last date of the year in the current context for the specified column of dates. TOTALYTD evaluates the year-to-date value of the expression in the current context.

12. **Answer C:** INTERSECT and NATURALINNERJOIN show rows that are in both tables. EXCLUDE is not a valid DAX function.

13. **Answer C:** The return value is a string-containing value formatted as defined by the format string provided.

14. **Answer D:** You can use a hidden column when creating a hierarchy.

15. **Answers A and C:** You cannot use an Implicit measure or an Excel table.

Chapter summary

- Some of the advantages of the data model over traditional Excel objects are:
    - Overcomes Excel row limitation
    - Data model can be as 1/10 the size of equivalent data in Excel due to compression
    - It is an in-memory engine which translates into high speed of processing
- The data model is composed of:
    - Tables
    - Columns from source systems
    - Calculated Columns
    - Measures
    - Relationships
    - Hierarchies
    - KPIs
    - Perspectives

- Other data model facts:
  - The data model is read-only.
  - A workbook can only contain one data model.
  - A data model can contain many tables.
  - This WorkbookDataModel is the name of the object in Excel that represents the data model.
- You can use the Table Import wizard from within Power Pivot to import data, although the options for sources are fewer than when using Power Query.
- You can manually enter data in an Excel table within the same workbook where the data model resides, then load that data to the Model. In previous versions of Excel, you could create this as a linked table. Now it is a refreshable table that operates the same as getting data using other objects.
- Relationships can be created automatically if the metadata exists in the sources to support them, or they can be manually created in the data model. No matter how relationships are created, care should be taken ensure they are: a) set up and b) set up properly, as this greatly influences the integrity of the data model.
- Only one relationship can be active at a time between two tables. Multiple relationships can exist and others will be set to inactive.
- A relationship has a direction. In the Excel data model, filters can only flow in one direction or what is called Single.
- Relationships enable bringing tables together in much the same way a VLOOKUP does, but with added performance and the ability to access the entire table.
- Requirements for Relationships are:
  - They are on a single column.
  - Data Types must be compatible.
  - They contain no blank values.
  - One side must contain unique values.
  - The Cardinality of a relationship in the data model can only be one-to-many.
- The DAX RELATED function is used to bring values from one table to another where the tables are related. If you need to use the inactive relationship, use the USERELATIONSHIP function. You also can use the LOOKUPVALUE function.
- Calculated Columns are generally used to create values that are used in slicers, filters, or as labels in rows and columns of PivotTables.
- Measures are created to aggregate data. You can create implicit measures by using a column from a table and dropping it into the values of a Pivot. The Implicit measure is only accessible by the PivotTable that created it. An explicit measure is created in DAX and is reusable across reporting solutions.

- There are two Evaluation Contexts in DAX: The Row and the Filter context. It is important to be aware of the Evaluation contexts that are present when building reporting solutions.

- The DAX language has over 200 functions within it. They are categorized as:
  - Date and Time Functions
  - Time Intelligence Functions
  - Filter Functions
  - Information Functions
  - Logical Functions
  - Math and Trig Functions
  - Other Functions
  - Parent and Child Functions
  - Statistical Functions
  - Text Functions

- It is possible to use DAX as a Query language. The EVALUATE clause is used is used to define and execute a query that returns a table. The general syntax for a DAX query is:

```
[DEFINE {  MEASURE <tableName>[<name>] = <expression> }
 {  VAR <name> = <expression>}]
EVALUATE <table>
[ORDER BY {<expression> [{ASC | DESC}]}[, …]
[START AT {<value>|<parameter>} [, …]]]
```

- Hierarchies offer a very convenient way for users to drill up and down within data sets in a pre-defined manner.

- Date Hierarchies are the most common type of hierarchy in analytics. You can create a date hierarchy as well as business hierarchies manually in the data model.

- KPIs gauge performance of a value as defined by a base measure against some form of Target value.

- If you use measures in KPIs, they can only be created on explicitly created measures in a data model.

- When you define a target, you need to do define the following:
  - Set a Target Value which can be a Measure or an Absolute value
  - Set Status Thresholds
  - Choose an Icon Style

Visualize data

Data in a transactional format is not very useful for spotting trends or identifying outliers in any reasonably sized set of information. Taking data and summarizing it so that a reader can more easily absorb a large amount of information is a highly important last step in the data analysis journey. Recently, as business users have started to experience a deluge of data, trends have been moving toward more visual means of presenting data as a starting point in analysis. A lot of focus has been put on building dashboards and scorecards that enable a user to start analysis at a highly aggregated entry point, and can then be guided through the process of drilling down to details as more "why" questions are asked.

This chapter covers the different ways to present data for end-user consumption. You start by looking at PivotTables to summarize data in a tabular format that enables the classic slicing and dicing of data. You then move to visualizing data using PivotCharts. And finally, in Skill 3-3 we look at the ever-growing and improving integration points between Excel and Power BI for both consuming and presenting data. Power BI offers some tremendous ways to share the work done in an Excel workbook that enables you to get around the traditional sharing challenges that have existed with Excel for some time now.

Skills in this chapter:

- Skill 3.1: Create and manage PivotTables
- Skill 3.2: Create and manage PivotCharts
- Skill 3.3: Interact with Power BI

Skill 3.1: Create and manage PivotTables

PivotTables have long been a staple in the Excel analysts' toolkit. With the advent of the Excel Data model, the ability to navigate over huge datasets has been made possible to extend the ability for a business user to quickly discover insights in their datasets to enable better decision making. And as we have seen, the Data Model also enables users to centralize logic in the form of Calculated Columns, Measures, Hierarchies, Formatting properties, etc. This enables reuse and consistency, which improves the quality and reliability of data products.

In this section, we take a deeper look at the many facets of a PivotTable that can be configured to help improve presentation and ultimately usability. There are many ways to format and interact with the PivotTable to influence this.

Format PivotTables

When you create PivotTables, you should always be thinking about what you would like your data product to look like once it is in your users' hands. As a designer, you have numerous options for formatting a PivotTable so that it is in the most usable state possible for users. Some formatting options can either be applied to the Data Model or made local to the Pivot-Table, and others can only be applied to the PivotTable. These will be highlighted as we move through the various options.

To begin looking at the options available, create a PivotTable so that you have something to format. There are two ways to create a PivotTable. The first is from within Excel, and the second is from within PowerPivot. The quickest way is to do it from within PowerPivot. If you do it there, Excel detects that you want to base the PivotTable in the Data Model, so you save some configuration options.

As a note, if you are basing the PivotTable on the Excel Data Model, you cannot use the Recommend A PivotTable functionality that is available from within Excel because it is not available when using the Data Model.

> **NOTE DEMO WORKING FILES**
>
> The Data Model as covered in Skill 3-1 Formatting.xlsx has had no Optimization performed on it. If this term is not familiar, go back to Chapter 2 "Model data" to review the section titled "Optimize models for reporting." This has purposely been done so that you can see how to format your model and what it takes to work your way toward a robust Data Model.

PivotTable overview

Let's first start by creating an empty PivotTable. To do this, perform the following steps:

1. Open the **\Chapter 3\CH03 Skill 3-1 Formatting.xlsx** workbook.
2. On the **Insert** tab, in the **Tables** group, click **PivotTable.** You will be presented with the **Create PivotTable** dialog as in Figure 3-1.

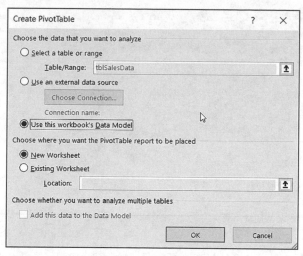

FIGURE 3-1 The Create PivotTable dialog box

3. Make the following selections below:
   ■ In the Choose The Data That You Want To Analyze section, select **Use This Workbook's Data Model.**
   ■ In the Choose Where You Want The Pivottable To Be Placed section, select **New Worksheet.**

4. Click **OK** when complete.

5. Save the workbook and leave it open for the next demo.

Alternatively, if you are already in Power Pivot, you can use the following navigation path:

1. On the **Power Pivot** tab, in the **Data Model** group, click **Manage**. This will open the Power Pivot window.

2. On the **Home** tab, click **PivotTable.** This option will not present you the Create Pivot-Table dialog box from Figure 3-1 because it assumes you want to use the Data Model as the basis for the PivotTable. You will, however, be asked if you want to create the Pivot-Table in a New or Existing Worksheet.

Using either method above for adding a new PivotTable to the existing worksheet will show you Figure 3-2. The **PivotTable Fields** pane is where you will add and configure many of the elements that you add to a PivotTable. It will appear whenever you click anywhere in the Pivot-Table. When you click out of the PivotTable, it will disappear since it is only relevant when the PivotTable is open. If you are in the PivotTable and do not want it on, you can toggle it on or off by doing the following. Under the **PivotTable Tools**, on the **Analyze** tab, in the **Show** group, click **Field List** to toggle it on or off.

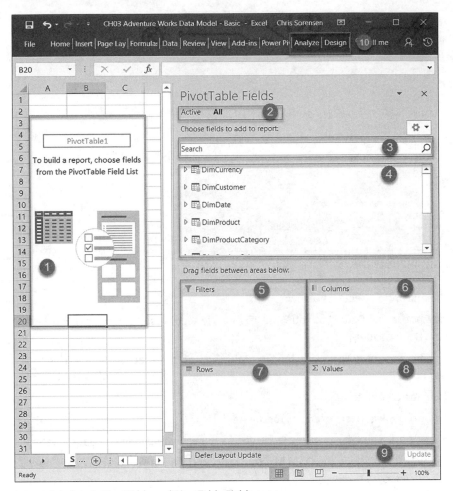

FIGURE 3-2 Empty PivotTable and PivotTable Fields pane

The areas of interest within the PivotTable Fields list are shown in this list, and the numbers correspond to the highlighted number areas in Figure 3-2.

1. **PivotTable** This is the area where data will be presented as you add items from the other parts of the PivotTable Fields pane.

2. **Table Status** This allows you to show either **All** the tables in the data model or only the ones that are **Active** in the PivotTable. All is desirable when building a report initially, but after you have it defined the way you want it, you can choose Active, which will only show the tables that are used in the Pivot. Optionally, you can Pin a table to the active tab, even if it's not currently being used, by right-clicking the table and selecting the **Show In Active Tab** option from the context menu. Once it is in the active tab you can remove it by doing the reverse of the previous step. Take note that you cannot remove a table from the active tab using this technique if it is being used in the PivotTable.

3. **Search**   Some data models, no matter how well-designed, can on occasion become large. In these instances, you can use the search function to find the field that you are looking for using the names that are assigned in the Data Model.

4. **Table List**   What appears in this window depends on the option that you have selected in the highlighted area shown in Figure 3-2. It will list tables that are in the Data Model if you have them All selected or only those in use if you have Active selected.

5. **Filters area**   Fields here are added to the PivotTable as a Report Filter. This option will be discussed in-depth in the section on Filtering data.

6. **Columns area**   Fields here are added to the columns axis as labels on the PivotTable. You have a great deal of flexibility, which will be discussed shortly.

7. **Rows area**   Fields that are added here are added to the rows axis as labels on the PivotTable. As with columns, you have a great deal of flexibility, which will be discussed shortly.

8. **Values area**   Fields that you add here are the things that you are trying to measure when using a PivotTable. You either use Explicit Measures that you created in the Data Model, or you can choose to add any fields here, and the PivotTable will choose the aggregation method that makes the most sense. If a default aggregation has been set in the Data Model, it will use that. You do have the option to override this within the PivotTable.

9. **Defer Layout Update**   When you add a PivotTable to a worksheet and begin to interact with it, the values are constantly being refreshed. With a Data Model that has lots of data, if you have an under-resourced machine, these updates can take time. If you know the structure of the PivotTable that you want to build, you can build it from the model definition and then manually refresh the data when you choose to.

10. **PivotTable Tools**   When you have a PivotTable highlighted, you will get two new context sensitive tabs in the ribbon. These are the Analyze and Design tabs, which are used to perform customizations on your PivotTable.

Populate the PivotTable

Now that you have had a walkthrough of the PivotTable Field pane, it is time to add to the empty PivotTable you created earlier so that you can see what can be formatted. There are many options available for formatting, and demos are best to show how to improve your model when you are ready for production consumption.

1. Open the **\Chapter 3\CH03 Skill 3-1 Formatting.xlsx** workbook, which you previously worked on and saved.

2. Using the empty PivotTable shown in Figure 3-2, add the following columns to the Fields pane:

- Columns area **CalendarYear** from **DimDate**.
- **Rows area SalesTerritoryCountry** and **SalesTerritoryRegion** from DimSalesTerritory. Ensure that SalesTerritoryCountry is listed first so that they nest properly.
- **Values Freight** from FactInternetSales.

3. The first thing is to name your PivotTable something meaningful. This will be helpful when you start working with multiple PivotTables, Slicers, Timelines, and PivotCharts in a Dashboard-like scenario. This enables you to easily find the object you are looking for when connecting objects together.

4. With the Pivot table highlighted, under **PivotTable Tools**, on the **Analyze** tab, in the **PivotTable** group, click on the **PivotTable Name** text box. Change the name from **PivotTable1** to **PTFreightByRegionAndYear**.

5. Your unformatted PivotTable should look like Figure 3-3. When you are done, save your work because you will need the PivotTable in this form for the next exercises. Between now and your next exercise, you will be experimenting with different layout, styling, and formatting options.

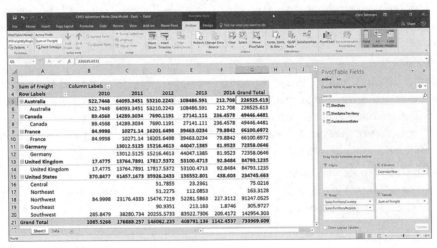

FIGURE 3-3 Unformatted PivotTable

Layout and styling

When in a PivotTable, Under **PivotTable Tools**, on the **Design** tab, you can see the formatting options as shown in Figure 3-4. In the **Layout** group, notice that you can control how Subtotals and Grand Totals are displayed, in addition to controlling the overall Report Layout, including the ability to insert blank rows between groups. Finally, there are additional options for styling the PivotTable through the style options and **PivotTable Styles** groupings, and each will be covered shortly. The styling options that are discussed in this section are made locally to the PivotTable and cannot be controlled by the Data Model itself.

FIGURE 3-4 The Excel ribbon

In the Layout group, you can configure how **Grand Totals** and **Subtotals** are displayed in the PivotTable. To control how Subtotals are displayed, you can experiment with the following steps.

1. Under **PivotTable Tools**, on the **Design** tab, in the **Layout** group, click **Subtotals**.

2. From the command drop-down, you can select from the options list below. Experiment with the options below to view their effects on the PivotTable display.

   - Do Not Show Subtotals
   - Show all Subtotals at Bottom of Group
   - Show all Subtotals at Top of Group
   - Include Filtered Items in Totals

Next, to control how Grand Totals are displayed, you can experiment with the following steps.

1. Under **PivotTable Tools**, on the **Design** tab, in the **Layout** group, click **Grand Totals.**

2. From the command drop-down, you can select from the options list below. Experiment with these options to view their effects on the PivotTable display.

   - Off for Rows and Columns
   - On for Rows and Columns
   - On for Rows Only
   - On for Columns Only

3. There is no need to save these steps.

Grand Totals can also be configured by performing the following actions:

4. Under **PivotTable Tools**, on the **Analyze** tab, in the **PivotTable** group, click **Options**.

5. In the **PivotTable Options** dialog, click the **Totals & Filters** tab. Then in the **Grand Totals** section you can choose to turn Grand Total off for rows and/or columns.

> **MORE INFO PIVOTTABLE OPTIONS**
>
> The PivotTable Options dialog box has a host of options that can be configured. For a list of options and explanations of each, please visit the following site: *https://support.office.com/en-us/article/pivottable-options-27c02eb7-27de-4b3f-9677-c48e3fe7637b.*

Once you have your PivotTable created, you may want to change the layout of the actual Pivot table based on your users' needs. There are three different **Report Layout** Forms that you can use to display a PivotTable. They are listed and described below:

- **Compact Form**   This is the default behavior for a PivotTable and can be seen in Figure 3-3. It displays items from different row area fields in one column and uses indentation to differentiate between fields. This takes up less space, which leaves more room for numeric data. Expand and Collapse buttons are displayed (which can also be turned off) so that you can display or hide details.

- **Tabular Form**   This displays one column per field, and fields are kept at the same level across the display. This is shown in Figure 3-5.

Sum of Freight		CalendarYear					
SalesTerritoryCountry	SalesTerritoryRegion	2010	2011	2012	2013	2014	Grand Total
⊟Australia	Australia	522.7448	64093.3451	53210.2243	108486.5909	212.708	226525.6131
Australia Total		522.7448	64093.3451	53210.2243	108486.5909	212.708	226525.6131
⊟Canada	Canada	89.4568	14289.3034	7690.1191	27141.111	236.4578	49446.4481
Canada Total		89.4568	14289.3034	7690.1191	27141.111	236.4578	49446.4481
⊟France	France	84.9998	10271.14	16201.6498	39463.0234	79.8842	66100.6972
France Total		84.9998	10271.14	16201.6498	39463.0234	79.8842	66100.6972
⊟Germany	Germany		13012.5125	15216.4613	44047.1385	81.9523	72358.0646
Germany Total			13012.5125	15216.4613	44047.1385	81.9523	72358.0646
⊟United Kingdom	United Kingdom	17.4775	13764.7891	17817.5372	53100.4713	92.8484	84793.1235
United Kingdom Total		17.4775	13764.7891	17817.5372	53100.4713	92.8484	84793.1235
⊟United States	Central			51.7855	23.2361		75.0216
	Northeast			51.2275	112.0853		163.3128
	Northwest	84.9998	23176.4333	15476.7219	52281.5863	227.3112	91247.0525
	Southeast			90.9351	213.163	1.8746	305.9727
	Southwest	285.8479	38280.734	20255.5733	83922.7306	209.4172	142954.303
United States Total		370.8477	61457.1673	35926.2433	136552.8013	438.603	234745.6626
Grand Total		1085.5266	176888.2574	146062.235	408791.1364	1142.4537	733969.6091

FIGURE 3-5 PivotTable in Tabular Form

- **Outline Form**   This is like tabular, but it displays subtotals at the top of every group because items in the next column are displayed one row below the current item. Figure 3-6 shows this format.

Sum of Freight		CalendarYear					
SalesTerritoryCountry	SalesTerritoryRegion	2010	2011	2012	2013	2014	Grand Total
⊟Australia		522.7448	64093.3451	53210.2243	108486.5909	212.708	226525.6131
	Australia	522.7448	64093.3451	53210.2243	108486.5909	212.708	226525.6131
⊟Canada		89.4568	14289.3034	7690.1191	27141.111	236.4578	49446.4481
	Canada	89.4568	14289.3034	7690.1191	27141.111	236.4578	49446.4481
⊟France		84.9998	10271.14	16201.6498	39463.0234	79.8842	66100.6972
	France	84.9998	10271.14	16201.6498	39463.0234	79.8842	66100.6972
⊟Germany			13012.5125	15216.4613	44047.1385	81.9523	72358.0646
	Germany		13012.5125	15216.4613	44047.1385	81.9523	72358.0646
⊟United Kingdom		17.4775	13764.7891	17817.5372	53100.4713	92.8484	84793.1235
	United Kingdom	17.4775	13764.7891	17817.5372	53100.4713	92.8484	84793.1235
⊟United States		370.8477	61457.1673	35926.2433	136552.8013	438.603	234745.6626
	Central			51.7855	23.2361		75.0216
	Northeast			51.2275	112.0853		163.3128
	Northwest	84.9998	23176.4333	15476.7219	52281.5863	227.3112	91247.0525
	Southeast			90.9351	213.163	1.8746	305.9727
	Southwest	285.8479	38280.734	20255.5733	83922.7306	209.4172	142954.303
Grand Total		1085.5266	176888.2574	146062.235	408791.1364	1142.4537	733969.6091

FIGURE 3-6 PivotTable in Outline Form

Often it is helpful to be able to have Blank Rows between groups of data in a PivotTable to help draw emphasis to the data. To do this, you can use the **Blank Rows** command to toggle the feature on and off. To do this, under **PivotTable Tools**, on the **Design** tab, in the **Layout** group, click **Blank Rows** after each item.

The PivotTable Style Options group in the Design Tab deals with styling the PivotTable with headers and banding. The following options can be toggled on and off based on preferences. Experiment with each of these to see their effects on the PivotTable.

- **Row Headers**   Highlights the row headers.
- **Column Headers**   Highlights the columns headers.
- **Banded Rows**   Shades every other row to make it easier to distinguish one row from another.
- **Banded Columns**   Shades every other column to make it easier to distinguish one column from another.

The final grouping option for formatting the PivotTable on the **Design** tab is **PivotTable Styles** group. Here you can change the coloring, formatting, and borders using the predefined Light, Medium, and Dark styles. In addition, you may create your own New PivotTable style as you determine an appropriate corporate standard. Once again, put your PivotTable in focus and try some of the styles out.

General Pivot Table commands

The following are a series of general commands that you can apply to your PivotTables. The styling options that are discussed in this section are made locally to the PivotTable and cannot be controlled by the Data Model itself.

Once you have a PivotTable formatted, you may wish to clear all of the formatting that you applied and start the process again. Under **PivotTable Tools**, on the **Analyze** tab, in the **Actions** group, click the **Clear** drop-down. From here you have two options: **Clear All** and **Clear Filters**.

The **Clear All** command resets your PivotTable, but does not delete it. The data connection, placement, and cache remain the same. If you have a PivotChart associated with the PivotTable, **Clear All** also removes related PivotChart fields, chart customizations, and formatting.

The other option is to use **Clear Filters** if you have any filters applied to the PivotTable.

To **Move** your PivotTable to a new or existing worksheet, you can do the following. Under **PivotTable Tools**, on the **Analyze** tab, in the **Actions** group, click the **Move PivotTable**. You may need to do this in an instance where you are arranging a series of Dashboards and the flow needs to change within the workbook.

The freshness of data is always important to manage. You can manually refresh your data for all sources or a single PivotTable. If you want to refresh all the sources in the workbook you use the **Refresh All** command. If you only want to refresh the connections of the current PivotTable, you choose **Refresh** while the PivotTable that you want to refresh is selected. Both commands can be found under the **Analyze** > **Data** > Refresh drop-down. Alternatively, you can set the PivotTable to Refresh data automatically when opening the workbook. This can be done by doing the following:

1. Under **PivotTable Tools** > on the **Analyze** tab > in the **PivotTable** group > click **PivotTable Options**.

2. In the **PivotTable Options** dialog, click the **Data** tab, and select **Refresh Data When Opening the File**.

When performing refreshes, it is also advisable to review how you want the layout and formatting to respond. This can be done by the following:

1. Under **PivotTable Tools**, on the **Analyze** tab, in the **PivotTable** group, click **PivotTable Options**.

2. In the **PivotTable Options** dialog, click the **Layout & Formatting** tab. Review the following two options:

   ■ Autofit column widths on update

   ■ Preserve cell formatting on update

If the source of your PivotTable needs to change, you can do so by editing the Connection Properties. To change these settings, do the following. Under **PivotTable Tools**, on the **Analyze** tab, in the **Data** group, click **Change Data Source** and select **Connection Properties**.

> **MORE INFO** **CHANGING THE SOURCE FOR A PIVOTTABLE**
>
> For more information on how to change the source of a PivotTable read the following article: *https://support.office.com/en-us/article/change-the-source-data-for-a-pivottable-ad8ed968-ada1-4dde-9f72-30e07782dccd*.

The last General commands you will review are used to change what you see when working with a PivotTable. Under **PivotTable Tools**, on the **Analyze** tab, in the **Show** group, you will see three options as in Figure 3-7. By clicking any of the items in the Show group, the corresponding number that matches within the PivotTable will react to the click. These are also described below and correspond to the numbers in Figure 3-7.

1. **Field List**   Will toggle the PivotTable Field list on and off.

2. **+/- Buttons**   Will turn the expand and collapse buttons on or off, should you have data in your PivotTable that enabled them.

3. **Field Headers**   Turns the Field headers on and off in the PivotTable.

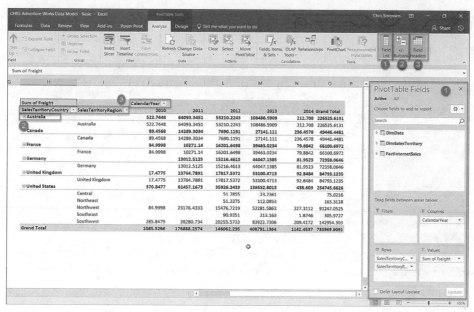

FIGURE 3-7 The PivotTable Interface and how it will react to the toggle commands in the Show groups

Formatting values in the PivotTable

Should you want to format the values that appear in the PivotTable, you have the option of making changes to the **Field Settings** on both the Rows and Column areas and the **Value Setting** on the Values area.

NOTE FORMATTING VALUES IN THE PIVOTTABLE

Keep in mind that when you make formatting changes here that they are local to the PivotTable you are working with. Should you want to make this formatting global, you are advised to move the settings into the Data Model. We will review how to do this in the next section, but for now let's focus on how to make local changes.

First let's look at the Values settings, in the **Values** area of the **PivotTable Field** pane.

1. With the PivotTable selected, click the drop-down arrow on the right side of the Sum of Freight column in the **Values** area of the **PivotTable Fields** pane.

2. Choose **Value Fields Settings**.

3. You will be presented with the **Value Fields Settings** dialog box as in Figure 3-8.

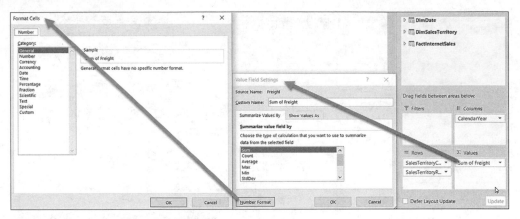

FIGURE 3-8 Formatting Values in a PivotTable

The first thing that you notice in the **Value Fields Settings** dialog is the **Source Name** for the column that you are evaluating. This is important to know when debugging calculation issues, especially if you are using a custom name in your reporting layer.

Users will often want to use a **Custom Name** for display purposes that may not match the source name. To change the name, you can type in a name of your choice in the text box.

Also notice that you have several ways to summarize the field you are working with on the **Summarize Values By** tab. These options are summarized and described in Table 3-1.

TABLE 3-1 Summarize values filed by options

Function	Summarizes
Sum	The sum of the values. This is the default function for numeric values.
Count	The number of values. The Count summary function works the same as the COUNTA worksheet function. Count is the default function for values other than numbers.
Distinct Count	The number of distinct values.
Average	The average of the values.
Max	The largest value.
Min	The smallest value.
StDev	An estimate of the standard deviation of a population, where the sample is a subset of the entire population.
StDevp	The standard deviation of a population, where the population is all of the values to be summarized.
Var	An estimate of the variance of a population, where the sample is a subset of the entire population.
Varp	The variance of a population, where the population is all the values to be summarized.

You can also format the actual number by clicking the **Number Format** button in Figure 3-8. This will give you the standard ways to format data as you would have seen in Excel.

The **Show Values As** tab in the **Value Field Settings** dialog lets you choose how you want to display a field's value relative to others in the PivotTable. The default value for this is no calculation, which will just show the summarized value for that given Row and Column intersection point.

> **MORE INFO** **SUMMARY FUNCTION OR CUSTOM CALCULATION OPTIONS FOR A FIELD IN A PIVOTTABLE**
>
> For more details on how to change summary functions and how to show values, refer to the following article: *https://support.office.com/en-us/article/change-the-summary-function-or-custom-calculation-for-a-field-in-a-pivottable-report-ea8945fb-9969-4bac-a16c-4f67b0f7b239.*

Next, you will look at the options to format the Rows or Columns with the **Field Settings** option. Perform the following:

1. Close the dialog boxes from Figure 3-8 if you still have them open.

2. With the PivotTable selected, click the drop-down arrow to the right of CalendarYear in the **Columns** area of the **PivotTable Fields** pane.

3. Choose **Field Settings** in the context menu. You will be presented with Figure 3-9.

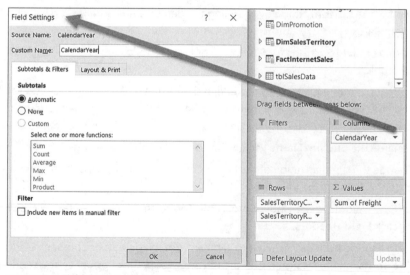

FIGURE 3-9 Field Settings dialog

4. In the **Subtotals & Filters** tab of the **Fields Settings** dialog, you can turn off subtotals for that Field or choose to use the Automatic value set at the PivotTable, as described earlier in this section. On this tab, you also have the option to include new items that come into the data set in any manual filters that have been set. This can be useful when you have a report set to filter data the way that you want, but the underlying values are changing, and you do not want to have them flow into the report.

5. In the **Layout & Print** tab of the **Fields Settings** dialog, you can change the following items:

    - Layout
    - Show item labels in outline form
    - Display labels from the next field in the same column (compact form)
    - Display subtotals at the top of each group
    - Show item labels in tabular form
    - Repeat item labels
    - Insert blank line after each item
    - Print
    - Insert page break after each item

Let's now go through a demo of Formatting a PivotTable.

6. Open the **\Chapter 3\CH03 Skill 3-1 Formatting.xlsx** workbook, which you previously worked on and saved.

7. In the **Field Settings** for SalesTerritoryCountry do the following:

    A. **Insert blank line after each item label** in the **Layout & Print** options.

    B. Modify the **Custom Name** by changing the default value of **SalesTerritoryCountry** to **Sales Territory Country**. Click **OK** when complete.

8. In the **Values Field Settings** for Sum of Freight do the following and then click **OK** when complete.

    A. Format the numeric values by modifying the format of the Freight values. Click the **Number format** button and then on the **Format Cells** dialog select **Currency** which is under the **Category** grouping. Leave all other selections as defaults.

    B. Rename the **Custom Name** value from Sum of Freight to **Average Freight**.

    C. Change the summarization of the field from sum to average by selecting **Average** from the **Summarize Values By** tab.

9. Turn off the Field Headers. Under **PivotTable Tools**, on the **Analyze** tab, in the **Show** group, click **Field Headers**.

10. Now let's change the Report Layout to Tabular from the default of Compact. Under **PivotTable Tools**, on the **Design** tab, in the **Layout** group, click **Report Layout** and select **Show in Tabular Form**.

11. In the rows bucket on the Pivot Table, swap the **SalesTerritoryGroup** and **SalesTerritoryRegion**.

12. Once complete, save your model, which should look like Figure 3-10.

Average of Freight		2010	2011	2012	2013	2014	Grand Total
⊟ Australia	Pacific	$87.12	$81.54	$45.60	$9.81	$0.64	$16.97
Australia Total		$87.12	$81.54	$45.60	$9.81	$0.64	$16.97
⊟ Canada	North America	$89.46	$84.05	$44.71	$3.95	$0.57	$6.49
Canada Total		$89.46	$84.05	$44.71	$3.95	$0.57	$6.49
⊟ France	Europe	$85.00	$73.37	$43.44	$8.09	$0.49	$11.89
France Total		$85.00	$73.37	$43.44	$8.09	$0.49	$11.89
⊟ Germany	Europe		$74.36	$41.35	$8.92	$0.57	$12.86
Germany Total			$74.36	$41.35	$8.92	$0.57	$12.86
⊟ United Kingdom	Europe	$17.48	$78.66	$42.12	$8.66	$0.54	$12.28
United Kingdom Total		$17.48	$78.66	$42.12	$8.66	$0.54	$12.28
⊟ United States	North America	$74.17	$79.81	$40.19	$7.21	$0.59	$11.00
United States Total		$74.17	$79.81	$40.19	$7.21	$0.59	$11.00
Grand Total		$77.54	$79.82	$43.00	$7.74	$0.58	$12.15

FIGURE 3-10 Formatted PivotTable

Optimizing the Data Model

Now that you have looked at some of the formatting options for the PivotTable itself, it is time to review implementing these changes at the Data Model level. As mentioned earlier, making formatting changes as we did directly in the PivotTable are local to that PivotTable and would need to be repeated for each PivotTable that you create that needs similar formatting. This is normal for some formatting options that are only available at the PivotTable level, but other formatting options should be centralized in the Data Model. Some of the things that you centralize will be demonstrated via an exercise where you will do the following:

- **Remove Columns from Data Model**   Remove those that are not useful in analysis or the Data Model.
- **Hide Table and Columns**   Hide those that are not useful in analysis but needed for the Data Model.
- **Naming Conventions**   Provide intuitive naming conventions for tables and columns.
- **Table and Column Descriptions**   For ease of maintenance, add table and column descriptions to each.
- **Data Types**   Choose the correct data type for columns.
- **Columns Formats**   Choose the appropriate formats for the values in a column.
- **Create Explicit Measures**   This will be done in the next section.
- **Column Sorting**   Enables sorting of columns by using the values in another column.

- **Data Categorization** Adds extra metadata to the columns that helps reporting tools better interpret data values.

- **Set Summarize By Property** This applies a default summary method for a column so that when it is used in a PivotTable, the proper summarization method is chosen by the PivotTable.

Each of these was explained in detail in Skill 2.1. In the following demos, we will drive these changes back to the Data Model so they are globally available to all PivotTables and PivotCharts that use the Data Model. We will go through each of the options above to prepare our model for general use.

1. Open the **\Chapter 3\CH03 Skill 3-1 Optimizing.xlsx** workbook.

2. Look at the Data Model and note that it is very rudimentary and has not been optimized. You should notice the tasks we outlined above have not been applied to this Data Model. These steps are usually completed as part of modeling, but we will perform them here to emphasize the process of optimization.

3. The first thing is to Remove columns from the Data Model that are not needed for Analysis to support the Data Model. From **Power Pivot**, ensure that you have the table you want to modify highlighted in either the Diagram View or Data View. Navigate to **Design**, and then click **Table Properties** to open the **Edit Table Properties** dialog as shown in Figure 3-11. From here, you exclude columns that you don't want imported into the Data Model by **Unchecking** the **Check box** next to each column name that needs to be excluded. Follow this entire procedure for each of the table and column pairings that are listed in Table 3-2, and click **Save** after you have completed each table. Note that you could have performed these steps when you did your initial import, per Skill 2.1.

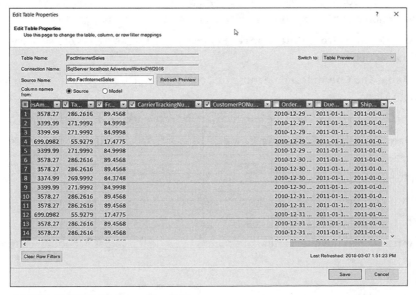

FIGURE 3-11 Edit Table Properties dialog

TABLE 3-2 Columns to remove from the model

Table	Column to Remove
FactInternetSales	DueDate ShipDate
DimCustomer	SpanishEducation FrenchEducation SpanishOccupation FrenchOccupation
DimDate	SpanishDayNameOfWeek FrenchDayNameOfWeek SpanishMonthName FrenchMonthName
DimProduct	SpanishProductName FrenchProductName LargePhoto FrenchDescription ChineseDescription ArabicDescription HebrewDescription ThaiDescription GermanDescription JapaneseDescription TurkishDescription StartDate EndDate Status
DimPromotion	SpanishPromotionName FrenchPromotionName SpanishPromotionType FrenchPromotionType SpanishPromotionCategory FrenchPromotionCategory

4. Now let's hide the ProductCategory and ProductSubcategory tables from client tools because they have no use in reporting. The columns that are needed from these two tables to support the H_Product Hierarchy been brought into the Product table using the DAX RELATED function. To hide a table in **Diagram View**, right-click on the **DimProductCategory** table, and choose **Hide from Client Tools** from the context menu. Repeat this procedure for **DimProductSubcategory**. You will notice that the tables are still visible but will become grayed-out in the diagram, which signifies that they cannot be seen in client tools but are still usable when performing modeling. If you now navigate back to the PivotTable, you will see that they no longer appear in the **Table List** on the **PivotTable Fields** pane. You do not need to do this, but to allow the tables to be seen again, you can go back to the table and choose **Unhide from Client Tools**. As a note, this can also be done from the Data View.

5. Now you will hide unneeded columns from each table from client tools. In **Diagram View**, find all fields that are listed in Table 3-3 and hide these from client tools. In **Diagram View**, right-click on each of the fields and choose **Hide From Client Tools**. Once you are done, they will become grayed-out in the model, which signifies that they

cannot be seen in client tools, but are visible and usable when forming modeling. As a note, you can choose multiple fields at once using the standard Windows multiselect commands. This can also be performed from the Data View, but is far easier to do in Diagram View.

TABLE 3-3 Columns to Hide From Client Tools

Table	Columns
FactInternetSales	ProductKey OrderDateKey DueDateKey ShipDateKey CustomerKey PromotionKey CurencyKey SalesTerritoryKey
DimCustomer	CustomerKey GeographyKey
DimPromotion	PromotionKey PromotionAlternateKey
DimCurrency	CurrencyKey CurencyAlternateKey
DimSalesTerritory	SalesTerritoryKey SalesTerritoryAlternateKey
DimDate	DateKey
DimProduct	ProductKey ProductSubcategoryKey

Now let's give the tables in the model friendlier names by renaming them in the Data Model. Note that if the tables had been imported using the Query Editor, you would need to perform these operations back in the Query Editor. In this demo, our tables were imported using PowerPivot so you can perform this as directed without error. If you had tried to rename tables that were imported using the Query Editor, you would receive the Error Message as shown in Figure 3-12.

1. In our case, you can right-click on the **Table Name** in either the **Diagram View** or **Data View** and then choose **Rename** from the context menu. When done, hit Enter so that the change takes effect. Do this for all the tables listed in Table 3-4.

FIGURE 3-12 Error message indicating that renames must be done Power Query

TABLE 3-4 Table Renaming

Original Table Name	New Table Name
FactInternetSales	InternetSales
DimCurrency	Currency
DimCustomer	Customer
DimDate	Dates
DimPromotion	Promotion
DimSalesTerritory	SalesTerritory
DimProduct	Product

2. Now let's give some of the columns names in the model friendlier names by renaming them in the Data Model. Once again, if the tables underlying the columns had been imported using the Query Editor, you would need to perform these operations back in the Query Editor. In this demo, our tables (and hence columns) were imported using PowerPivot, so you can perform this as directed without error. If you had tried to re-name columns that were imported using the Query Editor, you would receive the same error message shown in Figure 3-12.

3. In our case, in either the **Diagram View** or **Data View**, you can right-click on the **Column Name** that you want to change and then choose **Rename** from the context menu. When done, hit Enter so that the change takes effect. Do this for all the columns listed in Table 3-5.

TABLE 3-5 Column Renaming

Table	Original Column Name	New Column Name
Customer	EnglishEducation	Education
	EnglishOccupation	Occupation
Dates	EnglishDayNameOfWeek	DayNameOfWeek
	EnglishMonthName	MonthName
Product	EnglishDescription	Description
	EnglishProductName	ProductName
Promotion	EnglishPromotionName	PromotionName
	EnglishPromotionType	PromotionType
	EnglishPromotionCategory	PromotionCategory

4. Let's now examine the data types in the model and choose the correct data type for each column. The only column that does not have the correct data type (for this demo) is the DiscountAmount in InternetSales. Change this to currency by ensuring the **DiscountAmount** field is highlighted in the **Data View** and then navigate to **Home > Formatting > Data Type** and choose **Currency** from the drop-down list. You may get the **Data might be lost** error message as in Figure 3-13. If so, read the warning and understand what it is telling you and then click **Yes** to continue.

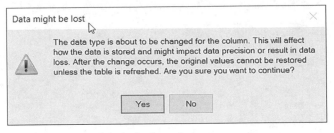

FIGURE 3-13 Data might be lost warning

5. Format the values in the UnitPriceDiscountPct column as a %. To do this, highlight the **UnitPriceDiscountPct** column in the **Data View** and navigate to **Home** > **Formatting** > **Format** and choose **Percentage** from the drop-down box.

6. If you require Explicit Measures to be created, you can do them here, but our model has enough in the way of Explicit measures. Notice that we have an **Average Freight** measure that we will format later. This can be used in place of the implicit measure named Average Freight that we have in the PivotTable.

7. Set Column Sorting on the MonthName column. In Data View, highlight the **Month-Name** column in the **Dates** table. Now navigate to **Home** > **Sort and Filter** > and click **Sort by Column**. In the **Sort by Column** dialog, ensure the **Sort Column** drop-down box has **MonthName** selected, and then in the **By Column** drop-down box choose **MonthNumberOfYear**. Click OK when complete.

8. Data Categorization adds extra metadata to columns of a certain type. Let's set two columns up to demonstrate. In Data View, ensure the **SalesTerritory** table is highlighted and then ensure the **SalesTerritoryCountry** column is highlighted within the table. Navigate to **Advanced** > **Reporting Properties** > **Data Category** > and choose **Country/Region**. It is likely that the Data Model has suggested that category for you already. Repeat the previous steps for **SalesTerritoryRegion** and choose **Continent** as its category. Setting these properties will help reporting tools understand that the text values in each column are not just any text, but that they represent geographical attributes.

9. And finally, set the Summarize By Property for our metrics. For each of the columns in Table 3-6, follow this procedure. Highlight the column in the **InternetSales** table and then navigate to **Advanced** > **Summarized By**, and choose the value in the drop-down box that corresponds to the Summarize By value in Table 3-6. Note that some of the values that the Data Model thought could be summarized, like the SalesOrderLineNumber, should never be summarized because it makes no sense to add up these values.

TABLE 3-6 Summarize By Properties

Table	Column	Summarize By
InternetSales	SalesOrderLineNumber	Do not summarize
	RevisionNumber	Do not summarize
	OrderQuantity	Sum
	UnitPrice	Sum
	ExtendedAmount	Sum
	UnitPriceDiscountPct	Do not summarize
	DiscountAmount	Sum
	ProductStandardCost	Do not summarize
	TotalProductCost	Sum
	SalesAmount	Sum
	TaxAmt	Sum
	Freight	Sum

Go to the PivotTable and add the **Average Freight** Explicit Measure from the **InternetSales** table to the **Values** area. At this point, take note of the fact that it has not been formatted. As opposed to formatting right in the PivotTable, go back to the PowerPivot and proceed with the next step.

10. Let's change the format of the measure from within Excel to demonstrate the different places where measures can be managed. Navigate to the **Power Pivot** tab, **Calculations**, **Measures**, and choose **Manage Measures**. In the **Manage Measures** dialog, choose **Average Freight** and then click **Edit**. This will open the **Measure** dialog box as shown in Figure 3-14.

11. In the **Category** selection at the bottom of the dialog, choose **Currency** and leave the **Symbol** and **Decimal places** values as their defaults. Click **OK** when complete.

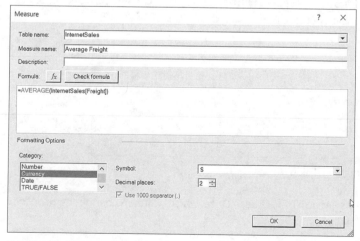

FIGURE 3-14 Measures management dialog

12. If you now return to the PivotTable, you will see that the new formatting has propagated to the model. If you had applied formatting at the PivotTable level first, the formatting you added to the model would not override what you did in the PivotTable. Despite the fact the formatting has been centrally set, you can override it in the PivotTable when necessary.

13. **Save** your work.

Format calculated measures

Once you create a Measure, it is advisable to provide it with a format you intend users to use when reporting. Formatting is a display setting only and does not affect how the data is stored in the Data Model.

Once the measure is created, you have the option to change the formatting to one of:

- Decimal Number
- Whole Number
- Percentage
- Scientific
- Currency
- Date
- TRUE/FALSE

Any Date formats that begin with an asterisk (*) will respond to changes in regional date time settings that are specified at the operating system level. To see which date formats are marked with an asterisk (*), do the following:

1. In **Data View**, ensure that the **Dates** table is highlighted and then highlight the **Full-DateAlternateKey** column.

2. From the Data Model, navigate to **Home** > **Formatting** > **Format**, and choose **More Formats**, which will open the Formatting dialog shown in Figure 3-15

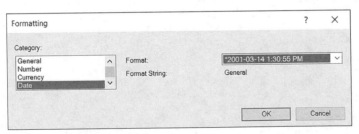

FIGURE 3-15 Formatting dialog

3. In the **Category** selection box, choose **Date**, which will then change the drop-down box to be a list of date formats.

4. In the drop-down, find a value with an asterisk next to it. The two options that are available are **General** and **Short**. In Figure 3-15 we have the General date format chosen.

As a reminder, you can also take advantage of the DAX FORMAT function to format a data field in an acceptable manner. To review how to achieve this, refer to Chapter 2 in the section on writing DAX queries where an example for the FORMAT function was presented. Do note that once formatted, numbers and dates become text strings and you can't perform calculations on them.

Let's take the measures in the Data Model and ensure that they are formatted properly.

5. Open the **\Chapter 3\CH03 Skill 3-1 Optimizing.xlsx** workbook you had been previously working with and navigate to the Data Model.

6. Format each of the measures in Table 3-7. Choose each **Measure** one by one in the **Calculation Area** and then choose **Home** > **Formatting** > **Format** and apply each format as indicated.

TABLE 3-7 Measure Formats

Measure	Home Table	Format
Most Recent Order Date	InternetSales	Date
Average Sales Amount Rounded	InternetSales	Whole Number
Average Freight	InternetSales	Currency
Sales over one million dollars	InternetSales	TRUE/FALSE
Total Sales	InternetSales	Currency
Total Cost	InternetSales	Currency
Profit Margin	InternetSales	Percentage

Filter data

Users often do not want to see an entire data set and are usually interested in smaller, more focused slices of data. If you want to narrow the data in a PivotTable based on criteria that has been specified, you can take advantage of filters. There are several ways to filter data that is contained within a PivotTable. You can use the following methods:

- Filter data using the PivotTable
- Add a PivotTable Filter
- Add a Slicer
- Add a Timeline

The first thing that we will do is add all of the filter types that we listed above to the Excel sheet so that we can demonstrate how to use them.

1. Open **\Chapter 3\CH03 Skill 3-1 Filtering.xlsx** workbook and ensure that you see the PivotTable that has been created for you.

2. With your **cursor** in the **PivotTable**, ensure that the **PivotTable Fields** pane is visible.

3. Next, from the **DimCustomer** table, drag the **MaritalStatus** column to the **Filter** area in the **PivotTable Fields** pane.

4. Now let's create a slicer. With your **cursor** outside of the PivotTable, navigate to **Insert > Filters**, and click **Slicer**.

5. In the **Existing Connections** dialog, click the **Data Model** Tab and ensure that **This Workbook Data Model** is selected and click **Open**.

6. On the **Insert Slicers** dialog, click the **All** tab and then find the **DimCustomer** table and check the **Gender** checkbox. Click OK when complete.

7. In the newly created Gender slicer, click **M** and then **F**. Notice that nothing happened. This is because the slicer has not yet been set up to interact with the PivotTable. To do this, right-click the **Gender** Slicer and choose **Report Connections** from the context menu. As a note, if you had your cursor in the PivotTable in step 4, the association would have been made for you automatically.

8. In the **Report Connections (Gender)** dialog, click **PivotTable1**. This will associate the slicer and PivotTable.

9. Now add a timeline. This time with your **cursor** inside the PivotTable, navigate to **Insert > Filters**, and click **Timeline**.

10. In the **Insert Timelines** dialog, find the **FactInternetSales** table and check the **Order-Date** field. Notice that the Insert Timelines dialog has only picked up on columns that have a date data type. Click **OK** when complete.

11. And finally, in the newly created timeline, click the **drop down** in the upper right corner that says **MONTHS** and choose **YEARS**.

12. When you are complete, your screen should look like Figure 3-16.

13. **Save** your work as **\Chapter 3\CH03 Skill 3-1 Filtering.xlsx**.

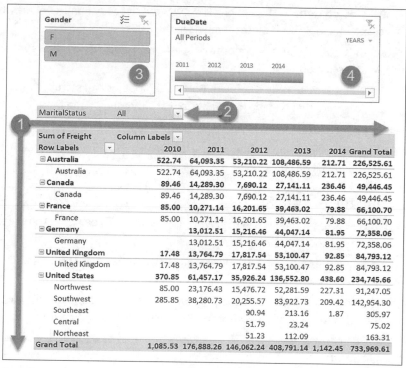

FIGURE 3-16 PivotTable with filter locations highlighted

In Figure 3-16 you will notice four distinct areas where filtering can be applied:

- Callout Bubble 1 on the X and Y axis of the PivotTable contains several areas where filters can be applied. We will cover these options in Filter data within the PivotTable.

- Callout Bubble 2 is the Pivot Table Filter.

- Callout Bubble 3 is the Slicer.

- Callout Bubble 4 is the Timeline.

> **IMPORTANT FILTER CONTEXT**
>
> Recall that in Skill 2.2, we introduced the concept of the Filter Context when writing DAX. The areas in Figure 3-16 are where filters can be applied that contribute to the Filter Context.

Filter Options

Let's discuss the Filter options that can be applied to a PivotTable. These can be found by right-clicking on any of the dimension members in the rows axis (or columns if we had a columns axis) in the PivotTable. Each of these will be shown shortly in an example. For now, right-click either **Australia** level member in the row axis and choose **Filter** from the context menu. You will be presented with the following options:

- **Keep Only Selected Items**   This option allows you to select any number of members at any level and then only keep those members in the PivotTable.

- **Hide Selected Items**   This is the opposite of Keep Only Selected and allows you to only hide what is selected.

- **Top 10**   This allows you to keep the Top or Bottom "x" (not just 10) member values. This is not just the measure that is in the PivotTable, but any measure in the Data Model.

- **Label Filters**   This allows you to filter on the member labels.

- **Value Filters**   This allows you to filter on measure values and not just the measure that is in the PivotTable, but any measure in the Data Model.

Filter data using the PivotTable

The first place that we will apply a filter is in the PivotTable itself. In this demo we will use the Top 10 filters.

1. Open the **\Chapter 3\CH03 Skill 3-1 Filtering.xlsx** workbook and ensure that the previous PivotTable is visible.

2. Place the cursor on the **Australia** member at the SalesTerritoryCountry level (as opposed to the value that is at the SalesTerritoryRegion level) of the row axis.

3. Right-click and in the context menu, choose **Filter**, and then navigate to the submenu and choose **Top 10**.

4. This will open the **Top 10 Filter (SalesTerritoryCountry)** dialog box as shown in Figure 3-17. Ensure that the dialog name does not have SalesTerritoryRegion in brackets, as that means you chose Australia at the incorrect level.

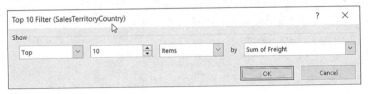

FIGURE 3-17 Top 10 Filter dialog box

5. In the dialog box you will have the following options that appear from left to right in Figure 3-17:

- In the first drop-down box, you can choose the following to decide where to start the ranking:

  - **Top**

  - **Bottom**

- In the second option box, you can choose a number to rank by. Examples are:

- Bottom 3 gives you the three worst performers for a metric.

- Top 5 gives you the Top five performers.

In the third drop-down, your options are:

- **Items** (default) Gives you the absolute number of items.
- **Percent** Gives you a percentage of data relative to the data set size.
- **Sum** Use to find the items that make up a specific sum.

6. Choose **Top 2 Items** by **Sum of Freight** and click **OK**.

7. You should only see the United States and Australia as in Figure 3-18.

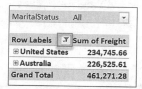

FIGURE 3-18 Filter Icon in the PivotTable

8. Now clear the filter by clicking the **Filter Symbol** next to **Row Labels** in the PivotTable, and then select **Clear Filter From "SalesTerritoryCountry"** from the context menu.

> **MORE INFO TOP 10 FILTERS**
>
> See the following article for more information and examples around using the Top 10 Filter
> *http://www.contextures.com/excel-pivot-table-filters-top10.html.*

Pivot Table Filter

These filters are added by moving one or more columns from the tables list in the PivotTable Fields pane to the Filters area. Note the following:

- If you have a field already in one of the other three areas (Rows, Columns, or Values), then the field cannot be placed in the Filter area without removing it from one of the other areas first.
- The PivotTable filter can only be used against the PivotTable it belongs to. If you want a filter to apply across multiple PivotTables, you will need to take advantage of Slicers and Timelines.

To use the filter, click the drop-down box next to the column name to be presented with a list of selectable items.

Slicer

Slicers provide highly visible buttons that you can click to filter data in your PivotTables and PivotCharts. In addition, slicers also indicate the current filtering state, which makes it easy to understand exactly which filters are being applied.

Timeline

Another option for filtering dates is to take advantage of a Timeline. A timeline enables you to filter by times and easily zoom in on the periods you want to see. Some notes are:

- A timeline is only useable with Date data types
- You can customize the slider to YEARS, QUARTERS, DAYS, and MONTHS
- It can be connected to multiple PivotTables and PivotCharts

Group and summarize data

You have already seen grouping and summarizing data from within a PivotTable by taking advantage of nesting fields in the Rows and Columns axis of the PivotTable. This is a manual way of grouping and summarizing data that is local to the PivotTable. Also, if you did this without using DAX Measures (explicit measures) then you will have created your own implicit measures that are summarized.

To make this centralized, you can add custom columns to your Data Model tables that can be used to group rows of data together. You can then use this alongside Hierarchies to improve usability.

IMPORTANT GROUP OR UNGROUP DATA IN A PIVOTTABLE

If you are accustomed to using the Group and Ungroup functionality, as found in traditional Excel, it is important to know that it does not work against the Data Model.

Skill 3.2: Create and manage PivotCharts

PivotTables are often a starting point for understanding data, but for general end-user consumption you often want to take advantage of using visuals for displaying data. Typically, when delivering solutions, you organize a collection of related visuals in the form of scorecards or dashboards that are used to tell a story for users in an "at a glance" fashion. If well designed and thought out, these solutions enable users to digest massive amounts of data in a very short period. Excel has many different visuals available, and you will review how to create and customize the major visuals in the remainder of this section. The intention of this book is not to make you an expert in how to design a well thought out and designed dashboard, but to show you the most common visuals and how to use and customize them as you prepare for the exam.

Select a chart type

Fact-based decision making is the foundation upon which successful businesses are built. Decision makers need to access data to help them make the right decisions quickly or to spot issues with a process so that corrective actions can be taken. The question on most decision makers' minds is "Do I need to do anything?"

As organizations grow, more and more data becomes available, so attempting to synthesize it all in a timely fashion can become a challenge. This is where visualizations that are properly selected and delivered can help provide that "at a glance" view of business performance across massive amounts of information. The Art and Science of Data Visualizations has taken off in recent years to help tame the deluge of data that inundates most organizations.

Building a well thought out Data Model that is friendly to use takes a considerable amount of time, but the efforts put in will pay dividends when you and your users are actively using the model in day-to-day analytic situations. The work done to Optimize the Data Model will make it easier to use, will help make the output more consistent between different users, and can help speed up time to delivery.

The Data Model only really becomes useful when you begin to consume the data for decision making purposes. As discussed in the earlier parts of this chapter, PivotTables are often the first stop when it comes to consuming data from the Data Model. Many Excel users have long been comfortable using PivotTables as their sole means of analysis. There comes a point, however, in the Analytics lifecycle where users that need to track multiple metrics or KPIs are better served by better means of visualizing their data. Tables of data and mountains of reports are hard to navigate when trying to understand performance. The current trend has been toward using the power of tools such as Excel to start with highly summarized visuals and providing users the ability to drill to details where needed. This is where Hierarchies that you would have built into the Data Model become useful.

So, the starting point when it comes to dashboard design is to understand the story that needs to be told with data while choosing appropriate visualizations arranged in an intuitive manner. It is beyond the scope of this book to discuss how to design well thought out dashboards that provide an at-a-glance view of data that is easily digestible and navigable, but it is worth pointing out its importance. The goal is to provide consumers of your data products the ability to find answers to questions themselves.

When building visualizations, is it is worth stepping back to see the big picture before selecting appropriate visualizations for what is being measured. There are four basic presentation types that you can use to present your data:

- Comparison
- Composition
- Distribution
- Relationship

Unless you are performing Data Science activities, you will primarily use the first two types in this list. In addition, Trending is something that is often broken into its own category as aspects of trending overlay both Comparison and Composition types.

For purposes of the exam, it is more important to get to an appropriate chart type because the specific categories are not likely to be tested. They are provided here to frame your thinking around the selection process.

Below are a few questions that you may ask yourself to help guide you toward selecting a proper visualization for your needs.

1. **Are you trying to compare values?** The following charts are useful for comparing one or many categories of data, as they can enable you to identify low and high points in the data:
   - Column
   - Bar
   - Line

2. **Do you want to show the composition of something?** The following charts are useful for showing how individual parts make up the whole:
   - Pie
   - Bar and variants of Bar
   - Stacked Column
   - Waterfall

3. **Are you interested in analyzing trends?** The following charts are useful if you want to know more about performance over time:
   - Line and variants of Line
   - Column and variants of column

4. **Are you trying to understand the distribution of your data?** The following Distribution-based charts are used to highlight outliers, display normal tendency, and show the range of data in your data set:

- Column
- Bar

5. **Do you want to better understand the relationship between value sets?** The following charts are useful for showing how one variable relates to one or more different variables:

- Scatter Plot
- Bubble
- Line and variants of line

> **MORE INFO** **RESOURCES TO HELP GUIDE APPROPRIATE VISUAL SELECTION**
>
> The following site has a tool called The Chart Chooser, which will help guide you toward an appropriate visual selection *https://extremepresentation.com/tools/*. In addition to this, Juice Analytics has an online chart chooser that uses the above flow to help you choose an appropriate chart. It can be found at *http://labs.juiceanalytics.com/chartchooser/*.

Excel has the following chart groupings. These chart types can use the Data Model or a PivotTable directly as a source.

- Column
- Line
- Pie
- Bar
- Area
- Surface
- Radar
- Combo

The following chart groupings cannot use the Data Model or a PivotTable directly as a source. To create these visuals, if you are using the Data Model as your primary source, you first need to create PivotTables and then convert them to Cube Functions or load the data to a traditional Excel table.

- Scatter
- Map
- Stock
- Funnel

The following chart groupings are new in Office 2016 and cannot use the Data Model or a PivotTable directly as a source.

- Treemap
- Sunburst
- Histogram
- Pareto
- Box and Whisker
- Waterfall

> **MORE INFO** **SIX NEW VISUALS IN OFFICE 2016**
>
> The six new charts types help you visualize common financial, statistical, and hierarchical data. You can learn more about these at the following location *https://www.makeuseof.com/tag/new-excel-charts/.*

Column

A Column Chart typically displays categories along the horizontal (category) axis and values along the vertical (value) axis. They are good for comparison-based analysis and are well suited if you have any negative category values, since negative values are often associated with having a downward direction. Each of the seven charts are shown in Figure 3-19 and Figure 3-20.

- Clustered Column and 3D Clustered Column
- Stacked Column and 3D Stacked Column
- 100% Stacked Column and 3D 100% Stacked
- 3D Column

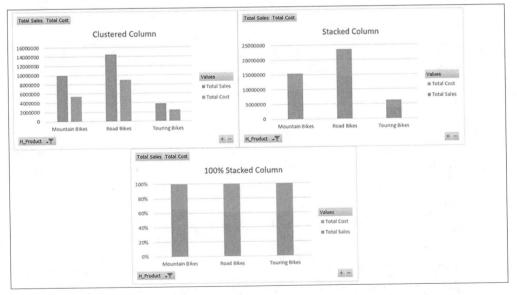

FIGURE 3-19 2D Bar Charts

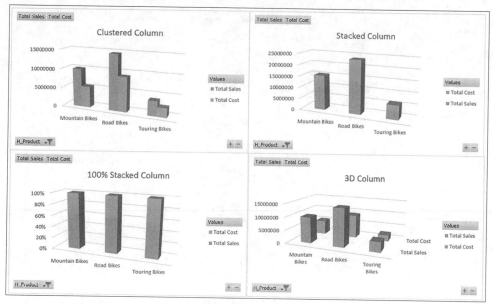

FIGURE 3-20 3D Bar Charts

Line

In a line Chart, category data is distributed evenly across the horizontal axis, and value data is distributed evenly across the vertical axis. Line Charts are good for showing continuous data over time. The charts that have markers are the same as the line charts shown in Figure 3-21 except for the fact that data point markers would be shown on the visual. Marker Charts are not separately shown but the only difference between each is that markers will show up on the visuals for each data point. Excel has the following seven chart styles as shown in Figure 3-21.

- Line and Line with Markers
- Stacked Line and Stacked Line with Markers
- 100% Stacked Column and 100% Stacked Column with Markers
- 3D Line

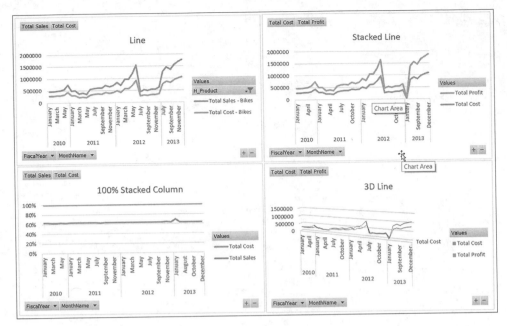

FIGURE 3-21 Line Charts

Pie and Doughnut

Pie Charts show the size of items in one data series, and the data points are shown as a percentage of the whole pie. There are five variants of the Pie Chart that also include the Doughnut. Figure 3-22 only shows the Pie and Doughnut Charts.

- Pie and 3D Pie
- Pie of Pie
- Bar of Pie
- Doughnut

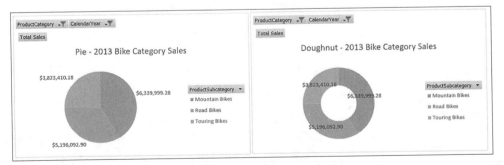

FIGURE 3-22 Pie and Doughnut Charts

Bar

There are six types of Bar Charts available in Excel. They are a good way to present data with long labels that would be hard to display below a vertical bar. They also work well if you are trying to display many categories on the category axis. The three 2D versions of the charts are shown in Figure 3-23.

- Clustered Bar and 3D Clustered Bar
- Stacked Bar and 3D Stacked Bar
- 100% Stacked Bar and 3D 100% Stacked Bar

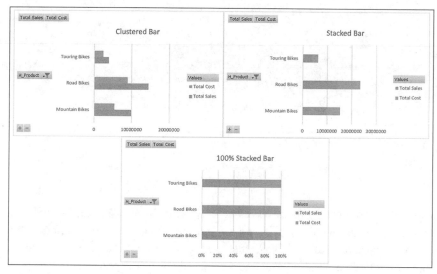

FIGURE 3-23 Bar Charts

Combo

Combo Charts enable you to combine two or more chart types to make relationships in your data easy to understand. You can combine charts from the groupings of Column, Bar, Line, and Area into a combo chart. You are also able to define a secondary axis, which is useful when plotting data sets with differing scales, such as we did with the chart labeled **Clustered Column-Line on Secondary Axis** in Figure 3-24. The three charts that are shown in Figure 3-24 are generally your starting point when building a Combo Chart. If any customizations are made to one of these visuals, Excel switches the chart type to a Custom Combination, which then allows you to make further customizations. The following four combo chart types are available:

- Clustered Column-Line
- Clustered Column-Line on Secondary Axis
- Stacked Area-Clustered Column
- Custom Combination

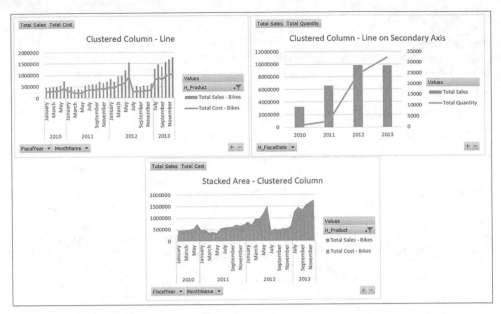

FIGURE 3-24 Combo Charts

Area

Area Charts are useful for visualizing time-series relationships (see Figure 3-25). Unlike line charts, they also visually represent volume by emphasizing the area with color or shading in the area between the Axis. Stacked Area Charts show the trend of the contribution of each value over time or other category data, and 100% Stacked Area Charts show the percentage trend that each value contributes over a category such as time. There are six different chart types that fall into this category in Excel:

- Area and 3D Area
- Stacked Area and 3D Stacked Area
- 100% Stacked Area and 3D 100% Stacked Area

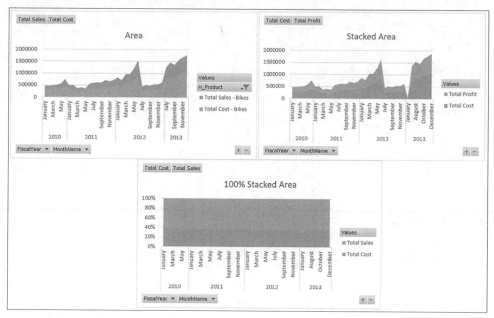

FIGURE 3-25 Area Charts

Scatter and Bubble

Scatter Plots are like line graphs (see Figure 3-26). A line graph uses a line on the X-Y axis to plot continuous data, while a scatter plot uses markers to represent individual data points. Scatter Plots are useful if you want to see how two variables are related to each other. There are seven different styles of Scatter Plots in Excel:

- Scatter
- Scatter with Smooth Lines and Markers
- Scatter with Smooth Lines
- Scatter with Straight Lines and Markers
- Scatter with Straight Lines
- Bubble and 3D Bubble

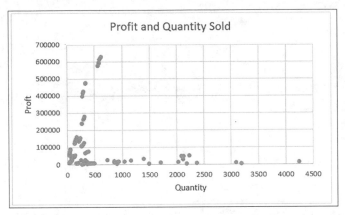

FIGURE 3-26 Scatter Plot

Stock

As the name implies, Stock Charts can show fluctuations in stock prices and other data sets that have high-low variability that you want to visualize. There are four different types of Stock charts:

- High-low-close
- Open-high-low-close
- Volume-high-low-close
- Volume-open-high-low-close

> **MORE INFO CREATE A STOCK CHART IN EXCEL**
>
> If you would like an example of how to create a stock chart in Excel, the following resource has some good demos *https://www.extendoffice.com/documents/excel/2138-excel-create-stock-chart.html*.

Map

Map Charts are useful when you want to plot data on a map to enhance the understanding of a data set across regionality. It is important to have geographical attributes in your data sets, as they are needed to help draw out the map visualization. Figure 3-27 contains a map of the Adventure Works sales across all time. Notice that the default map as created here varies; the color shades go from darkest to lightest, where the highest sales are shown using the darkest colors. This helps to further emphasize patterns in the data.

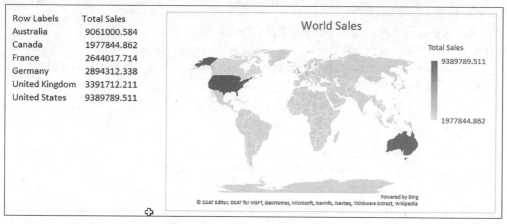

Row Labels	Total Sales
Australia	9061000.584
Canada	1977844.862
France	2644017.714
Germany	2894312.338
United Kingdom	3391712.211
United States	9389789.511

FIGURE 3-27 Map Chart

> **MORE INFO FORMAT A MAP CHART**
>
> There is quite a bit that you can do with a Map Chart to customize and emphasize data points. The following site has some good examples and details on the things you can do: *https://support.office.com/en-us/article/format-a-map-chart-2c744937-a1cc-48f7-bc5e-776497343a29.*

Radar

As defined by Wikipedia, a Radar Chart is "a graphical method of displaying multivariate data in the form of a two-dimensional chart of three or more quantitative variables represented on axes starting from the same point." In Figure 3-28, we display Total Profit and Total Sales across the Accessories Product Subcategory.

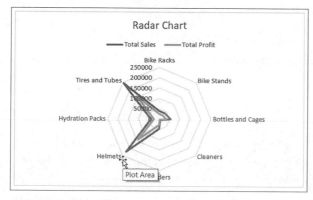

FIGURE 3-28 Radar Chart

Funnel

Funnel Charts are typically used to show multiple stages in a process, such as movement through a sales pipeline or a registration process for a school. They use horizontal bars that are arranged in the same order that a process flows, to show progression though the process. They are also useful for displaying data across categories as well, since the bars are sized relative to each other on display. In Figure 3-29 we are displaying the ranked Total Sales of the Accessories Product Subcategory.

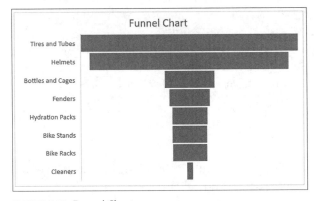

FIGURE 3-29 Funnel Chart

Treemap

A Treemap is a Hierarchical Chart that is useful for comparing parts to a whole, or when several columns of a category form a hierarchy. It provides an easy way to compare different levels of categorization. It displays categories by color and proximity and can display lots of data easily.

Remember that this visual cannot be sourced directly though the data model. If you try, you will see a message that says the following.

You can't create this chart type with data inside a PivotTable. Please select a different chart type or copy the data outside of the PivotTable.

To solve this, we will first create a PivotTable and then will convert the PivotTable to Cube Function calls. Once we have the data in this format, you will build the PivotChart off that data set. Let's create a demo around building out the Treemap by performing the following steps:

1. Open the **\Chapter 3\CH03 Skill 3-3 PivotChart Demo.xlsx** workbook.

2. From **Excel** > click the **Insert** tab > **Tables** > **PivotTable**.

3. In the **Create PivotTable** dialog, in the Choose the data that you want to analyze, **Use this workbook's Data Model**, and then in the Choose where you want the PivotTable to be placed, choose **New Worksheet**. Click **OK**.

4. In the PivotTable Fields pane, do the following:

   A. Drag **Total Sales** from the **InternetSales** table into the **Values** area.

   B. Right-Click on the **SalesTerritoryGroup** in the **SalesTerritory** table and choose **Add to Rows Labels** on the context menu. Do the same for **SalesTerritoryCountry** as well. Once complete, ensure that SalesTerritoryCountry is nested under the SalesTeritoryGroup. Note: Do not use the hierarchy for this exercise but the field itself which is under the **More Fields** folder.

5. At this point, your PivotTable should look like Figure 3-30.

Row Labels	Total Sales
Europe	**8930042.263**
France	2644017.714
Germany	2894312.338
United Kingdom	3391712.211
North America	**11367634.37**
Canada	1977844.862
United States	9389789.511
Pacific	**9061000.584**
Australia	9061000.584
Grand Total	**29358677.22**

FIGURE 3-30 Treemap PivotTable

6. We now need to change the Layout of the PivotTable so that the data is in the necessary state to support the visual. With the cursor in the PivotTable, navigate to the **Design** tab, **Layout** group, **Report Layout**, and click **Show in Tabular Form**.

7. Now make the data labels repeat down the rows by navigating to the **Design** tab > **Layout** group > **Report Layout** > click **Repeat All Item Labels**.

8. Remove the Subtotals by right-clicking one of the subtotal labels in the PivotTable and choose **Field Settings** from the context menu. On the **Field Settings** dialog, ensure the **Subtotals & Filters** tab has focus and then under **Subtotals**, choose **None**.

9. Remove the Grand Totals by navigating to Cube formulas so that it can be used as the source for the Treemap. For this, navigate to **Design** > **Layout** > **Grand Totals** > click **Off for Rows and Columns**.

10. Now insert a Slicer so that you can interact with the data. To do this, ensure that the cursor is inside the PivotTable and the navigate to **Insert** > **Filters** > click **Slicer** to open the Insert Slicers dialog. Note that since we said to insert the slicer while we were in the PivotTable, a few things were done for us that we may need to otherwise do manually. First, Excel knew to base the slicer on the Data Model. If you had done this operation outside of the PivotTable, you would have been asked what source to use for the slicer. Secondly, Excel knew to associate the slicer to the PivotTable, which is what signals the slicer values to be passed to the PivotTable when you interact with the slicer.

11. From within the **Insert Slicer** dialog, ensure that the **All** tab is open and then in the **Customer** table, check the **Gender** field to create the slicer based on this. Click **OK** when complete.

12. Finally, we need to convert the PivotTable to Cube Functions since the Treemap PivotChart type cannot use a PivotTable. To do this, navigate to **Analyze** > **Calculations** > **OLAP Tools** > and click **Convert to Formulas**.

13. At this point your data worksheet should look like Figure 3-31. Notice that it is no longer a PivotTable, but has been converted to a series of Cube Function calls that get the equivalent data to the PivotTable.

FIGURE 3-31 Data formatted for Treemap consumption

14. Use the newly converted set of data as the source for the Treemap chart. To do this, highlight the rows and columns in the worksheet in Figure 3-30, including the column headers.

15. Next navigate to **Insert** tab, **Charts** group, **Insert Hierarchy Chart** command and then click **Treemap** in the drop-down.

16. You should then be presented with the default Treemap chart as in Figure 3-32. Notice that this screenshot was taken immediately after you clicked Treemap so that data points in the table are still highlighted.

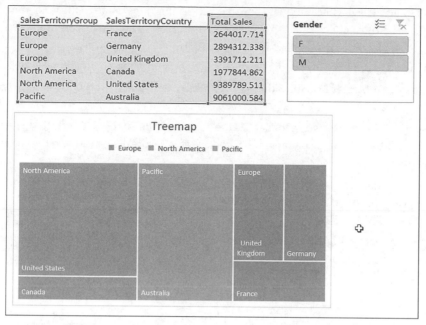

SalesTerritoryGroup	SalesTerritoryCountry	Total Sales
Europe	France	2644017.714
Europe	Germany	2894312.338
Europe	United Kingdom	3391712.211
North America	Canada	1977844.862
North America	United States	9389789.511
Pacific	Australia	9061000.584

FIGURE 3-32 Default Treemap Chart

17. Interact with the slicer values and watch the chart and data table change with the different filter values.

18. **Save** the file, as you will use what you have done so far to build a Sunburst Chart next. You will also come back to the Treemap in a later demo to format it.

> **MORE INFO CREATING TREEMAPS**
>
> For more information on creating Treemap visuals see the following article *https://support. office.com/en-us/article/create-a-treemap-chart-in-office-2016-dfe86d28-a610-4ef5-9b30- 362d5c624b68*.

EXAM TIP

Knowledge of MDX syntax is not examinable outside of what is needed when working with the CUBEFUNCTIONS. Some knowledge is helpful if you find yourself getting into more advanced reporting using the Data Model, PivotTables, and PivotCharts.

Sunburst

The Sunburst Chart is useful for displaying hierarchical data. Each level of the hierarchy is represented by one ring or circle with the innermost circle as the top of the hierarchy. A Sunburst Chart with only one level of categories resembles a Doughnut Chart. However, a Sunburst

Chart with multiple levels of categories shows how the outer rings relate to the inner rings. The Sunburst Chart is most effective at showing how one ring is broken into its contributing pieces.

Even though the data for the previous example may not be the best for display in a Sunburst Chart, let's use the data as a matter of convenience to show creating an additional visual.

1. Open the **\Chapter 3\CH03 Skill 3-3 PivotChart Demo.xlsx** workbook that you previously saved.

2. Use the newly converted set of data as the source for the Sunburst Chart. To do this, highlight the rows and columns in the worksheet in Figure 3-31, including the column headers.

3. Next, navigate to **Insert** tab > **Charts** group > **Insert Hierarchy Chart** command and then click **Sunburst** in the drop-down.

4. You should be presented with a Sunburst Chart as shown in Figure 3-33. Take note of how the chart is effective at showing how one ring is broken into its contributing pieces.

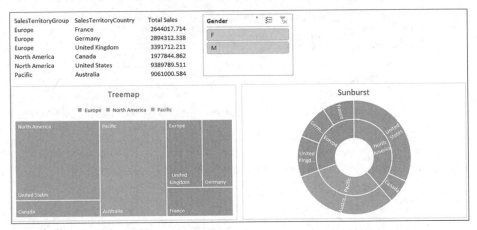

FIGURE 3-33 Sunburst Chart

5. Interact with the slicer values and watch the chart and data table change with the different filter values.

6. **Save** the file, as will you use what you have done so far. You will also come back to the Treemap in a later demo to format it.

MORE INFO CREATING SUNBURST VISUALS

For more information on creating Sunburst visuals see the following article *https://support. office.com/en-us/article/create-a-sunburst-chart-in-office-2016-4a127977-62cd-4c11-b8c7-65b84a358e0c*.

Histogram

Histograms show distributions of data. They are used to plot data with ranges of the data grouped into bins or intervals. Often Histograms are described as bar charts, which is a mistake. Bar charts are used to plot categorical data and are used to compare values across categories.

Let's look at creating Histogram by looking at how our customer base is distributed across commute distance. The Customer has a Bin already included in the data set, which is useful. All that we will do is perform a count in the CustomerAlternateKey so that we can see the number of customers in each bin. To do this, follow these steps:

1. Open the **\Chapter 3\CH03 Skill 3-3 PivotChart Demo.xlsx** workbook.

2. Navigate to the Histogram worksheet. Once this worksheet is open, you will notice that a data set has already been created for this demo to save you the steps of data preparation.

3. Highlight the rows and columns in the worksheet, including the column headers.

4. Next navigate to **Insert** tab > **Charts** group > **Insert Statistic Chart** command, and then click **Histogram** in the drop-down.

5. You should then be presented with a new Histogram chart as shown in Figure 3-34.

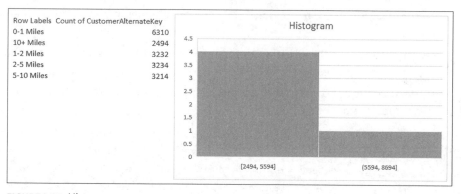

FIGURE 3-34 Histogram

6. This is a good start, but it is not quite what we had intended. We wanted to see the distribution across the Bins that we had in our data set, which is what we will see in Figure 3-34 after we configure the next step.

7. To get your Histogram to look like this, do the following steps. Highlight the **x-axis** as shows by Callout Bubble 1 on Figure 3-35 and then double-click it. Then in the context menu, select **Format Axis**. When the **Format Axis** pane appears, ensure that **Axis Options** (Callout Bubble 2) is highlighted, and choose **By Category** in the **Bins** options, which is Callout Bubble 3. This will put the counts in the appropriate bins.

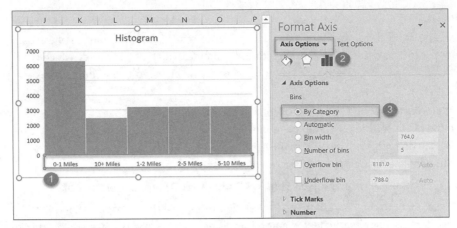

FIGURE 3-35 Histogram

For completeness, you have the following options for configuring bins:

- **By Category**   You specify the categories for the bins.
- **Automatic**   Excel will automatically determine the number of bins.
- **Bin Width**   Use this to specify the range of each bin.
- **Number Of Bins**   Use this option if you know the number of bins you want to show in the chart.
- **Overflow Bin**   Use this to define an upper limit value for bins. Values that are above this number are put into another bin.
- **Underflow Bin**   Use this to define a lower limit value for bins. Values that are above this number are put into another bin.

> **MORE INFO   CREATING HISTOGRAM AND PARETO CHARTS**
>
> For more information on creating histogram charts, please see the following sites: *https:// support.office.com/en-us/article/create-a-histogram-in-excel-85680173-064b-4024-b39d-80f17ff2f4e8* and *https://support.office.com/en-us/article/create-a-pareto-chart-a1512496-6dba-4743-9ab1-df5012972856*.

Box and Whisker

Box and Whisker plots are used to compare distributions because the center, spread, and overall range are immediately apparent. In contrast to a Histogram, it does not show a distribution in as much detail, but is useful for indicating whether a distribution is skewed or not.

Waterfall

Waterfall Charts are useful for visualizing positive and negative values and how they impact a subtotal or total. They are often used when visualizing financial statements data such as net income or profit, and how accounts, business units, or divisions impact these overall values. Figure 3-36 demonstrates this.

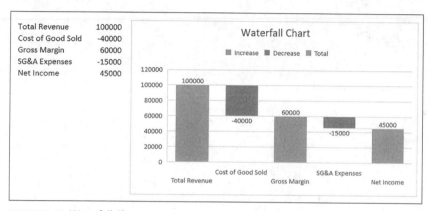

FIGURE 3-36 Waterfall Chart

Format PivotCharts

When building PivotCharts, you typically start out by getting the PivotChart functioning properly from a data perspective. Once you have it displaying the data that you want, and perhaps even alongside some other visuals, the time will come to give your PivotChart a professional look and feel.

Each of the Chart Types have many elements in common, such as Titles, Axis Labels, and Legends. There are some elements that are unique to each visual. In this section, we will focus on the common things that can be done to format your PivotCharts to make them look visually appealing. There are many formatting options, and it is beyond the scope of the exam to go into details around all options.

The first thing that you need to be familiar with is the **Format Selection** pane. There are numerous ways to have it appear. In Figure 3-37, the chart area is highlighted and then we navigated to **Format**, **Current Selection**, and clicked **Format Selection**, which made the **Format Chart Area** pane appear as shown.

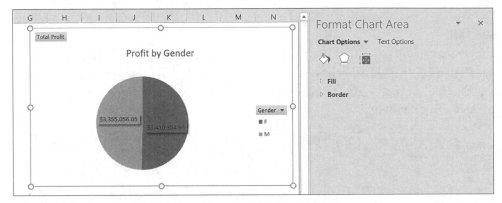

FIGURE 3-37 Pie PivotChart with Format Chart Area visible

In the Current Selection group, as shown in Figure 3-38, you will notice the drop-down with the word **Chart Area** selected.

FIGURE 3-38 Current Selection group

If you click the **Chart Elements** drop-down box, you will see all the chart elements for a Pie Chart as is shown in Figure 3-39. You will know what can be formatted once you click on an element and then see what is available in the Format Selection pane.

FIGURE 3-39 Pie Chart customizable chart elements

As you have seen, when you have a PivotChart in focus, you will get the following tabs that show up in the Ribbon under PivotChart Tools.

- Analyze
- Design
- Format

The tabs that we are concerned about in this Section are the Design and Format tabs. In the Design tab, as shown in Figure 3-40, you will notice the following options, which are used to change the styles of your PivotChart.

- **Add Chart Element** Lets you add and modify valid elements for a given Chart Type.
- **Quick Layout** Has predefined styles for you to change the overall layout of your chart.
- **Change Colors** Allows you to customize your colors and styles.
- **Gallery** Allows you to choose from many predefined styles that are applied to all the elements of a given visual.
- **Change Chart Type** From here you can change your chart to many different types.

FIGURE 3-40 PivotChart Tools Design tab

In the Format tab, as shown in Figure 3-41, you will notice the following options, which are used to change the format of your PivotChart. Below are the most commonly used commands on this tab.

- **Chart Elements** As mentioned earlier, this is where you can pick chart elements from the drop-down.
- **Format Selection** Opens the Format Selection pane that has formatting options for each element.
- **Reset to Match Style** Clears the custom formatting of the selected chart element back to the overall style applied to the chart. This helps to ensure that the selected chart elements match the overall theme of the document.
- **WordArt Styles Gallery** Customizes fonts on the visual.
- **Height** Adjusts the height of the selected chart element, if applicable.
- **Width** Adjusts the height of the selected chart element, if applicable.

FIGURE 3-41 PivotChart Tools Format tab

Listed below are some of the Chart Elements that can be formatted:

- Chart Area
- Chart Title
- Axis Title
- Axis
- Plot Area
- Data Labels
- Data Series
- Data Point
- Legend

Formatting a chart can be a time-consuming task as you work to get every aspect of the design and format just right. So, once you have your chart formatted the way you like, you may find yourself wanting to use a similar set of formatting styles on other charts. To do this, you can save your chart as a template for reuse in other workbooks.

> **MORE INFO** **SAVE A CUSTOM CHART AS A TEMPLATE**
>
> For more information on how to save a custom chart as a template, visit the following site *https://support.office.com/en-us/article/save-a-custom-chart-as-a-template-259a5f9d-a9ec-4b3f-94b6-9f5e55187f2a.*

Filter data

Filtering data can be done on the PivotChart or it can be done using an external object such as a Slicer or a Timeline. This is done in the same manner as we did with PivotTables. You have already seen Slicers and Timelines, so let's focus the discussion around filtering PivotCharts to the filters on the chart itself. Figure 3-42 shows the three filters that are available to be applied to the PivotChart.

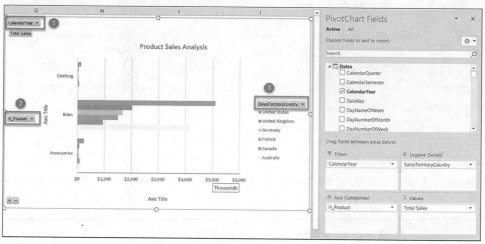

FIGURE 3-42 PivotChart with filters

Callout Bubble 1 is the CalendarYear filter that has been designated in the Filter area of the PivotChart Fields pane. This filter can only choose specific values from the list of valid members. Callout Bubble 2 has the filter options that can be applied to the Axis (Categories) and Callout Bubble 3 is for the Legend (Series). Both Callout Bubbles 2 and 3 allow for extended Filtering on Labels and Values in the chart.

Skill 3.3: Interact with Power BI

Excel has arguably been one of the top, if not the top, BI tool for many years. However, Excel has several shortcomings that needed to be addressed. Some of the largest pain points with Excel have been sharing, collaborating, and maintaining version control of an Excel workbook. For years, users have been creating wonderful insights that they have had a tough time sharing in a consistent and secure manner.

In recent years, Power BI has gained in popularity, largely in part due to its ability to overcome the sharing and collaboration barrier. In conjunction with the evolution of the Office 365 and Azure suite of products, we now have many options that allow for easier centralization of data and sharing of those data products in the form of the Data Model or Excel Visualizations.

> **This section covers how to:**
> - Import Excel data from Power BI
> - Manipulate Excel data in Power BI

Power BI overview

Before we dive into the options that you have for interactions between Power BI and Excel, we will do a quick overview of Power BI and its components.

Power BI desktop

Power BI desktop is the tool where most of the development work to create Power BI models and visualization is done. The tool has capabilities to connect to data sources, load, cleanse, and model data for end-user consumption. It then allows you to build visuals and then consume this content in the Power BI service. Fundamentally it does many of the same things that you have already done in Excel using PivotTable and PivotCharts, using the Excel data model and Get & Transform data. Power BI originally launched as part of Office 365 back in July 2013 and in July 2015 it became its own product that was disconnected (from a product development lifecycle) from the Office suite of products.

It comes in two versions: Power BI Desktop and Power BI Desktop optimized for Power BI Report Server. The latter is meant to be used against Power BI Report server.

Power BI Service

The Power BI Service is where content that is developed using Power BI Desktop is published for more widespread sharing and collaboration using the Internet. From here it can be accessed anytime, anywhere, by any device. It is also possible to import data using the service and then build reports from it, but the functionality is not nearly as rich as the desktop tools. The Power BI Service interface is shown in Figure 3-43.

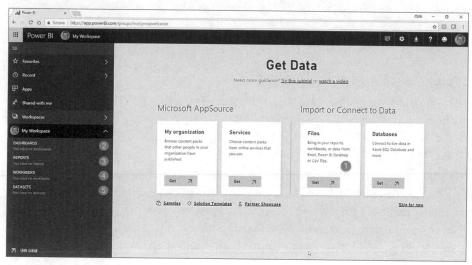

FIGURE 3-43 Power BI Service interface

The relevant parts of the service for purposes of this book are shown in the following list. Note that each number in the list corresponds to a numbered Callout Bubbles on Figure 3-43.

8. **Import or Connect to Data**   We will be navigating to Files, Get to publish data from Excel to the Power BI Service so that content can be shared using this interface.

9. **DASHBOARDS**   This is where Power BI Dashboards are housed and managed once they are created.

10. **REPORTS**   This where Power BI Reports are stored, managed, and created.

11. **WORKBOOKS**   This is where any Excel workbooks that have been published to the Power BI Service will be housed and managed.

12. **DATASETS**   This is where Power BI stores datasets that are used to build reports.

Power BI Mobile

Once content is published to or built in the Power BI Service, it is made available almost instantaneously in Power BI Mobile. It allows you to securely access and view live any dashboards and reports on any device, with native mobile BI apps for Windows, iOS, and Android.

Power BI Embedded

Microsoft Power BI Embedded is targeted at application developers to use so that they can embed fully interactive reports, dashboards, and tiles into applications without the time and expense of building their own data visualizations and controls from the ground-up. Power BI, on the other hand, is a software-as-a-service analytics solution that gives organizations a single view of their most critical business data.

Import Excel data from Power BI

There are multiple ways to get data and objects from Excel into Power BI. The terminology differs depending if you're using Excel or Power BI as the starting point.

Publish from Excel

With Excel 2016, you can publish Excel workbooks to Power BI right from Excel. This enables you to harness the power and skills you have with Excel and then benefit from the interaction and distribution capabilities from within Power BI. For years, one of the largest challenges with Excel has been how to share workbooks while maintaining versions. With Office 365 and Power BI you now have the capabilities to avoid what has traditionally been one of the largest challenges.

You have two options for publishing to Power BI from within Excel and each has differing outcomes. You can:

- Upload your workbook to Power BI
- Export your workbook data to Power BI

To get to the Publish location from within Excel, navigate to **File**, to >**Publish** and you will see Figure 3-44.

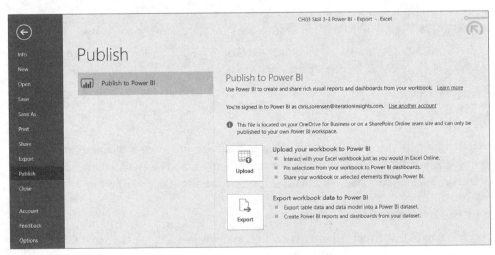

FIGURE 3-44 Excel Publish Interface

First Let's look at what each option offers by first looking at the **Upload Your Workbook To Power BI** option, which has the following functionality. As a note, these functions are active once you publish:

- Interact with your Excel workbook just as you would in Excel Online.
- Pin selections from your workbook to Power BI dashboards.
- Share your workbook or selected elements through Power BI.

There a few things that you need to be aware of before you publish:

- Before you can publish to Power BI, your workbook must be saved locally, in OneDrive for Business or on a SharePoint Online team site. If the file is saved locally, only Excel 2016 with an Office 365 subscription will see the experience to publish with local files. If you are using an Excel 2016 standalone installation, you will still have the Publish behavior, but this requires that the Excel workbook be saved to OneDrive for Business or SharePoint Online.
- The account you use to sign in to Office, OneDrive for Business, and Power BI must be the same account.
- You cannot publish an empty workbook or a workbook that doesn't have any Power BI supported content.
- You cannot publish encrypted or password-protected workbooks, or workbooks with Information Protection Management.
- Publishing to Power BI requires modern authentication be enabled (default). If disabled, the Publish option is not available from the File menu.

If your Excel work book is stored on OneDrive for Business or on a SharePoint Online team site, you will only be able to publish to your own Power BI workspace per the below message in Figure 3-45.

 This file is located on your OneDrive for Business or on a SharePoint Online team site and can only be published to your own Power BI workspace.

FIGURE 3-45 File Location Message

If your Excel workbook is stored locally, you will able to **Select Where You'd Like To Publish To In Power BI**. This is any workspace that you have permissions for as shown in Figure 3-46. To generate this screenshot, simply move the Excel file that you want to publish to your desktop.

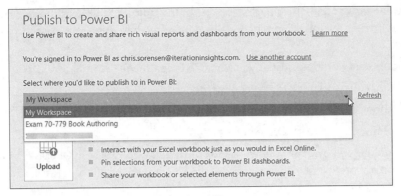

FIGURE 3-46 Publish to Power BI via a local file

Let's now publish a file to Power BI using the Upload option. To do this, perform the following steps:

1. Open the file named **\Chapter3\CH03 Skill 3-3 Power BI–Upload.xlsx**. In this demo, the file was stored in OneDrive for Business.

2. Observe that the file has the following characteristics:

   - It has a Data Model that has been populated using the Query Editor
   - It has an Excel Table named tblLetters on Sheet2
   - It has several reporting objects such as a Timeline, PivotCharts, and PivotTables

3. Navigate to **File** > **Publish** > and then click **Upload.** Once you click **upload**, you should see the status bar at the bottom of the screen as appears in Figure 3-47.

FIGURE 3-47 Publish to Power BI status

4. Once the Publish is complete, Excel will display the message in Figure 3-48 below the Ribbon. Click the **Go to Power** BI button.

FIGURE 3-48 Publish to Power BI success message

5. In Power BI you should see the following, as in Figure 3-49. You will notice that it is Excel Online and that the name of the workbook **CH03 Skill 3-3 Power BI–Upload** shows up under the **WORKBOOKS** area. Here are a few important points:

   - The entire workbook has been published.
   - You cannot edit the workbook in Power BI.
   - You can edit it by clicking **Edit** and then choose to **Edit in Excel Online** or **Edit in Excel**.

- No data has been uploaded to Power BI because nothing shows up in **DATASETS**. This means that the data is still in the Excel Data Model. Any additional visuals need to be created in Excel.

- If data changes in the workbook on OneDrive for Business, it can take up to one hour for the changes to be reflected in Power BI.

- You can Pin the visuals, including the PivotTable to a Dashboard.

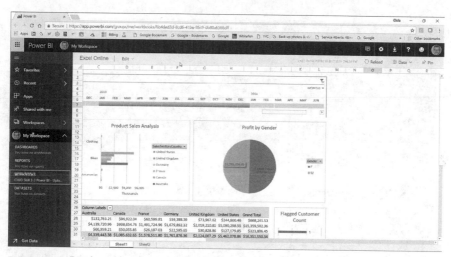

FIGURE 3-49 Excel workbook content hosted in the Power BI Service

Let's now publish a file to Power BI using the Export option. To do this, perform the following steps:

1. Open the file named **\Chapter3\CH03 Skill 3-3 Power BI – Export.xlsx**. In this demo, the file was stored in OneDrive for Business.

2. It has the same characteristics as the Upload file but was given a different name to add clarity to the demo.

3. Navigate to **File** > **Publish** > and then click **Export**. Once you click upload, you should see the status bar at the bottom of the screen appear as in Figure 3-47.

4. Once Publish is complete, Excel will display the message in Figure 3-48 below the Ribbon. Click the **Go to Power** BI button.

5. In the Power BI service, you will notice that this time the only the Data Model tables have been imported in the **DATASETS** section as shown in Figure 3-50.

   - Any supported data in tables and/or the Data Model are exported to a new dataset in Power BI. Note that if you have Data Model data and Excel tables, only the Data Model tables will come over. In our case, the Excel table name tblLetters was not brought over. Had there been no data model in the workbook, the table would have come over.

   - If you have Power View sheets, they are re-created as Power BI Reports.

■ When you edit your workbook and save it in OneDrive for Business, your changes are synchronized with the dataset in Power BI within an hour. If you need it faster, you can Publish again.

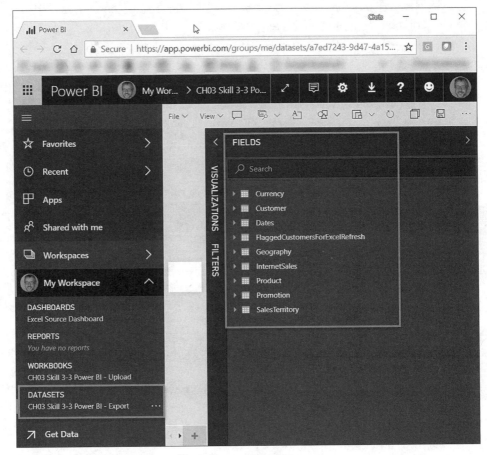

FIGURE 3-50 Excel DATASET hosted in the Power BI Service

6. If you click on the Ellipses next to the **CH03 Skill 3-3 Power BI–Export** dataset you will notice the following, as in Figure 3-51, which indicates when the last data refresh occurred.

FIGURE 3-51 Last dataset refresh time

Import from Power BI

From within Power BI you can effectively perform the same action:

- Import a workbook to Power BI (like Export within Excel)
- Connect to the workbook to navigate its data and content (like Upload from Excel)

As a note, My Workspace in Power BI was cleaned out completely so that we can demo the same actions from above, but this time using Power BI as the interface to bring in Excel content.

If your current Power BI screen does not look like Figure 3-52, you can click **Get Data** in the bottom left of the Power BI interface as shown with Callout Bubble 1, because this will show up in all Power BI screens. Once you have the full screen as in Figure 3-52, navigate to **Import** or **Connect to Data**, and click **Get** (Callout Bubble 2).

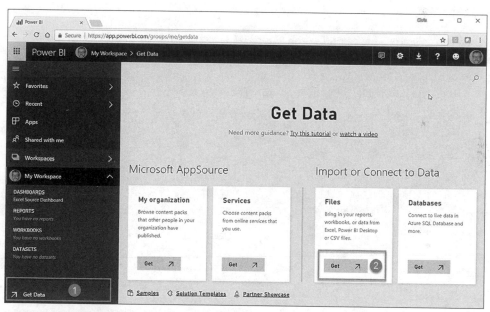

FIGURE 3-52 Get Data from Excel using the Power BI Service

You are then presented with the following screen as in Figure 3-53. Here you will see that Power BI allows you to bring files in from several other locations as well.

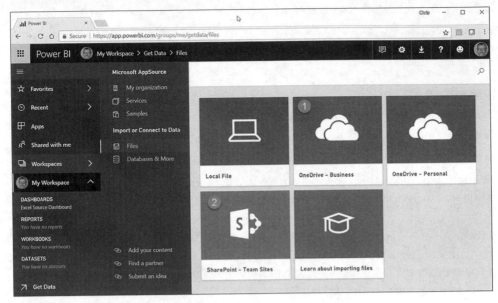

FIGURE 3-53 Import or Connect to Files

When you select one of the options on Figure 3-53, you get the navigation screen for OneDrive for Business. Here you navigate to the file locations (same as where they were for Excel) and then click Connect. Once you have done this, you will be presented with Figure 3-54, where you decide how you want to connect your Excel workbook.

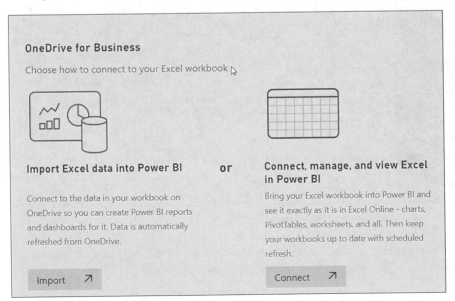

FIGURE 3-54 Choose how to connect to your Excel workbook dialog

From this point forward, you will end up with the same result as when we published from Excel. Once again, if you choose to **Import** a workbook to Power BI, it will function like Export within Excel. If you choose to **Connect** to the workbook, it will function like Upload from Excel.

Power BI Publisher for Excel

Power BI publisher for Excel enables you to take snapshots of Excel objects such as PivotTables and PivotCharts and pin them directly into Power BI.

You first need to download the Power BI publisher for Excel. The easiest way to do this is to navigate to Power BI and click on the download icon in the upper right part of the screen as in Figure 3-55. From here you will be taken to the download site.

> **MORE INFO POWER BI PUBLISHER FOR EXCEL DOWNLOAD**
>
> To download the Power BI publisher for Excel, you can also navigate to *https://powerbi. microsoft.com/en-us/excel-dashboard-publisher/* and then choose the correct bit version that needs to be installed.

FIGURE 3-55 Download location for Power BI publisher for Excel

Once you have done the install of the Power BI publisher for Excel, you will have a new tab in Excel named **Power BI,** as shown in Figure 3-56.

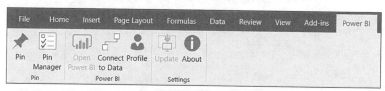

FIGURE 3-56 Power BI Publisher for Excel tab

> **MORE INFO POWER BI PUBLISHER FOR EXCEL**
>
> For more information and examples, see the following article: *https://docs.microsoft.com/ en-us/power-bi/publisher-for-excel*.

Manipulate Excel data in Power BI

Once your data is in Power BI, you can create Reports and build Dashboards as you would if you were building Power BI objects off an existing Power BI model. The tutorial that is in the MORE INFO reader aid below does an excellent job explaining how to:

- Get data
- Start exploring your dataset
- Continue the exploration with Q&A (natural language querying)

> **MORE INFO GETTING STARTED WITH THE POWER BI SERVICE**
>
> For more information and examples on how to use the Power BI Service, see the following article *https://docs.microsoft.com/en-us/power-bi/service-get-started*.

Thought experiment

In this thought experiment, you will test your knowledge pertaining to visualizing data. As a practice for the exam, eliminate answers that you know are incorrect first as to narrow the smallest set of most correct answers first.

1. Which of the following is not an area in the PivotTable Fields pane?

    A. Values

    B. Slicers

    C. Rows

    D. Filters

2. You have a Data Model with one table in it, and data for a PivotTable you are building is sourced exclusively from the Data Model. If the Data Model gets its data from a SQL Server via the Query Editor, what sequence of steps needs to happen to get refreshed into your PivotTable if you know that data at source has changed? Assume that the Query Property named Refresh this connection on Refresh All is checked. Choose all that are correct.

    A. From the PivotTable Tools menu, click Refresh

    B. From the PivotTable Tools menu, click Refresh All

    C. From the Query Editor, click Home, Query, Refresh All

    D. All the above

3. Which set of steps will connect a slicer to a PivotTable? Assume one PivotTable and Slicer are in the workbook. Choose all that apply.

   A. With a cell in the PivotTable selected, choose Insert, Filters, Slicer

   B. With a cell selected outside of the PivotTable, choose Insert, Filters, Slicer

   C. With a cell selected outside of the PivotTable, choose Insert, Filters, Slicer. Right-click on the Slicer and choose Report Connections from the context menu and then associate it with the PivotTable

   D. All the above

4. Which filter types can be connected to many PivotTables and PivotCharts? Choose all that apply.

   A. Slicer

   B. Timeline

   C. Dicer

   D. Filter in the Filters area of a PivotTable

5. Which Filters are available when filtering on a member that is in the Rows of Columns of a PivotTable? Choose all that apply.

   A. Top 10

   B. Label Filters

   C. Value Filters

   D. All the above

6. Which is not an available chart type in Excel?

   A. Histogram

   B. Combo

   C. Radar

   D. Card

7. Which chart type is best to illustrate comparisons among individual items where there are many individual items? Choose the BEST answers.

   A. Bar

   B. Pie

   C. Column

   D. Waterfall

8. Which chart types cannot connect directly to data that is house in the Data Model?

   A. Pie

   B. Bar

   C. Funnel

   D. Waterfall

Thought experiment answers

This section contains the solutions to the thought experiment.

1. **Answer B**: The Slicer is a separate object from the PivotTable.

2. **Answers A** and **B:** The Refresh preview in the Query Editor only refreshes the data preview for the Query Editor and does not load the data to the Data Model.

3. **Answers A** and **C:** Step B is incomplete. You would need to go through the steps of choosing where to source the Slicer from and then you would need to connect it to the PivotTable

4. **Answers A** and **B:** A Dicer does not exist. The Filter in the Filters area of a PivotTable is local to one PivotTable.

5. **Answer D:** All these filter types are available.

6. **Answer D:** There is no Card Chart type in Excel.

7. **Answers A** and **C:** Pie Charts would become too difficult to interpret with many individual items. Waterfall Charts are useful for understanding how an initial value is affected by a series of positive and negative values, such as in Financial Statements.

8. **Answers C** and **D:** The Funnel Chart and Waterfall Chart cannot connect to data directly in the Data Model.

Chapter summary

- PivotTables are a great way to start analysis. They summarize data into a grid format as defined by the PivotTable Fields pane.

- It is a good idea to give your PivotTable a name once it is created. This is useful as most reporting solutions end up with multiple reporting objects; this helps keep them organized.

- With a Data Model that has lots of data, you can use the Defer Layout Update to defer data updates as you define a PivotTable.

- You have options to format aspects of your PivotTable locally or in the Data Model. Making changes to the Data Model allows them to be available to all PivotTables.

- The default Report Layout is Compact. There are two other Report Layout types:
    - Tabular
    - Outline

- Measures that are created in the PivotTable are known as Implicit Measures and are local to the PivotTable they are created in. To create globally available measures, you will create Explicit Measures that become part of the Data Model.

- Grand Totals can be removed from PivotTables in the following ways:
  - Off for Rows and Columns
  - On for Rows and Columns
  - On for Rows Only
  - On for Columns Only
- Subtotals can be configured in the following ways:
  - Do Not Show Subtotals
  - Show all Subtotals at Bottom of Group
  - Show all Subtotals at Top of Group
- Blank Rows can be added to your PivotTables between groupings to help add clarity to your PivotTables.
- Refreshing data in your PivotTables can be done in several ways:
  - Manually for each PivotTable
  - Manually for all PivotTables
  - Automatically when opening the file
- Values in a PivotTable can be summarized and formatted locally to a PivotTable using the Value Field Settings set of properties. These override any formatting that has been done in the Data Model.
- When done building a Data Model, it should be optimized by doing the following:
  - Remove Columns from Data Mode that are not useful in analysis
  - Hide Tables and Columns that are not useful in analysis but are needed in the Data Model
  - Naming Conventions should be intuitive for tables and columns
  - Table and Column Descriptions should be added to each
  - Data Types - choose the correct data type for columns
  - Columns Formats should be set to appropriate formats for the column
  - Create Explicit Measures
  - Column Sorting
  - Data Categorization, which helps reporting tools better interpret data values
  - Set Summarize By Property, which applies default summary method for a column
- Filtering data the is displayed in your PivotTable can be done in the following locations:
  - In the PivotTable itself
  - By adding a PivotTable Filter
  - By adding a Slicer and connecting it to the PivotTable
  - By adding a Timeline and connecting it to the PivotTable

- Excel Has the following chart groupings. These chart type can use the Data Model or a PivotTable directly as a source:
    - Column
    - Line
    - Pie
    - Bar
    - Area
    - Surface
    - Radar
    - Combo
- These chart groupings cannot use the Data Model or a PivotTable directly as a source:
    - Scatter
    - Map
    - Stock
    - Funnel
- The following chart groupings are new in Office 2016 and cannot use the Data Model or a PivotTable directly as a source:
    - Treemap
    - Sunburst
    - Histogram
    - Box and Whisker
    - Waterfall
- When you upload a workbook to Power BI using the Excel Publish to Power BI, you can:
    - Interact with your Excel workbook just as you would in Excel Online
    - Pin selections from your workbook to Power BI dashboards
    - Share your workbook or selected elements through Power BI
- When you Export workbook data to Power BI:
    - Excel table data comes as long as there is no Data Model. If a data model is present, only it is exported into a Power BI dataset
    - You can create Power BI reports and dashboards from your dataset

- With Power BI Publisher for Excel, you can take snapshots of PivotTables, charts, and ranges and pin them to dashboards in Power BI.
  - Specifically, you can select:
    - A range of cells from a sheet or table
    - PivotTables
    - PivotChart
    - Illustrations and images
    - Text
  - You cannot select:
    - 3D Maps
    - Power View visualizations

Index

A

Access
  connecting to 12
actual-to-target values 162
actual value calculation 160
Add Conditional Column dialog box 72–73
Advanced Editor 45, 49
AdventureWorks2016 Database 5
aggregate functions 126–127
ALL 147
Analysis Services 13–17, 141
AND 129
Append transformation 55–57
area charts 206–207
arithmetic operators 123
automatic relationships 104–105
AVERAGE 126
AVERAGEX 128
Azure
  data sources, connecting to 24–26
  subscription 24
Azure Data Lake 25–27
Azure SQL
  connecting to 24
Azure SQL Data Warehouse
  connecting to 24

B

bar charts 202–203, 205
Blank Query 30
box and whisker plots 216–217
bubble charts 207
business hierarchies 156–157
business rules
  applying 71

C

CALCULATE 135–136, 147
calculated columns 90, 116–118, 128, 158
Calculation Area 89
CALENDAR 130
CALENDARAUTO 130
cardinality 101, 102
categorization 113, 190
charts. *See* PivotCharts
child functions 140
Clear All command 179
column charts 202–203
columns
  adding 43–44, 56
  calculated 90, 116–118, 128, 158
  conditional 72–73
  extracting values from existing 47–48
  formatting 112–115
  formatting, in PivotTables 183–184
  from examples 71
  from source systems 90
  hiding 110–111, 187–188
  index 73
  merging 48–49
  rearranging 42–43, 61–62
  related 101
  relationship 105
  removing 46–47
  renaming 44–45, 189
  Sort By 111–112
  sorting 190
  splitting 66–67
Combine Files tranform 53–55
combo charts 205–206
Compact Form
  for PivotTables 178

P

Q

Hear about it first.

Get the latest news from Microsoft Press sent to your inbox.

- New and upcoming books

- Special offers

- Free eBooks

- How-to articles

Sign up today at MicrosoftPressStore.com/Newsletters